JAMES CAMERON'S
STORY OF
SCIENCE FICTION

JAMES CAMERON'S
STORY OF
SCIENCE FICTION

WRITTEN BY

RANDALL FRAKES, BROOKS PECK, SIDNEY PERKOWITZ,
MATT SINGER, GARY K. WOLFE, AND LISA YASZEK

FOREWORD BY
JAMES CAMERON

PREFACE BY
RANDALL FRAKES

AFTERWORD BY
BROOKS PECK

INSIGHT EDITIONS

San Rafael, California

CONTENTS

SCIENCE FICTION HAS ALWAYS ASKED THE GREAT AND PROFOUND QUESTIONS: What is it to be human? What is our place in the grand scheme of things? Are we alone in that vastness or part of a great community? What does it all mean? What will happen next? Are we doomed, or destined for greatness? It's a genre that's not afraid of the deepest philosophical abyss. This thematic depth hooked me as a teenager after the flashy robots and slavering monsters lured me in as a kid. I started as a rabid consumer of sci-fi novels, films, and television. I gorged myself on every pulp paperback and magazine I could find with a spaceship or robot on the cover (usually juxtaposed with a voluptuous maiden woefully underdressed for the hazardous environment of space or alien worlds.) I stayed up till the wee hours for every Friday night *Creature Feature*. I knew the black-and-white B movies of the 50s by heart. I had an encyclopedic knowledge of every alien invasion strategy—every pod or spore or meteor-borne blob of goo by which they came to walk among us. I was familiar with every monster-creation method, whether by lab accident or nuclear testing or the electrical energizing of stitched-together corpses. I attended high school in a nearby city with an hour-long bus ride each way every day. And on those rides I read a science fiction book a day (well, *Dune* took a few days)—everything from the pulps of the '30s and '40s to the grand masters like Bradbury, Clarke, Heinlein, and Asimov, to the New Wave iconoclasts of the late '60s.

It wasn't until college that I realized there were actually other genres of fiction, and I began to read more widely and see cinema as a broader art form. But the fix was in. I had already genetically engineered my brain to be a science fiction storyteller.

And when it came my turn to stand and deliver, the first scripts I wrote were space operas and alien-invasion stories. The first to be made was *The Terminator* in 1984. When I was finishing the film on a crushing deadline, I met with the head of marketing for Orion Pictures, the distributor. I gave him my ideas for how we would sell it as a science fiction story. He said, "It's not a science fiction movie. That would be misleading." I gaped at him. A movie about time travel *and* killer robots not a science fiction movie? It took me a while to realize that his understanding of science fiction consisted only of *Star Wars*. It was only when George Lucas's epic neo-myth had come along that science fiction had entered the mainstream in the minds of Hollywood power brokers. Before that it was a niche genre—the redheaded stepchild of commercial filmmaking—low-budget B movies that went straight

to the drive-in, think pieces that always lost money (*2001: A Space Odyssey* took twenty-five years to break even), and tales of bleak dystopias and apocalyptic futures whose downbeat themes never exactly got the crowds lining up around the block.

It was only in the few years immediately before *The Terminator* that the genre burst into mainstream success. In 1977, *Star Wars* somehow—impossibly—became the highest-grossing film in history. Then *E.T. the Extra-Terrestrial* repeated that inconceivable feat in 1982. These days, science fiction blockbusters are not the exception, but rather the films dominating the list of the highest-grossing movies. If you include Marvel movies—whose heroes have robotic exo-suits (Iron Man) or were bombarded by gamma rays in a lab (the Hulk) or were bitten by a radioactive mutant spider (guess who?)—and *Transformers*—whose heroes and villains are alien robots—then eleven out of the top twenty highest-grossing movies of all time are science fiction. These stories are neo-myths told in terms of an age of science, not superstition and fantasy. And they are not only science fiction but also the most profitable form of entertainment in the world. Science fiction is now the majority, not the minority.

Science fiction hasn't always reigned supreme. For most of the twentieth century it struggled to find acceptance and was regularly dismissed and marginalized, often ridiculed. But before the iconic movies and TV shows of the present, there were the pioneering shows of the '60s (*Star Trek*, *The Twilight Zone*, *The Outer Limits*, *Lost in Space*), and before that, the B movies of the '50s and the pulp magazines and comics of the '30s, and before them, the great literary pioneers—Jules Verne and H. G. Wells. I embarked on the AMC original series *James Cameron's Story of Science Fiction* because I believe we need to honor the early writers and artists upon whose shoulders the economic giants of pop culture stand today. I want the casual fan of science fiction to understand the debt we owe those early pioneers, and that begins with tracing back the DNA of the ideas. Who first thought up these crazy concepts? How did others run with and develop them? And how did that lead to the iconic films that the world celebrates now? *Star Wars* didn't pop up out of nowhere. It was the result of a rich legacy of ideas and images from decades of science fiction literature, comics, and movies. I wanted to mine these historic cultural veins to honor and elevate the seminal writers and artists of the genre.

I also wanted to show how science fiction is a way for us to both dream about the promise of the future and exorcise the demons of our present angst. In these uncertain times, rife with fear of nuclear war, social unrest, and ecological disaster, science fiction allows us to explore our greatest hopes and fears for the future. It also allows us to address our uneasy relationship with humanity's technological prowess, along with our growing understanding of the universe and our possibly insignificant place in it. Science fiction is our way of dealing with these fears.

In *Story of Science Fiction* we take a deep dive into six broadly grouped subgenres—Dark Futures, Monsters, Time Travel, Intelligent Machines, Outer Space, and Alien Life—to show how they emerged from scientific progress and an understanding of the natural world, and also from the angst and paranoia of the times.

To get further perspective, I personally interviewed six titans of science fiction filmmaking for the show: Guillermo del Toro, George Lucas, Christopher Nolan, Arnold Schwarzenegger, Ridley Scott, and Steven Spielberg. This book reproduces those wide-ranging conversations in full, providing in-depth insight from the creative minds behind some of the most notable science fiction movies of all time. Also featured are essays by several science fiction experts on the key themes explored in the show. These pieces offer additional historical context and a deeper understanding of the crucial elements of the genre.

Science fiction is not just about monsters and rocket ships. Science fiction looks directly into the human soul. It explores how a bunch of tool-using apes have taken over the world, creating the Anthropocene era, for better or worse. The human race is careening down a highway at night, about to skid off the road at every turn, driven forward by technology that both enables and threatens our existence. Science fiction serves as our headlights, a way to see down the road so that we might be able to swerve in time. Or so that we can get a glimpse of the consequences if we don't. Understanding the incredible body of work left for us by generations of science fiction creators is a step toward taking control of our own fate as a species.

This is the story of science fiction. We get to decide the ending.

JAMES CAMERON'S
SCIENCE FICTION FAVORITES

LISTS PRESENTED IN NO PARTICULAR ORDER:

FILMS

2001: A Space Odyssey (1968) – Dir. Stanley Kubrick

Metropolis (1927) – Dir. Fritz Lang

Blade Runner (1982) – Dir. Ridley Scott

Close Encounters of the Third Kind (1977) – Dir. Steven Spielberg

Alien (1979) – Dir. Ridley Scott

Forbidden Planet (1956) – Dir. Fred M. Wilcox

A Clockwork Orange (1971) – Dir. Stanley Kubrick

The Road Warrior (1981) – Dir. George Miller

Planet of the Apes (1968) – Dir. Franklin J. Schaffner

The Day the Earth Stood Still (1951) – Dir. Robert Wise

The Matrix (1999) – Dir. The Wachowskis

Star Wars (1977) – Dir. George Lucas

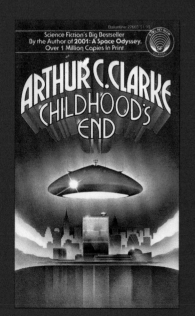

BOOKS

Fahrenheit 451 (1953) – Ray Bradbury

Childhood's End (1953) – Arthur C. Clarke

Dune (1965) – Frank Herbert

The Hyperion Cantos [*Hyperion* (1989), *The Fall of Hyperion* (1990),
Endymion (1996), *The Rise of Endymion* (1997)] – Dan Simmons

Neuromancer (1984) – William Gibson

The Forever War (1974) – Joe Haldeman

The Stars My Destination (1957) – Alfred Bester

The Moon Is a Harsh Mistress (1966) – Robert A. Heinlein

Starship Troopers (1959) – Robert A. Heinlein

Solaris (1961) – Stanislaw Lem

The Time Machine (1895) – H. G. Wells

Ringworld (1970) – Larry Niven

I FIRST MET JAMES CAMERON IN 1972 when we were both students at Fullerton College in Orange County, California. I was taking drama classes; he was studying physics, psychology, and the origins of myth. But what created a lifelong bond between us was our mutual passion for sci-fi—the works of masters like Robert A. Heinlein, Joe Haldeman, Arthur C. Clarke, Alfred Bester, Stanislaw Lem, Larry Niven, and the founders of modern sci-fi, H. G. Wells and Jules Verne.

Jim and I were voracious readers—vampires, in a way, drinking up words like they were blood. (Jim regularly read a book a day.) We were hooked on the great wonder and scope of the sci-fi universe, the unfettered imaginations of its great minds and the infinite possibilities they proposed. We also devoured sci-fi TV shows. We'd laugh at the ludicrous nature of some and celebrate the audacity and creativity of others. One of our favorites was *The Outer Limits* (1963–1965), a series brimming with fantastic ideas that inspired many fans to become sci-fi storytellers themselves.

Jim was inspired to create his own science fiction by the stories he consumed as a teenager. It was easy to see his talent and ambition, but what was uncommon in a eighteen-year-old was his uncompromising vision for the stories he wanted to tell. The son of an engineer father and artist mother, Jim looked at the world by breaking it down and examining its constituent parts, and then reassembling them into engaging, hyperreal fiction. He would get excited by the ideas in a novel, film, or TV show, and then take them further than the original creators had dared, extrapolating in ways that were compelling, far-thinking, and always surprising.

The first thing I ever read by Jim was the first five chapters of his *Necropolis*, a postapocalyptic novel he had handwritten on a legal pad in pencil. His instinctive skill as a prose writer was evident, his dynamic ideas leaping off the page with dramatic intensity. Just sitting there in his small rental in humble suburbia, I was transported to a vividly different place and time and exposed to concepts I had never encountered before.

Early on, Jim told me that most science fiction books and films didn't connect with a mass audience because they focused too much on the head and not enough on the heart. Jim had studied myth and read James George Frazer's *The Golden Bough* (1890) and Joseph Campbell's *Hero with a Thousand Faces* (1949); he was on a mission to find the universal story underlying his sci-fi, something that all audiences could relate to.

OPPOSITE An early James Cameron piece typical of the transcendental, apocalyptic themes he was exploring as a young science fiction artist. In the image, the transcendent couple has returned through a dimensional portal from a distant time or place with a revelation too terrifying for the unevolved humans.

RIGHT A portrait of Randall Frakes by James Cameron.

Heavily influenced by the kind of hard science fiction popularized by authors like Clarke and Lem, Jim wanted to make highly cerebral notions universally understandable while maintaining their punch and power.

Jim was also able to bring elements of his personal life into his sci-fi, further grounding the stories in humanity. When writing *The Terminator* in the early '80s, Jim was living with a girl who worked as a waitress. Hearing what she went through each day on the job, Jim took that insight and worked it into his screenplay. His heroine in the story, Sarah Connor, became a waitress, a believable "everyperson" whose reaction to the mind-boggling news that she is being pursued by a mechanical killing machine is entirely relatable.

One of the most haunting aspects of the Terminator films is the idea that humanity is on the verge of a nuclear apocalypse brought on by misuse of science—namely, the creation of the malevolent artificial intelligence known as Skynet. Although the films seem to have a dark vision of the future, Jim has always incorporated rays of hope into his sci-fi stories. In his 1991 sequel *Terminator 2: Judgment Day*, Sarah Connor decides to destroy Skynet by blowing up the company where it was generated and therefore changing the course of history, a strategy she borrows from the malevolent AI itself. Although human beings created the problem, in Jim's world, human beings can also solve it using science, strategic

thinking, and sheer grit. So, while Jim sharply condemns the worst aspects of humanity, he simultaneously celebrates its best qualities. Above all, he empowers his characters and, by design, his audience: If we created the problems, then we can solve them. His sci-fi stories are gauntlets flung at the viewing public's feet, challenging people to take responsibility for the world around them and encouraging them to be on the right side of history. To explore, not exploit; to give, not take.

Jim has always believed that audiences have the potential to respond to sci-fi themes in ways that might inspire human progress in real life. Following his second major feature, *Aliens* (1986)—a sequel to one of Jim's favorite films, Ridley Scott's *Alien* (1979)—he got a taste of just how true this notion might be. After putting extensive work into designing the Power Loader that protagonist Ripley uses to battle the film's big bad, the Alien Queen, Jim received a phone call from a major hydraulics company. The company was looking to manufacture a commercial version of the Power Loader, unaware that the device was an elaborate special effect. Jim had thought up something that seemed like it *could* exist and in fact *should* exist, and to this day robotics experts continue to work on similar robotic exoskeletons as a means of artificially enhancing human abilities.

Jim's next film, the deep-sea sci-fi epic *The Abyss* (1989), saw his imagined worlds bleed into real life once again. Not only was Jim required to build real diving equipment and fully functional remote-operated vehicles (ROVs) for the movie—creations that would form the basis of the "bots" he would later use to explore the *Titanic*—but his vision for the science fiction elements of the film would actually help force a seismic shift in movie technology. Jim needed to show that the film's deep-sea alien civilization was able to use water as a communication tool, but traditional visual effects methods proved

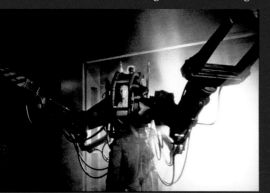

RIGHT An early concept sketch by James Cameron for the Power Loader seen in *Aliens*. Cameron envisioned the controls for manipulating the arms to be similar to grasping a baseball bat and drew this sketch to help communicate the idea to the *Aliens* crew.

LEFT Sigourney Weaver as Ripley pilots the final version of the Power Loader in *Aliens*.

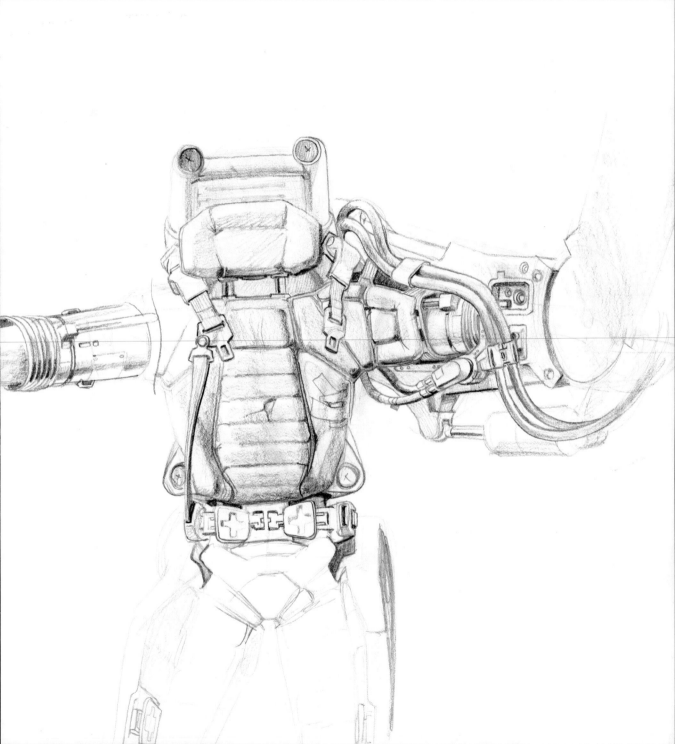

inadequate. To solve the issue, Jim worked with VFX house Industrial Light & Magic to create the "water tentacle." This lifelike, digitally generated creature effect was entirely new to audiences in 1989. There had been nothing like it before and there wouldn't be again until two years later when Jim took the technology to a whole new level with his liquid-metal T-1000 character in *Terminator 2*. A key aspect of Jim's contribution to science fiction has always been his ability to push the limits of what's possible in the real world to accommodate his own relentless imagination, a quality that has delighted audiences and greatly benefited the filmmaking industry. When he imposes his will on a project, the end result broadens our minds and forces technology to make a giant leap forward.

Jim's investment in new technologies, including new filming methodologies and 3-D camera systems, was necessary to create *Avatar*, an epic sci-fi film featuring a detailed and entirely realistic alien world—the ultimate dream for a science fiction fan weaned on stories of interstellar travel and contact with otherworldly races. Pandora, an alien moon, would be a world of ecological balance and the celebration of nature. Jim developed a sound scientific basis for all its creatures, technology, and biospheres. Nothing broke the laws of physics. Pandora became a place that *could* actually exist somewhere in the universe.

I remember visiting Jim late at night on the motion-capture stage where the digital parts of *Avatar* were being shot. Everyone had gone home but Jim, who was sitting under a bright beam of light on a stool on the vast stage, playing with the control of his virtual camera. He showed me how he was manipulating digital images of the scene where the film's hero, Jake Sully, touches a mushroom-like plant that suddenly collapses like an umbrella, revealing the hammerhead titanothere creature about to charge him. Jim

OPPOSITE A James Cameron concept sketch for the Thanator seen in *Avatar*.

BELOW The Thanator in a final frame from *Avatar*.

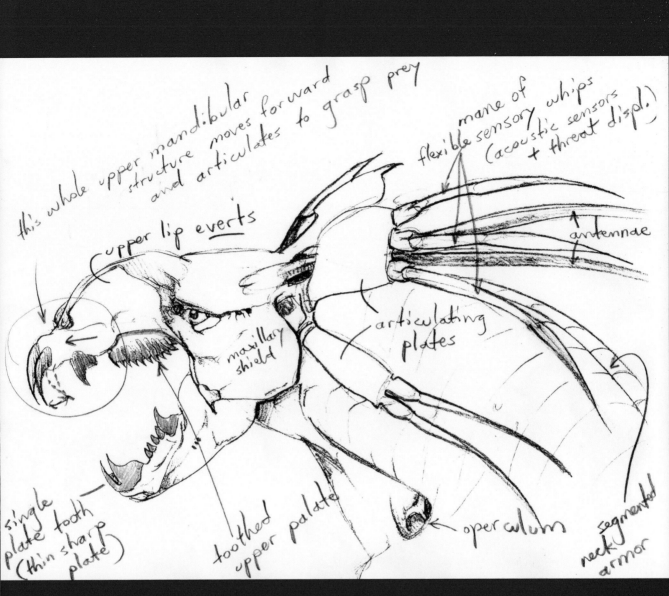

this whole upper mandibular structure moves forward and articulates to grasp prey

upper lip everts

mane of flexible sensory whips (acoustic sensors + threat displ.)

antennae

maxillary shield

articulating plates

single plate tooth (thin sharp plate)

toothed upper palate

operculum

segmented neck armor

was adjusting the speed of the plant's collapse so it would walk the line between real physics and dramatic impact. He had pushed the technology to the point where his virtual world could be filmed in real time, his actors' motion-capture performances instantly turned into previsual renders of the alien Na'vi characters on a digital set. Within this virtual Pandora, he could control the framing and the direction of the light, and even manipulate the plants and other elements.

Jim had envisioned a whole new world in *Avatar*, digitally recreating it down to the finest detail and manipulating it to his exact specifications. I thought back to the time I first met him, when he was scribbling stories on his legal pad. What an incredible journey he's taken. He had the courage to dream worlds, make them real, and inspire us all, breaking through seemingly insurmountable artistic and technological boundaries along the way.

In *James Cameron's Story of Science Fiction*, Jim sits down with sci-fi greats to share insight on where science fiction has been and where it's going. There are no better guides to the genre's importance and limitless appeal than Jim and his peers. Welcome to their universe.

JAMES CAMERON

INTERVIEW BY RANDALL FRAKES

RANDALL FRAKES: As a young man and aspiring writer and filmmaker, what were the key science fiction books or films that really inspired you to create?

JAMES CAMERON: Well, there is an inherent flaw in the question because it was as a kid and a preteen, a teenager, that I was an enormous fan of science fiction. As I became an aspiring filmmaker, I was reading a lot less science fiction and writing science fiction. So, I had gone from input to output.

In the input phase as a kid, it was initially, I guess, television. So, every B science fiction [movie], B monster movie, and some of the A stuff. *Fantastic Voyage*, that was in '66. I would have been twelve. *Planet of the Apes* (1968) a few years later. But there was nothing I loved better than going to the movies—nothing I loved better than seeing a fantasy or science fiction movie. So whether it was *The 7th Voyage of Sinbad* (1958) or *Jason and the Argonauts* (1963) or on television—again, Harryhausen films, *Earth vs. the Flying Saucers* (1956), *20 Million Miles to Earth* (1957), things like that. I would die to see anything space-themed in a movie theater or on television. Then that led to reading science fiction, and once I started reading science fiction I just went supersonic

then ultimately hypersonic. When I was in high school I had a one-hour bus ride both directions, so I had two hours a day on a bus. Then I had as much class time as I could get with my books hidden behind my math text—you know, hunched down and propped up behind the text. I'd read about a book a day or, if it was a long book, a book every couple of days.

RF: Would you follow authors like Isaac Asimov then? Or were you reading anybody?

OPPOSITE James Cameron on the set of *James Cameron's Story of Science Fiction*. Photo Credit: Michael Moriatis/AMC

ABOVE Illustration of a figure in a spacesuit navigating a giant alien forest created by James Cameron while he was in eleventh grade, circa 1970. This is likely the earliest piece of artwork related to what would eventually become *Avatar*.

JC: I would read anybody. For me, it was a question of how interesting was the cover on the paperback.

RF: You must have read a lot of Ace Double books.

JC: I read a lot of Ace Doubles. I think I read every Ace Double. Now after a while you start to realize some authors are better than others and some authors get anthologized like Arthur C. Clarke and Ray Bradbury, so you start to pay attention to authors. Then, once I started figuring out an author was worth it, I'd start burning through that author. I'd just start going through everything they had written. But you know, it's not like we had Amazon. I couldn't order any book I wanted. It was kind of what showed up on the bookstand at my local A&P market.

RF: Did you regularly read science fiction magazines?

JC: I never really read the magazines that much. You know, I'd buy some *Analog*s and things like that. But it was mostly anthology books and novels, from the high grades to the low grades. To me, there wasn't a whole lot [of difference]. I mean, I understood that Clarke was better, smarter, that his ideas were bigger, his themes were grander than some of the guys writing for the Ace Doubles. But I loved the Ace Doubles; I thought they were fantastic. And I loved some of the—they didn't even have YA [young adult] classification back then—but the stuff that was written back then for younger audiences, like Andre Norton's stuff.

RF: *Daybreak.*

BELOW James Cameron concept art for a spaceship from *Xenogenesis*. The idea of the engines being extremely hot black-body radiators was later used for the ISV Venture Star spacecraft seen in *Avatar*.

OPPOSITE Two phone doodles created by James Cameron while on long calls.

JC: Sure. *Daybreak—2250 A.D.* (1952) and, you know, the stories about the guy with the space cat and stuff like that. And Heinlein, *Have Space Suit—Will Travel* (1958). Those were YA sci-fi before there was such a category.

RF: You liked movies, you were a moviegoer, but when you saw a fantasy or science fiction film you got an extra kick?

JC: Absolutely.

RF: Why do you think that was? What was it that delighted you so much more than any other kind of film?

JC: I don't know. If you're born with a kind of strong visual imagination, you're stimulated by other artist's imaginations. To me that was the most imaginative stuff. You know, *Mission: Impossible* (1966–1973) was cool, but it was ultimately a bunch of people standing around talking. But *The Outer Limits* (1963–1965)? That was interesting stuff. They had rocks that melted and turned into parasitic creatures that controlled your mind and all kinds of crazy stuff. . . . I even liked *Lost in Space* (1965–1968) a lot until it got silly. I had a very low tolerance for silliness. And so, you know, the robot waving its arms around and Dr. Smith twirling his mustache took me out of that show eventually and I just stopped watching it.

RF: Because you wanted to take your sci-fi seriously?

JC: And I was very dogmatic about genre boundaries as a kid, and not because I was part of some fan group or had other kids to talk to

this stuff about. I made a very clear distinction in my mind between *Outer Limits*, which was hard science fiction, and *Twilight Zone* (1959–1964). Which was whimsical and fantasy and sometimes fantasy-horror, and it would sort of skirt around fantasy ideas. But it was kind of all over the map. Now, the average person liked *The Twilight Zone* better than *Outer Limits*, and *Outer Limits* failed after a couple seasons, but I couldn't imagine a better show. I collected the trading cards. There were *Outer Limits* trading cards, believe it or not, and they always got the descriptions wrong. I could never understand that there was this completely cheesy aspect to publishing, especially with stuff like trading cards, and they would just make up some stupid description for an alien from *Outer Limits* that had nothing to do with the episode, and I felt so outraged by that.

RF: Sociologically and historically, why do you feel it's the right time to tell the story of science fiction? Spielberg said science fiction used to be the dessert but now it's the steak on the plate.

JC: Yes, well you know, I think what he is referring to is that science fiction has been legitimized as arguably the most commercial film genre. The biggest movies of recent years have been science fiction or fantasy films. You have *Lord of the Rings*, *Transformers*—

RF: What was the pivot point?

JC: *Star Wars* (1977) was the one that reversed a trend of declining commercial returns for science fiction that had been going on for twenty years at that time. It had gotten more and more dystopian, and then *Star Wars* came along and

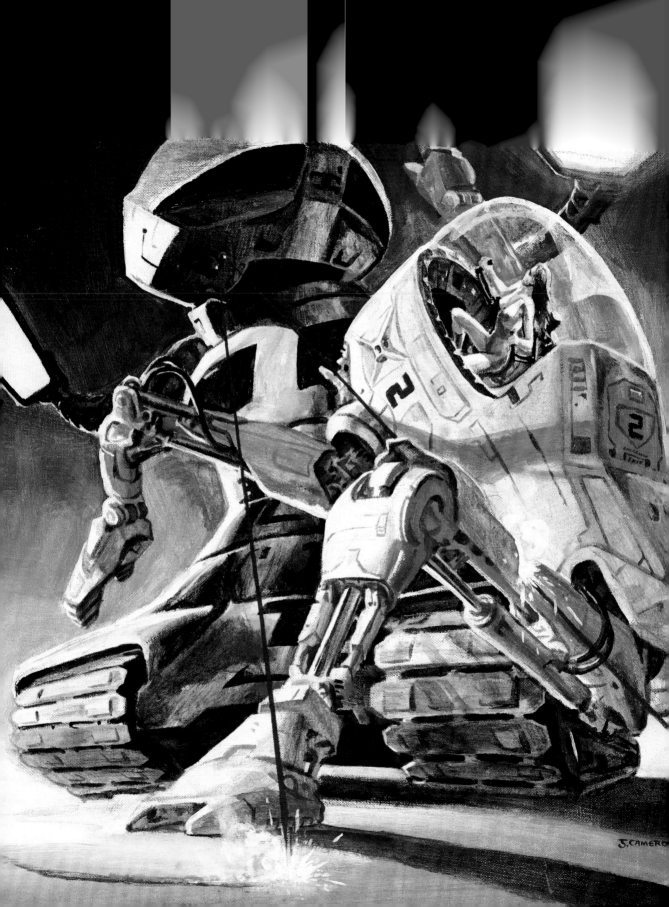

went *boom*! It just blew the doors off everybody's perceptions of what science fiction could be. Now it didn't legitimize science fiction artistically, I mean, we are still struggling to do that to this day, but it certainly pivoted everybody 180 degrees on whether science fiction could be commercial. So I think that's what Spielberg meant about it being the steak on the plate now. But I think in terms of its timeliness or its value to human survival at this point, we live in an age where it's almost impossible to predict from year to year what the ramifications of our technology are going to be. And so all of these science fiction stories that explore, What happens if we create a pathogen that takes out half of the human race? What happens if we create a strong artificial intelligence that actually challenges us for dominance on this planet? What if? What if? What if? Asking these questions now in a science fiction framework is really just a way of anticipating what may be happening in ten, twenty, or thirty years.

Now, traditionally, science fiction has been pretty terrible at predicting exactly what is going to happen. We were supposed to be sending a manned mission to Jupiter in 2001. Now that didn't happen, and we weren't supposed to have a global internet, essentially a global electronic neural net that connects all people everywhere. And even at the moment of the internet's inception, most science fiction writers were talking about big mainframes. They weren't talking about individualized computing. And the time from the personal computer to the internet was pretty darn quick—a couple of years—and the personal computer didn't exist in science fiction. It was always big centralized mainframes, whether they were alien, human, futuristic, or whatever it was. So, here you have the thing that has truly revolutionized human civilization and culture and our trajectory as a conscious species, and it was not predicted by science fiction.

RF: Some people think that science fiction's primary purpose is to predict the future, but it's not true, is it?

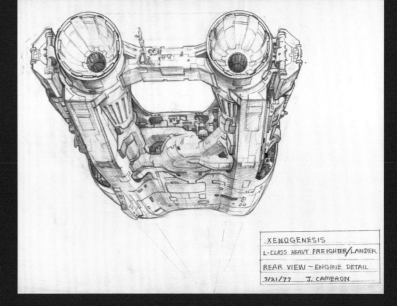

XENOGENESIS
L-CLASS HEAVY FREIGHTER/LANDER
REAR VIEW ~ ENGINE DETAIL
3/21/77   J. CAMERON

JC: No. Science fiction never predicts the future, but it can prevent the future if we listen and pay attention.

RF: So why has science fiction filmmaking become so popular? Is it essentially the revenge of the nerds?

JC: No. I mean, science fiction was very nerdy for a long time. It was basically written and read by nerdy white American males. That was pretty much it, and there were a few females, but they basically went under ambiguous names like Andre Norton that everyone assumed was a guy. Or they went under a pseudonym or just under their initials. D. C. Fontana—everyone just assumed she was a guy when she was writing *Star Trek* episodes. At the time it was just not ripe for women, so it was all about the male technological domination of the world, and the universe—conquering space, conquering atomic energy, fighting robots. It was a very male fantasy. There were some very good female writers, but they were sort of in the shadows. Then they came forward in the '60s or '70s, and science fiction became much more egalitarian from a gender perspective, both in its themes and the number of writers and readers. So, science fiction is much more mainstream than it was when I was growing up and before that.

OPPOSITE James Cameron concept art for *Xenogenesis*. The tank-like automaton on the left would form the basis of the design for the Hunter-Killer tanks in *The Terminator*.

ABOVE A Cameron concept sketch for an "L-Class Heavy Freighter/Lander" from *Xenogenesis*.

JC: I think it's a great thing, and I think *Star Trek* did a lot to help with that. It did a lot to show people that science fiction could be about sociological things and not just big ideas and hard science stuff.

RF: Things that could affect the people watching the show.

JC: It could be about race. It could be about gender. It could be about the things that are forbidden and that are suppressed in society. I think that was a real eye-opener for a lot of people.

RF: One of the things science fiction can do is dress up aliens and spaceships with social commentary and criticism that would otherwise be rejected by people.

JC: Sure, and every time an alien is your friend or your lover or someone equal to you, someone you would die for, then it doesn't matter what someone looks like. So then all of a sudden, you've taken appearance out of it, you've taken gender out of it, you've taken skin color out of it, and that's what *Star Trek* did. *Star Trek* also showed a vision of the future that was not dystopian but hopeful and heroic, and I think that people needed that in the '60s.

RF: Is it easier to write science fiction where you have a positive future, or a dystopian novel with a negative vision of the future? What do you think is easier for people to accept?

JC: I think you can easily write in either direction. You can show how exciting new developments are and how that can swerve us into some kind of sociological developments that we don't expect. But I think in terms of popularity, people always want the Cassandran warning first because they want a dire circumstance. Action, tension, and drama all come from some kind of dire circumstance. I think that's why most writers tend to gravitate toward some kind of darker vision of the future.

RF: Where the conflict is?

JC: Yes, but let me add a little detail to that because there is a certain hopefulness that says we are going to have robots that can talk like people. We are going to have spacecraft that can go to other planets. Civilization is going to keep the wheels on long enough for us to get all the cool shit that we can now write an adventure story around. But then we are very cynical and sardonic about how bad things are as we write that adventure story. And that is what I would say most pop culture science fiction literature is. You take all the shiny new baubles, put it together into a world. There is an inherent hopefulness in all that because it says we are going to be around and we are going to continue to invent and continue to innovate. But then we are going to make it a really bad place to live and dangerous and have lots of dark characters in it, so you are kind of giving and taking away with the same hand. But that is not bleak the way *A Canticle for Leibowitz* (1959) is bleak. That book says we are not going to go forward and that we are going to go back to a dark age, and all the things that we have now are going to be swept away forever by a human state of mind that collapses to dogmatism. That to me is a terrifying future. Because we may have nefarious creatures in the back alleys of some *Neuromancer*-type future, but there is still something innately optimistic about the fact that we are going to have

BELOW Leonard Nimoy as Mr. Spock in the original *Star Trek* series.

OPPOSITE Concept art by James Cameron for *Xenogensis* gives a closer look at the wind-sharks. Although the wind-shark was a design precursor for the banshees seen in *Avatar*, the only detail that would ultimately be kept was the sharp teeth that could extend and retract.

an interne... ...nd that we are going to have these advanced AI systems and so on. Where it really goes dark for me is when the human mind goes against progress and against innovation and against science. And that is happening. It's happening in our world right now.

RF: Fear rules the day.

JC: I think we need more fiction discussing the inherent conflict between faith and science because, to me, faith is superstition and science is the path to truth. That is me personally. I don't necessarily project my personal views in my work that much, other than I have a positive science character in *Avatar* in Sigourney Weaver's Grace. But I think that is going to be the ultimate test of human consciousness as an experiment: Do we turn our backs on that which we have learned about the world just because the universe is vast and it doesn't give us easy answers? We want to collapse it down to some simple manual for life, like you just bought a new lawn mower and you want to learn how to make it work. You're going to have a manual for your life and it is going to tell you everything you need to know, and you never have to do any research or innovation and you never have to look out into the universe because all of the answers are right there. Because if humanity settles for that, then we are fucking doomed and the whole human experiment was a waste of time. That is my own personal projection. Could I write science fiction about that? If I was a science fiction author primarily, working as a literary author, I would write the hell out of that theme. That would become the dominant theme of my work for my whole adult life, I guarantee it.

RF: It certainly seems to be a subtheme in a lot of your earlier work. Like in *Terminator 2* you have the Terminator telling John Connor, "It's in your nature to destroy yourselves."

JC: I think it is in our nature to acquire power and protect our in-group. The problem is, how wide a net do you cast for your in-group? Now, for us to survive, we have to cast that net on a global scale. Our in-group is the human race. But people don't know how to do that. I think there are a few enlightened people out there, but human beings are terrible at that. They create false divisions when we don't even need them. My team from my city is better than your shitty team from your shitty city. Oh, come on, really? Are we twelve years old?

BELOW Early concept sketch by Cameron for *The Terminator* showing the title character after receiving critical damage in the film's final scenes. In the finished film, the character would not wield a knife.

OPPOSITE TOP A pre-*Xenogenesis* Cameron pencil sketch from 1977 typical of the science fiction action scenarios he was drawing at the time. Along with foreshadowing elements of *Xenogenesis*, such as the Hunter Killer–style tank and the spider vehicle, the robot's mantis-like arms would later be echoed in Cameron's design for the Alien Queen in *Aliens*.

OPPOSITE BOTTOM Phone doodle by Cameron.

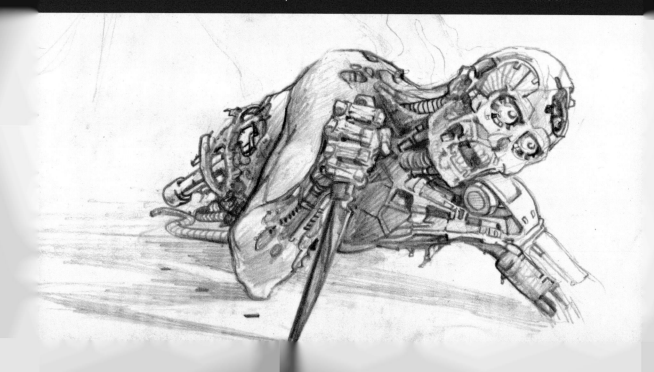

RF: Isn't a lot of that being driven by political motivations?

JC: Of course, but political motivations are driven by innate aspects of the human psyche. We tend toward tribalism. Our tribe is good, your tribe is bad—unless you've got something we want to trade with. In which case, we will tolerate you. But that is how we have evolved. That is how we have lived for hundreds of thousands if not millions of years—with a tribal perspective. And so people are seeking tribalism. That's why they align with sports teams. That is why they align with causes and with principles and to a certain extent, religions, too. It creates an in-group and an out-group.

RF: So can science fiction break that logjam conceptually?

JC: Absolutely. That is where science fiction challenges you to think differently. It can't *make* you think differently, but it can offer ways to look at things through a different lens; a different perspective. And if you can do that through an alien culture that you've just encountered that is potentially threatening and doesn't see the universe the way you do, then why can't you do it with other humans that don't see the universe the way you do?

RF: An example is Guillermo del Toro's new film, *The Shape of Water*, which is basically about a relationship between a human and a nonhuman.

JC: It's about love being where love is. There was a science fiction story—and I wish I could remember what it was—that I read as a kid that was basically about homosexuality. And the line I remember from the story is, "Love strikes like lightning." And so, that is what Guillermo is saying, and that is why he has the main character's best friend be gay, because that is what the story is about. The story is about—when someone is in love, they are in love. You don't get to judge it.

MOLOCH

RF: When I was a kid, what attracted me to science fiction was a sensitivity or a mind-set—whatever you want to call it—to perceived injustices, imbalances, things that weren't working right in the culture around us, and these science fiction stories were saying yes, you're right, and here's some possible fixes—

JC: Or here's how bad this could get if we keep going this way. But ultimately, you could have fantasy do that. You can have sociological science fiction do that. The hard science fiction tends to be more about our human relationship with technology. Humans are inextricable from their technology. We are dominant on the planet, above the animal kingdom, and everything that we have accomplished, at least from the perspective of the control of our environment—our food supply, energy, and so on—all comes from technology. And it comes from our ability to coevolve with our technology. We walked upright so we could use our hands for something besides locomotion. That allowed us to chip pieces of chert, make sharp edges, and carry them around

with us, and we now had claws when we needed claws, even though we weren't born with them. We could kill something and carry it with us indefinitely. We could pick something up and then carry it with us, or dig something up, a tuber from the ground, and carry it with us because we were bipedal. So the whole history of human descendants is about technology influencing our actual physical evolution, meaning our brains got bigger, which then influenced the technology in a positive feedback loop that, in a funny way, led inevitably to where we are right now.

So science fiction really is the most comprehensive human fiction because it deals with us and our technology and how we coevolve with it. We evolve our technology and it evolves us. And that has been happening for a million years or longer. I mean, the first stone tools go back at this point at least 1.5 million years, maybe as early as two million years ago. So this has been going on for a long time, but it is a long curve. It's accelerated, you know? Ten thousand years ago, we had rope and woven baskets, and I don't think we were quite at the wheel yet. And we didn't get metals until five thousand years after that, and we are on a long curve that's accelerating to where we can't even predict where we are going to be twenty

RF: Unless you read science fiction, maybe.

JC: Well, look, science fiction authors are always out ahead kind of poking around trying to figure out what it all means. But it has all collapsed to the point that some of the things that are being announced coming out of Silicon Valley are beyond what science fiction writers could imagine or have imagined. So the problem is the window between the future you imagined and the future in which you are living has consistently shrunk over time. And yet, the things that were accepted by science fiction in the '40s, '50s, '60s, and so on—interstellar travel, faster-than-light travel—all those things, they still elude us completely. So, it's our near-term, day-to-day coevolution with our technology that's gone ballistic, and it's the grand old themes of science fiction, of conquering the galaxy, that still elude us. We aren't any closer to conquering the galaxies now than we were in the 1930s when Hugo Gernsback and John W. Campbell were imagining what that would be like. We got to the Earth's orbit, we got to the Moon, a few times in the '60s and '70s, and haven't been back there since. We haven't had people travel off the planet to a destination since 1972. So, in a funny way, we've peaked and collapsed back. Now our robots are going out and doing amazing things. We made it to the edge of the solar system and actually well beyond if you consider the Voyagers making it out to the heliopause and all that stuff.

RF: You personally interview six people in the show *James Cameron's Story of Science Fiction*: Guillermo del Toro, George Lucas, Christopher Nolan, Arnold Schwarzenegger, Ridley Scott, and Steven Spielberg. Why did you pick those particular people?

JC: I think we were lucky enough to be granted interviews by some of the top practitioners of science fiction in pop culture. . . . For me the obvious go-to people to comment and give something back to a genre that had made them very successful were George, Steven, Guillermo and the rest of our list. It's like, okay guys, we've all played in this genre for a significant part of our careers, not all of our films are obviously science fiction, but as a group, we've certainly done an awful lot and made milestone films in the genre and made a lot of money doing it. So, let's try to share with people how that started for us, how that hooked us as kids. What were the themes that intrigued us as kids and teenagers when we were sort of coming up as artists? Why did these ideas mean so much to us? And I think the results of the interviews speak for themselves. You really see a common thread that people like George and Steven and the others, they don't dabble in it, they *have* to do it. They have to do it because these ideas and these images are bursting in their minds. They've got to get it out.

RF: It's like a vision they have, an artistic vision.

JC: Sure. And it is something that they want to share with the world. It's in their heads and they have to get it out as filmmakers. And writers do the same thing. Some writers are more visual in the way they write, and they can conjure a moment so clearly in the prose that you can imagine it in your mind. And then maybe even years later when you see that translated into a movie, you say, "Ah ha. That's what I saw in my head." Or, as my sixteen-year-old, Claire, says, "I'm not even going to see that movie, it won't be right. It won't be what I see."

RF: In the AMC series, there is a lot of conversation about the definition of science fiction in relation to other genres, like fantasy. Why is that so important to make the distinction, and what does science fiction offer that other comparable genres do not?

JC: Well, first of all, if you are reading something or you're watching a film and you are enjoying it, I don't think it is important to classify it down to its genre or down to its subgenre. But, I do think it is important for the average person to understand the distinction between science fiction and horror, which often overlap each other, but are also quite distinct. You can have science fiction horror, and *Alien* is a beautiful example of that, but I would classify it as a

science fiction film first. It takes place on a spaceship, in deep space, so that immediately makes it, in my mind, a science fiction film. Is it important? No, I don't think so. If you're enjoying something, it doesn't matter. Is *Transformers* science fiction or fantasy? Who cares? It's *Transformers*.

RF: It seems to me that *Blade Runner* (1982) is the science fictional variation of *Frankenstein* regarding the Roy Batty character, especially—

JC: Yes, as in a lot of the android or synthetic human stories, the synthetic human is more charismatic, more interesting than its creator. And in the original *Frankenstein* story, the monster was much more interesting than Victor Frankenstein, I thought. And in the various incarnations of that story, that's been the case.

RF: It's the living incarnation of the idea of, What is human?

JC: That is absolutely one of the most fundamental themes of science fiction. What is human? I think the way a science fiction writer defines it is, to be human is to believe you're human. Even if you are a machine, even if you are an intelligent dog! The point is, what is human? And what is an emotive consciousness equal to or greater than a human that must be afforded the same rights and respect and dignity? But ultimately, I don't think that science fiction writers, for the most part, are writing about what it would really be like to meet an alien species, because that is kind of irrelevant to our lives right now. The real question is how to tell a story about meeting an alien species and learning to understand them or accommodate them and interact with them. How does that inform our process when dealing with, let's say, a culture you don't understand?

RF: Like the movie *Arrival*.

JC: Exactly. So what are cultures we don't understand? We certainly didn't understand the ultra dogmatic religious terrorist culture behind the September 11 attacks, or we would have imagined it was possible and we would have prevented it. That was like being attacked by aliens. I had two reactions the day after that. One I wanted to bomb them into oblivion. The other one was I wanted to learn Arabic and really just like stop what I was doing as a filmmaker and try to understand the world from their perspective, because I felt that it was the only way to prevent something like that from being inevitable again. And I realized we simply didn't understand them. I think we have a much greater understanding of them now. The "them" is now obviously highly factionalized to the point it would require a constant effort to continue to understand the individual differences between these factions and these sects and all that sort of thing. But, I think for the American public at large, there was very little understanding. Now you read a book like *Dune* and you realize that it's all in there. Frank Herbert was writing about the mujahideen and their struggle against Russia probably—I don't know the exact timing of it—but there was certainly a series of events in the nineteenth and twentieth centuries where desert nomadic Bedouin Arabic culture was at odds with imperial forces, whether it was the English, you know, whoever it was.

TOP Kyle MacLachlan as Paul Atreides in director David Lynch's *Dune* (1984).

ABOVE Novel cover for *Dune* by Frank Herbert, published by Ace Books.

RF: The "spice" from *Dune* is oil.

JC: Yeah, *Lawrence of Arabia*, right? So then it ultimately became about oil. So, spice is oil. Herbert was probably commenting on the carving up of the whole Mesopotamian Valley arbitrarily by the Americans and the Brits. Carving it up into different countries, not along sectarian or tribal lines, which has led to all the problems that we have right now because nobody understood those cultures. But that is what Herbert was doing with *Dune*. He was saying the Fremen were the mujahideen. The Fremen were the kind of guys that are Afghan warlords or terrorists now. If you read *Dune* now you get a completely different perspective. Also, let's look at *Star Wars*. Guys from a desert fighting a great empire with ad hoc weapons, a bunch of scrappy rebels. It's the mujahideen against Russia; at that time that would have been a reference point. And by the way, I'm sure *Dune* fed into *Star Wars* quite a bit. But ask yourself, how can I cheer for the rebels in *Star Wars* when I actually work for the Empire? Because as an American, you are working for the Empire. It's pretty much that simple. You might not be wearing a white Stormtrooper outfit and actually be a janitor on the Death Star, but, you know, you are working for the Empire.

RF: That may be the important aspect of science fiction as a genre, which is that it can teach us to see ourselves the way aliens might look at human beings.

JC: That's right. So then everybody can relate to those scrappy rebels in *Star Wars* blowing up the Death Star. But I think the limitation is you can put it before you, but if you can't make the translation to your own life, ultimately you've just read a pleasing yarn or seen a fun movie. It hasn't resonated through. I think only a small percentage of the audience actually goes, "Oh, well that would mean that I'm the bad guy." Very few people can get to that place.

RF: If you watch the prequel *Star Wars* trilogy, that becomes pretty obvious.

JC: That's right. "This is how democracy dies— with thunderous applause."

RF: Yep.

JC: I think we just saw that about a year ago.

RF: Do you see any point to writing and directing to inspire humanity as a whole to be better versions of themselves and to show possible paths to betterment?

JC: Look, this is an entirely rhetorical question because that is obviously exactly what I am doing. That's what *Avatar* was and the intention of the Avatar sequels. The bigger question is, so you actually think it will work? I don't know. I don't know if *Avatar* worked. I mean, the message was there. It worked for some people. I think that 90 percent of the people just enjoyed the beauty, the adventure, and that sort of thing. I think 10 percent took it to heart as a call to action or at least a wake up call about our intolerance of each other and about our lack of respect for nature and so on—the things that are basically plaguing our civilization right now and threatening our survival.

Avatar threw such a broad net in terms of its viewership that even if there was only microscopic change per person, there must be some measurable change globally because millions and millions of people saw that film. So, maybe it's only one more grain of sand that has to be added to many others that causes people to change the way they view the world, change their perspective, become more tolerant, maybe not vote so stupidly, then it's done some good. I think it's not measurable whether the film actually does real good, but as an artist, you have to try.

The other thing is, you can also throttle your artistic effort in the crib by making it too preachy, too didactic. On the first *Avatar*, they didn't see it coming. It was just a big, glossy, colorful spectacle that had all this other stuff in it. Next time the pundits will be on guard looking for those lefty, tree-hugging themes. I'm sure Trump will tweet about it.

RF: That's the measure of success.

JC: So it may do less good because it may be less successful. It was a bit of a Trojan horse the first time. We'll see. But I'm not backing off the throttle. I'm also not hammering the throttle down and trying to ram a message down people's throats. I'm trying to tell a good story that exists within a thematic framework that people can either buy into or not buy into, and if they don't buy into it, they'll still enjoy the story. I don't believe in the values of Don Corleone but I still love *The Godfather*. So, you don't even need to buy the values to go on the ride and follow and care about the characters.

RF: Should a science fiction writer feel a moral imperative to get the science correct and address real-world issues?

JC: I'd say that the moral imperative to get the science right is less important than the moral imperative to comment on our times and our political and sociological situation through a lens of entertainment. Or at least a lens that is somewhat removed or askance so that people can see things with a new perspective. We are certainly seeing, in what we thought were more enlightened times, that people are incredibly prejudiced and dug-in and dogmatic. The current size of populism and isolationism around the world shows that we are actually moving backward in that regard. Or, at the very least, deeply entrenched dogmatic perspectives are being revealed to us in harsh terms in our liberal bubble, which may have been a bubble of illusion, so that our sort of path of social revolution and enlightenment has not been nearly as effective as we thought it was. Which basically means we have got to double down, because whatever progress we have made can be somewhat attributed to people being able to see past the prejudices that they grew up with or were indoctrinated with, or that they learned in their schools or that they learned from their parents. One of the many inputs to that kind of social

evolution has been science fiction, which does request and demand that people look outside their immediate bubble, their immediate reality.

RF: Yeah, it seems to me that Carl Sagan's mission in life was to popularize science so that people could appreciate its value for them in their daily lives. It's very similar to what a science fiction writer does. Same thing. Bring science home.

JC: Well, I think that Carl Sagan tried to popularize science and make the universe accessible mentally or intellectually to a broad audience, but I think we are in a different time now. That was at a time when space travel saw us landing *Viking* on Mars and sending *Voyager* up to Jupiter. We are in a different time now. Sure there are space enthusiasts, but we're also in a time where the pendulum is swinging back the other way. There is a broad mistrust of science, and there is a well-funded disinformation machine that is actively attacking science. Science is under assault from multiple directions in our current post-truth age that is rife with every type of humbug and fake news out there. Science is on the ropes and we collectively, as a society, do not have enough respect for scientific method. We believe in the same kind of superstitious, supernatural mumbo jumbo that we always have. The problem is that, more and more, we live in a scientific age in which the crises that we face must be solved through an understanding of science, climate change being a perfect example. If we don't understand it and don't respect the source of our information and our analysis, then we cannot possibly make correctly informed decisions and policies at a global level to prevent the worst effects of climate change. And we are currently ill-prepared, sociologically, psychologically, and politically, to meet that kind of threat because we are not putting enough faith in science.

So, science fiction is a way for the average person to find an understanding and respect for science. Unfortunately, the more popular science fiction has become, the more it's become divorced from its own respect for science. Now you have what is essentially science fantasy. Spaceships whipping around, traveling to other planets in hours or minutes or instantaneously—no respect whatsoever for the laws of physics. Space travel is just a catch-all for any kind of adventure fantasy that you can imagine, whether it's essentially a samurai movie, a Western, or a sorcery story. There is very little science left in science fiction, with a few notable exceptions in recent years like *The Martian*, which was wildly popular. The main character says that in order to survive he has to "science the shit out of this," and he does, and people were intrigued enough to turn that film into a hit. It's not a metaphor, it's the situation we are in. We need to science the shit out of this. We need to come to grips with what it means to be tinkering with the genome, what it means to create pathogens that could wipe us out, what it means to be changing our planet's climate so much that pathogens are moving out of places where they have been typically restricted into other territories. Plant species are dying out of one area and moving to other areas, and animals are migrating or dying out, and we are essentially precipitating the sixth great extinction in the natural history of this planet. We have essentially created a new era that scientists are now recognizing and calling the Anthropocene. So, you know, it's science and technology got us into this and it's only science and technology that will get us out of it.

RF: Is literary science fiction also getting more divorced from the science, or do you think we are still seeing a lot of respect for science in the medium?

JC: It varies by author and subgenre whether there is respect for or even interest in the science. I think there is much more interest in technology and in the ramifications of technology especially around artificial intelligence, the internet, virtual reality, and things like that. I think there is much less of the old "The Cold Equations" [written by Tom Godwin, 1954] type of hard science fiction

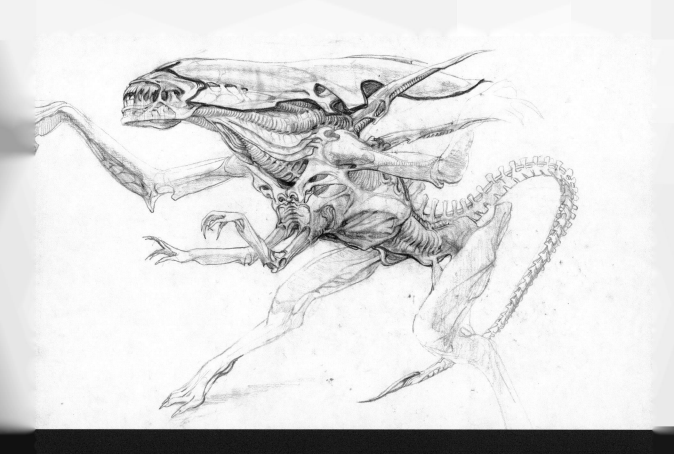

story or even the Arthur C. Clarke type of hard science fiction story with notable exceptions like *The Martian* and *Interstellar*. *Interstellar* I don't believe was based on a literary source, but that is a pop culture example.

RF: Okay, let's talk about monsters for a little bit. What do you think makes a truly great sci-fi monster?

JC: Well, I think that a truly great sci-fi monster has to be literally that: It has to be a science fiction monster. It has to come from our misuse of technology or our misunderstanding of science or natural laws and our own hubris in thinking that we can be godlike in creating some better version of ourselves or that we can control that which we barely understand when we unleash it on the world. So you take something in the real world such as GMO foods and you extrapolate that to say well what if we tinker with the genome and it gets away from us. What horrors might come out of the laboratory? So it's always

kind of a slap at human error or human hubris which, of course, goes all the way back to *Frankenstein*, to the original science fiction monster. In a way it's always sort of extolling human frailty or our inability to understand, and that's been the nature of science fiction monsters for the most part. It's our inability to really truly understand the unknown.

I think even the xenomorph from *Alien* (1979) would fall into that category. You come up against something so unknowable, so it's about the limitations of human consciousness or human knowledge. Which is interesting in the sense that science fiction is often about using the surgical instrument of our science to understand our universe better. The monsters come from our fear of the outcome of that process. The monster comes from the demonstrable effects of science on the world when it does go awry, such as nuclear weapons. So many of the science fiction monsters emerged in the late '40s, '50s, and early '60s, and it was all a result of nuclear angst. It was all around the sense of doom that comes

from having essentially learned too much and become too powerful without the wisdom to go with it. People often say that it's the idea of a chimpanzee with a machine gun. Our technological evolution has become too powerful for our sociological, emotional, and spiritual evolution.

RF: You've been responsible for creating a couple of iconic monsters yourself. How did you go about adapting Swiss artist Hans Rudi Giger's iconic xenomorph for *Aliens* and creating the Alien Queen?

JC: Well, obviously I was inspired by Giger, but as a lover of monsters and creatures, and a designer of them myself, I wanted to have my own go at it. So I took the biomechanoid concept, which was very phallic in the creature created for *Alien*, and turned it around and tried to make it female. So, I gave her very long, elegant, tapering legs and almost a kind of a high-heel look at the foot, and then she just kind of turned into this creature that was hideous and yet somehow beautiful. There were so many gestures that Giger had just created out of whole cloth: the tubes coming out of the creature's back, the long phallic head that was just pivoting on the central neck and that reminded me a little bit of a triceratops. So I took the back part of the triceratops skull with the armor frill and just ran with it and mixed it with many of Giger's biomechanoid gestures. It's not like it came to me in a dream or something. It was fairly methodical. The series of

ABOVE Early conceptual design by Cameron for the iconic battle between Ripley and the Alien Queen in *Aliens*. This piece was created before Cameron wrote his *Aliens* script.

OPPOSITE An early concept for the Alien Queen by Cameron shows its egg sack in very a different configuration from the elevated egg sack seen in the final film.

spines sticking out of its back form a kind of threat-display structure, but that is just purely an extrapolation from the tubes sticking out of Giger's alien, which I came to call the Alien Warrior.

I had to create a society or a hierarchy and a life cycle that made some sense, so if the queen was like a termite queen with her big egg sac and ovipositor creating all those eggs that Ridley Scott or Giger never account for in the original film—in fact, they did account for it, but they cut it out of the film. They had some kind of strange life cycle where some of the human hosts were encapsulated and then turned into the egg from which the facehugger emerged, but that never made a damn bit of sense to me. I figured it was fair game to chuck it out because they didn't put it in the movie. So the idea was that it was a parasitic, insect-like creature, like a digger wasp that will paralyze caterpillars or some other host and inject its eggs into them, then the eggs would hatch out. Yet it had a different life cycle. It had a two-part life cycle because the egg would give birth to a facehugger, which would then inject a second egg inside the host. So the big egg was a container for the facehugger. The facehugger would then inject its egg into a host and give birth in a parasitic way—much like a digger wasp's larva would emerge from a dead caterpillar—to the actual alien itself that would become an adult. So, presumably, somewhere in there an alien queen would emerge in the same way that bees can use hormones or some other signal to generate a queen when they need a queen. That added a layer to the life cycle that I don't think was really contemplated by Ridley and Giger, but that made sense to me. And I saw the tail as being a stinger that could be used to paralyze the prey as well.

Then the other question is: Why would you have a two-part life cycle like that? And the answer is adaptation. The digger wasp's larva does not adapt to its host, but the next generation of wasp should be more effective at attacking that species of caterpillar. So, my idea for the two-part life cycle was that when the facehugger laid its egg or embryo inside the

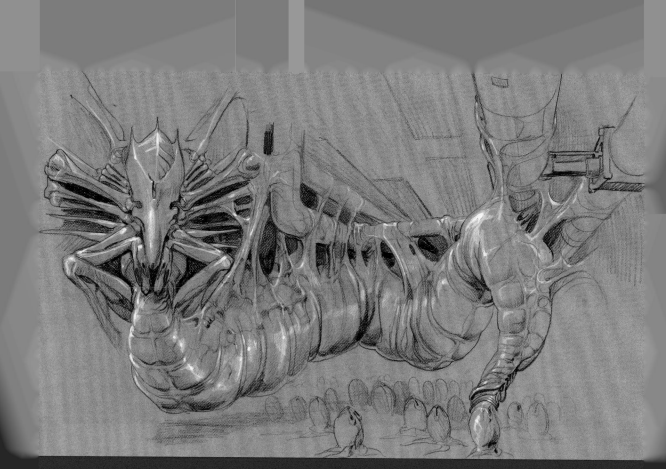

host, that allowed a process of adaptation where the emerging creature would take on aspects of the host. In the case of the alien, it came out with fingers and hands and legs and arms that were jointed with elbows and actually quite human in the general architecture of the body, but quite inhuman in the development of the head. I know the idea used in some of the subsequent films was the dog version of the alien, and I think even a cow version at one point. So the purpose of that kind of intergeneration or intermediate phase of the lifecycle was adaptation, and theoretically the creature was either genetically engineered or had just evolved naturally to adapt well to hosts anywhere. So, if you think about how you are going to take over a galaxy, that is how you do it. You have to be able to adapt to the chemistry and the morphology of any potential host population, and if you are going from planet to planet, those hosts are going to be organisms you have never seen or been exposed to before. You can't possibly show up perfectly adapted to prey on that host population without having that intermediate stage in the lifecycle. So, that was the concept.

RF: Well, your answers are a perfect example of what sets you apart from other science fiction filmmakers: You clearly know your science. You've done the research and you use commonsense application of that knowledge.

JC: Yes, it's common sense and informed by science and an understanding of biology. It's also informed by science fiction literature. I mean these are not new ideas in literature. Most of these ideas seem so revelatory to the average viewer who was not raised on science fiction literature. But for fans of science fiction literature it's more like, What took so long?

RF: It's not just the science you bring to science fiction, it's also good storytelling. I want to talk about that briefly in regards to the unity of opposites in both *The Terminator* and

Aliens. You have this incredible unity of opposites where the two main characters, in this case, the Queen Alien's and Sigourney Weaver's characters, are two mothers defending their young. And you can't find a stronger unity in opposites than that. In *Terminator* it's a pregnant woman fighting for her life and that of her unborn child against a Terminator that symbolizes death.

JC: Right, exactly. He's a skeleton, a classic death figure. And by the end, she is the mother of the future. So, those films both have this motherhood theme and this idea of the mother as the sort of avatar protector of life, or the life principle, against a death figure. And what is more of an implacable death than the Terminator or the alien? They both have that in common. The alien has the added effect of being the unknowable—the X-factor, that thing which is so strange that we can only encounter it from outside our world. Whereas the Terminator, in a way, feels very human. He is sort of the reductio ad absurdum of us and our quest to use our technology to kill better. So what better symbol of that than a mechanical skeleton? But in Ridley's film at least there was a different unity of opposites. Yes, it was a woman who was the final opponent of the alien and she prevails, but she wasn't a mother figure, she was definitely a female warrior. The alien was this kind of male, phallic, Freudian, psychosexual invader, and so really, at a subconscious level, it worked on our fear of rape, violation, and impregnation. So it all made sense. There was a beautiful unity of opposites in *Alien* itself, the first film. And I was not oblivious to all that stuff. I chose to take it into a slightly different area that was more about both mothers fighting for their own life principle. Which has nothing to do with rape or violation or any of that. That was just a different choice. I mean, you don't make the same movie twice.

RF: You told me once that the fiercest force in the universe is maternal instinct.

JC: Well, I think so. Because a mother fighting for her young will sacrifice herself. She'll take every iota of energy in her body, every defensive skill and tooth and claw that she has, and she will use it and expend herself unto death to protect her young. That is just how mothers have been hardwired throughout evolution. Whereas men will fight for other reasons. Sometimes it's pride; sometimes it's territory; sometimes it's dominance. And they'll stop if it hurts too much.

RF: Let's move to dark futures. As a writer and filmmaker, what issues does dystopian fiction allow you to explore? And what do you think is the significance of dystopian fiction to the genre as a whole?

JC: I think dystopian fiction has been a huge part of science fiction. It's always been a part of the genre, and if you think about some of the earliest works of science fiction, they were warnings about the future. H. G. Wells was warning us about the future. He was warning us about social-psychological trends and the misuse of technology in many of his stories. Where it went off the rails is when *Star Wars* came out because dystopian science fiction had been the mainstay in the '60s and '70s, and we can name all of our favorite dystopian science fiction films from that time period, many of them postapocalyptic. Then *Star Wars* came along and said, let's not do that, that's no fun. Let's just turn it all around into a big kind of neomythic Western adventure with princesses and lightsabers and instantaneous travel and make it upbeat and optimistic, even though we are fighting against an oppressive empire. It's all good clean fun and it blew up into the biggest film in movie history, and then all of a sudden science fiction was viewed completely differently by mainstream media. And you couldn't get a dystopian film made to save your life for about twenty years after that.

On the one hand, George Lucas did an enormous amount for visual effects and for science fiction in general, but he knew exactly what he

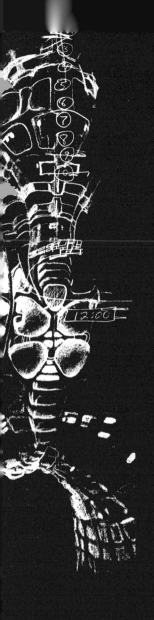

was doing. He was doing space opera. He had already done his dystopian science fiction film, *THX 1138* (1971), and it didn't make any money. So he said, I'm not going to do that again. I think *Star Wars* did an enormous service to science fiction in barging it into the mainstream pop culture and at the same time did somewhat of a disservice in that it made it less of a spotlight on that which is wrong with our present society, which is really what dystopian science fiction is about. It's about saying, what if this trend continues? What if the trend of machines watching us continues? What if the trend of weaponization continues? What if the trend of surveillance and genetic manipulation continues? You get *Brave New World*, you get *1984*. And what if the trend of out-of-control development of nuclear weapons or other weapons systems continues? Then you get *On the Beach* and any of the post-nuclear, postapocalyptic stories.

RF: When we make contact with life from other planets, do you think they'll be closest to the Na'vi of *Avatar*, the xenomorphs of *Aliens*, or the benign extraterrestrials of *The Abyss*?

JC: I don't think they will be any of the above. I think they will be colonial. I think they will be imperialists. I think they will take what they want. I think they will be superior to us. If they have a reason to come to Earth, it probably won't be us. We will probably just be in the way.

RF: So what will be the best defense against that?

JC: Well, don't broadcast. Don't let them know we are here until we get strong enough to defend ourselves. I'm not worried about some nonintelligent, nontechnological monster like the xenomorph. And the Na'vi are perfectly happy in their own jungle. They have no reason to go roaming and taking. But the history of cultural contact on Earth has always ended badly for the technologically inferior culture. They may be culturally superior, they may be spiritually superior, they

may be much better-adjusted human beings but if you have a bunch of gap-toothed, scurvy-riddled Portuguese guys that show up with cannons, armor, ships, and gunpowder, then they become ascendant, not because they are better people, but just because they have the tech. Nine times out of ten it's not even tech they've invented. There is this sense that just because aliens show up and they have the smarts to build their interstellar technology, that the guy driving the ship is the guy that had the smarts to build the technology, but that is not likely the case. Chances are the technology was developed by some benign civilization ten thousand years earlier and is ripped off by some rapacious conquering warriors. Look at the Romans. Romans didn't invent mathematics and geometry and philosophy and all that. They ripped it off from the Greeks. In fact, they just waltzed into Greece and took over. They grabbed a bunch of philosophers and mathematicians and inventors and dragged them all back to Rome and beat the crap out of them until they did what they wanted.

RF: Like we did to German scientists after World War II.

JC: It's an absurd assumption that because the aliens have evolved their technology that they must have evolved their sociology, philosophy, and spirituality that far. These guys might have ripped it off. It could be some teenager that took his dad's car keys. You don't know what the fuck you are going to deal with just because somebody steps out of a spaceship. Think about your own life. You drive a car, you might know how a car works, but most people don't. Most people don't know how a cell phone works. Most people don't understand the basics of electronics, and yet they use all this stuff all the time. It doesn't make them better people. Usually, it makes them worse people.

RF: Going back to the technology in *The Terminator*. Are you aware that the US military establishment now calls their systems for minimizing targeting error in their experimental combat fighters the Terminator Syndrome?

JC: Yes, the Skynet Syndrome and the Terminator Syndrome are things that are actually actively discussed now. At DARPA (Defense Advanced Research Projects Agency) and the Department of Defense they are having to grapple with things that were pure science fiction when I wrote *The Terminator* back in 1982. It's now imminent. Are you going to give an independent kill capability to an autonomous machine like an aerial drone or an underwater drone? Are you going to give it kill authority? And there are a lot of drivers that might cause either our military or another nation's military or terrorists to say "hell yeah" because in some situations the command and control chain might be too attenuated or you might have lost contact with the machine or you are in radio silence and you may just want to set it loose and have it do that. You may want to develop that weapon as a counter weapon to what you assume North Korea or Russia is developing. Do you think Russia is asking themselves whether or not they should do that? I don't think so. Putin has already stated publicly that the nation that develops strong artificial intelligence first will rule the world. Quote, unquote. So, it's not even whether you want to develop it or not. You have to develop it to be able to compete with the other guy. So it's pretty inevitable that every good idea and every new piece of technology that's created always gets weaponized, if there is a way to weaponize it.

RF: Did you ever imagine your ideas could have a real-world influence when you were writing that script?

JC: The fact that they actually used the term Skynet and the term Terminator? No, and I don't take a great deal of pleasure in it.

RF: Or the idea that your scenario is coming to pass in real life?

JC: Right, which begs the question, what do we do for a new Terminator movie that the world isn't already doing? The interesting thing is the areas where the world is becoming closer to what used to be science fiction and, conversely, the areas where we are just as far away as we always were. We are no closer to interstellar travel than we were back in Hugo Gernsback's day. But we are a hell of a lot closer to *Terminator*.

RF: Do you think we are doomed to a self-made apocalypse, or is there no fate but what we make for ourselves?

JC: Well, there is no fate but what we make for ourselves, but the question is, what is that fate? Science fiction can sometimes simultaneously extol the best virtues of human beings and show our worst attributes. So, what are our best attributes? We are inventive; we can science the shit out of this. We can invent our way out of this. We have that ability. We're empathic. We are compassionate. And that is part of who we are, of what we evolved to be. We have the ability to function socially together as a group, and that has been part and parcel of our rise on the planet because evolving toward a larger brain hit a wall when it got to be the maximum size that could pass through the female birth canal. And so the solution to that problem that evolution selected was postpartum development of brain size. None of the other animals do it but us. And once you understand that, you understand everything about the human species. We had to learn to be socially cohesive so that we could raise children and essentially develop their brains outside the womb—as opposed to a baby deer, which drops out, gets up on its wobbly legs, and keeps up with the herd in a couple hours. A human is keeping up with the herd in a couple of years. That's an enormous difference. And so that forced us to become socially bonded, socially cohesive, altruistic, empathetic, compassionate, oriented toward justice and conflict resolution, and all those things. The only problem is we haven't yet evolved to the next level, which is to take it beyond a tribal, internal cohesiveness. We

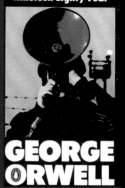

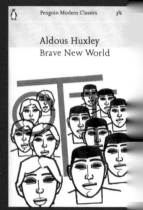

haven't evolved to be globally inclusive to all humans and we are either going to crack the code of that or we die.

RF: So you think science fiction can bridge that gap and help us?

JC: I think it can show us how it might be possible, and it can remind us that there is hope. That we innately have the ability to do it. We innately have the questing, curious, problem-solving, analytical mind and consciousness to do it. We innately have built into us the desire, and even the need, to be altruistic and compassionate. But it can also show how technology goes awry, it gets weaponized. It turns around and bites us. And so, I think science fiction, better than any other genre, can show the hope and the fear for the future.

RF: In your Terminator films, what was your biggest influence in the way you portrayed time travel? In particular, the way that Kyle Reese had to travel back in time in order for the leader of the resistance, his comrade, to be born.

JC: I would say probably Heinlein. Heinlein had written some serious and some not so serious time-travel stories that were seminal, including "'—All You Zombies—'" (1959), which is the ultimate time-travel story. In it, the main character becomes both his own mother and father through time loops. You can't beat that one. And it takes a big blackboard with a giant flowchart going in both directions to show how that all worked in that one short story.

But I think I took a classic Heinlein/Clarke time paradox approach for the time travel in *The Terminator*. Which is, somebody really smart in the future, an artificial intelligence, powerful enough to have conquered the human race, thought it was a viable idea to tinker with the time stream for its own benefit. So that is an interesting premise right there. You never meet Skynet, and the Terminator doesn't have much opinion about time travel—he is just on a mission and

doesn't care whether he gets delivered to that kill zone by a helicopter or a time machine. Kyle Reese doesn't understand the technical stuff and Sarah never really gets her mind around it. At the end of the film she is contemplating it and running in circles saying, "Well, if I don't tell you then you'll never send Kyle, then you can never be. A person can go crazy thinking about this stuff."

So, it does a very brief touchtone to the kind of grandfather paradox idea and ultimately says, "Hey, it doesn't matter. We can't know that and that is above our pay grade. All we have to do is do what makes sense to us in the moment." And, I think that ultimately all time-travel stories boil down to one thing: Is there free will or not? Are things preordained or not? I think that things are not preordained, but is that a human fantasy? Is that a delusion that we all live under? Is that our satisfying answer to sort of sing ourselves a lullaby so we don't have to worry about it? The Hindu religion believes in a kind of ultimate fatality, that everything is preordained unto the end of the universe. Then there's not fuck-all you can do about it. I don't find that to be very satisfying. Because then you are just like pixels in a giant CG movie. You don't have any choice, you are just part of the show. So, who created the show and who is it being shown to? And who is appreciating this great work of art? Or is it all just fucking pointless?

RF: Well, we don't want to think that, especially in storytelling.

JC: Well, exactly. So, the whole nature of the Judeo-Christian, Abrahamic God approach to theology is you have a choice. God gave you a choice. You have free will. Now, you are probably going to fuck it up and you're probably going to go to hell, but you are going to exercise your free will and you're going to pay the consequences. So, that is kind of a profound idea. And that is what we all grew up with and it sort of gives us comfort, and we'd feel that suddenly we were in a totalitarian state versus a democratic system if our free will was taken from us.

16

REESE LEAPS INTO FRAME, STOPS FOR A MOMENT BEHIND A PIECE OF STANDING WALL AS A SEARCHLIGHT SWEEPS STRAIGHT TOWARD CAMERA.

AS SEARCHLIGHT PASSES, REESE DARTS FORWARD, EXITING LEFT

— NO EFFECTS

17

DOLLY W/ REESE AS HE PASSES WINDOW A MOMENT BEFORE SEARCHLIGHT BEAM STABS THROUGH.
REESE REACHES A BREAK IN THE WALL AND PAUSES FOR HIS TEAM-MATE TO CATCH UP.
— NO EFFECTS

RF: When I was writing the novelization for *The Terminator*, it occurred to me that you were creating a situation dramatically where there could be a dance between human will and fate. That they were both influencing each other and that one was not necessarily dominant over the other.

JC: Well, look. The moment in *Terminator 2* where Sarah stabs the knife into the table after she has just carved "no fate" into the table is the moment that she goes off script—the moment that she is no longer fulfilling her destiny. Her predestination was to be the mother of John, to train him and keep him safe. That was her job and that was all she was supposed to do. But the moment she stabs the knife into the table and goes to assassinate Dyson, she is exercising free will.

She fucks everything up. In the process of which she actually changes the world.

RF: In the original film, there's a moment where she decides that she wants to fight the Terminator and not keep running from it. It's an aspect of the story that was reduced in the finished film but was in the novel.

JC: Right, and it became the nucleus of the second film. The whole thing of her going to Cyberdyne and trying to blow it up was originally part of the first film. In the movie, Sarah and Kyle just randomly wind up in a computer factory, and the remains of the Terminator just randomly fall into the hands of the computer experts and they pass it down to the guys that you see in the second film. But obviously, you and I know there is a lot more to that. She actually looked up

Cyberdyne Systems in a telephone book. The same way the Terminator looked up her number. And that's why they were making the pipe bombs. She was going to Cyberdyne and she was going to blow it up. She was going to flip the script and play the same trick on Skynet that Skynet had tried to play on John Connor, which is, I'm going to take you out before you are born. So there was a symmetry in that story. Now, I wasn't able to pull it off, I didn't have the budget. The scenes sucked. We wound up taking them out of the movie, and we made a much simpler story where we just left her in this kind of existential state at the end where she didn't quite know what she was supposed to do. But by *Terminator 2* we see that she ultimately made the right decisions.

Going back and amending something I just said, at the end of *Terminator 2*, we took out the fact that she actually did successfully prevent judgment day. So we don't know at the end what the film says about free will. There is no resolution on whether it exists, but she has hope. She

has hope because not only did she exercise free will, but she saw the Terminator exercise free will. And if a machine can understand the value of human life enough to change and act in accordance with that belief, then it has free will. Which I think is very interesting because up until then the Terminator had no free will. It could have been sent to kill John Connor and would have done so without batting an eye. On the other hand, it was captured by John Connor in the future and reprogrammed to be a protector. In which case, it did the task with no particular emotional attachment. But it was a learning computer, and because it was learning and copying human behavior, at what point does the copying become its reality? At what point does the Terminator actually act on his own? It's the point where he creates a workaround to his own programming that says he can't self-terminate. He basically saves the human race from the rise of Skynet by handing Sarah the controls to put him into the molten steel. That is his moment

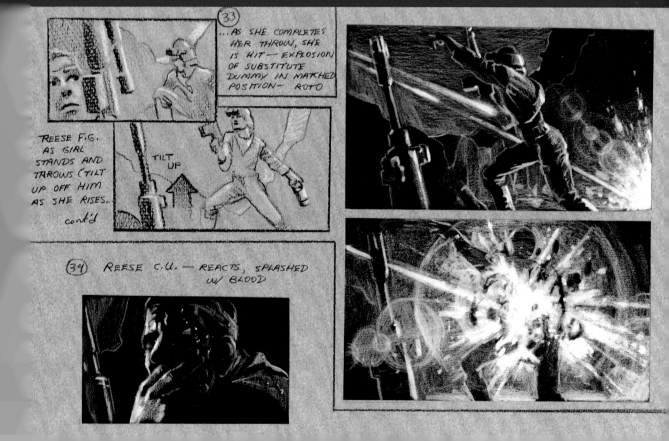

33 ...AS SHE COMPLETES HER THROW, SHE IS HIT — EXPLOSION OF SUBSTITUTE DUMMY IN MATCHED POSITION — ROTO

REESE F.G. AS GIRL STANDS AND THROWS (TILT UP OFF HIM AS SHE RISES.. cont'd

TILT UP

34 REESE C.U. — REACTS, SPLASHED W/ BLOOD

where he defies his fate. And I think that is pro-found, at least as profound as a movie should ever be.

RF: Do you think that darker representations of artificial intelligence in science fiction could make the public overly cautious about AI and its potential benefits for humanity?

JC: I don't think you can be overly cautious. We have this tendency to run these enormous social experiments with no control group. It's not like there is a second Earth where people aren't developing AI that we can go back to. We just run these experiments on ourselves, and it's not like there is even anybody running the whole thing. It's just a bunch of companies competing with each other, mindlessly charging ahead at accelerating rates toward what might be a cliff. There is no caution, no mechanism in place to control it, no government that wants to take on the gigantic tech companies that are driving the economy and rein them in. I've talked to AI scientists, and they all sound like atomic scientists from the thirties. They were going to create unlimited energy for the human race and solve poverty and solve starvation and all that. They were not thinking that within five years, the energy they were developing would be used to incinerate humans.

RF: Do you think robots should be made to look human like in *Blade Runner* (1982), or should arti-ficial life always look functional and inhuman so that people don't emotionally connect with machines as real personalities?

JC: I think there are so many roboticists right now that are working on creating a human emo-tional affect in machines so that they can perform functions such as caregiving for the elderly, the sick, for children, and for teaching and things like that. It's inevitable that machines will resemble us. We are going to create them to look like us, be smart enough to act like us, and be emotional enough to emote like us. So they will basically be us, but they will be slaves. What we want is

another disposable, discountable population. We want slaves. We want humans that we can con-trol. That is where all this is going, and I confronted a couple of top AI scientists about it at this very high-level conclave. Somebody asked the ques-tion, "What is your goal?" And one of the scientists answered, "Our goal, simply stated, is to create a person." So I put up my hand, and they all knew I was the Terminator guy, right? So, immediately they start to laugh the minute I put up my hand. I said, "Look, I don't want to be stereotypically negative here, but what I'm hearing is that you want to create a machine that has personhood. A machine that has not only an analytical con-sciousness, but a sense of identity. An independent being in its own right. And I think you've also stated that your goal is to make it at least as intelligent as we are if not more so." And he said, "That is correct." I said, "How do you keep it from turning against us?" And of course, every-body laughed. I said, "No, I'm serious. How would you keep it from having its own agenda and that agenda being counter to our own agenda?" And he said, "It is very simple. We just give it the goals that we want it to have." I said, "Oh, well, this is not a new concept. We've had this concept for thousands of years. We have a name for it. It's called slavery. How long do you think that a machine that is more intelligent than us is going to want to be a slave?" Man, they didn't like that.

RF: I can imagine. But those are good questions. Those are questions that they should be asking.

JC: Yes, it's a good question, especially because my prior question had been about emotions. I said, "Do you think it is necessary for a machine that has a sense of its own *ego logus*, its own sense of survival and identity, to have emo-tions?" And I said, "Before you answer, let me say specifically what I mean by that. We don't have emotions because they are flaws, we have emo-tions because they serve a purpose. Nature has selected emotions for a reason: to create cohe-sive social bonds, interactions, interdependences that have benefited us. They are adaptive. They make us who we are, and who we are is the

In the Year of Darkness, 2029, the rulers of this planet devised the ultimate plan.
They would reshape the Future by changing the Past.
The plan required something that felt no pity. No pain. No fear. Something unstoppable.
They created 'THE TERMINATOR'

THE TERMINATOR 18

ABOVE Theatrical poster for *The Terminator*.

ascendant consciousness on the planet. Do you think that you can create such a consciousness with a sense of identity, purpose, and the will to survive that will not just shut itself off or become suicidal or depressed without emotions? And they said, "No, we think it has to have emotions." So, now you have an emotional slave. Not only are you taking its freedom but it can feel the consequences of that.

RF: Did you ever seriously consider embarking on an outer space exploration?

JC: Oh, absolutely. Well, not an exploration, but I wanted to make a film in low Earth orbit at the Mir space station. I pursued that and went into contract with Energia, the Russian state-owned company that was in charge of that at the time. I actually had a contract to go into cosmonaut

training and to train to go to the Mir space station. I was going to take my 3-D camera with me and do an extended stay and even an EVA [spacewalk], believe it or not. I said, "When I'm on an expedition I don't sit on a dive boat for two months and watch everybody go into the water but me. I go in the water. I'm helmet trained. So, I'm good to go, just train me and I'll jump in that Orlan suit and I'll go on an EVA and I'll film it." And they were fine with that. They added a lot of money to the contract, but I made the down payment and I started my cosmonaut training. Then they ran out of money, and the Mir space station deorbited because they didn't have the funds to pay for the reboost mission.

So, the Mir came down but the Russians still had their hooks deep into NASA because they built half the International Space Station and they still operate it jointly. So the Energia guy said, "Hey no problem, you can't go to Mir, but you can go to our side of the International Space Station." So, then I just went to NASA and said, "Hey, I'm going up on the Russian side. Do you guys want to be in on this? I'm going to make a film about how great the Russians are. I'd rather make a film about how great the international cooperation is. I can't do that if I can't get past the hatch into your part of the space station." And they came back and said, "Ah, yeah, we can support that mission. What do you have in mind?" So it actually went along pretty far down the line until the *Columbia* disaster in 2003, and at that point everybody just retrenched. It's like the elastic band snapped and all the fantasies of civilians being taken into space by NASA or the Russians or whoever got shut down. And then, you know, it relaxed over time when they started flying again, but by then I had already started moving on to *Avatar* and I just never went back to it.

RF: One of the other things you do besides film-making is deep-sea diving. You've gone to the deepest place in the ocean, the Mariana Trench, but you also do skin diving at shallower depths. You once told me that it's the closest you can come on Earth to exploring an alien planet.

JC: Absolutely. All you have to do is look at a reef and imagine all the creatures bigger, and you're in an alien world. I mean, you *are* in an alien world. You don't even have to imagine the creatures bigger. You look at a cuttlefish or a polychaete worm or a Christmas tree worm or any of these animals. They are stunning. They are amazing. They communicate with light. They're biolumi-nescent. They are multicolored, multilimbed. They operate differently than us. They live in a different medium than us. They breathe differently than us and they share our world with us. And they are much older than we are. We are the Johnny-come-latelies up here breathing air and walking around on the land. So, to me, you can experience an alien world anytime you want just by holding your breath or slapping on a scuba tank.

RF: Some suggest that to be a good story-teller you have to write about firsthand experiences: "Write what you know." This is difficult but not impossible with science fic-tion. For example, many sci-fi writers are actual scientists, a few have actually been in space. Is it harder to write good science fiction than any other genre?

JC: No, I don't think so. I think it is as hard to write good sci-fi as it is to write good crime drama or good legal drama, if you don't know your stuff. Now you don't have to be a scientist to understand science. Anybody that can afford a subscription to *Scientific American* can become a well-rounded layman who understands sci-ence. In fact, I would even submit that, in a world in which most of the major policy deci-sions require an understanding of science, our democracy is at risk if our legislatures don't know science and we as a citizenry don't know science. So, we all need to fucking know some science. So, with that as a given, the science fiction writer only needs to know a little bit more science, or the same science, as the read-ership, but be a little bit better at putting the pieces together from a story perspective to show people something that they hadn't thought of before.

But I think another significant point is the number of people who went into science careers as a result of being influenced by science fiction. Because the same type of curious, extrapolating consciousness that allows you to imagine, as Arthur C. Clarke did, the geosynchronous satellite or the space elevator or whatever, is the same type of mind that allows you to imagine a new type of technology or a particular type of mole-cule or chemical bond or physics equation and be good at theoretical science. The same type of curious mind that would have loved that type of fiction as a kid is the same kind of curious mind that makes a good lab scientist or field scientist who wants to go out and find an answer. They are detectives. They are curious. They want to put the pieces together. They want to bring back a little piece of the unknown and show it to

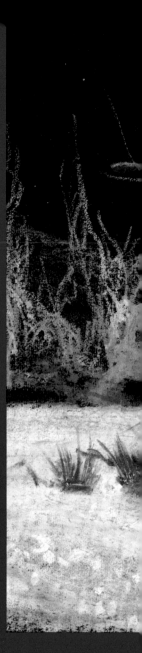

ABOVE This early concept by a nineteen-year-old James Cameron features bioluminescent flora and fauna reminiscent of *Avatar*.

everybody and say, "I've figured this out." And so that type of mind often gravitates toward reading science fiction as a kid or as a teenager and then is actually attracted to working in space science or astronomy or any of the sciences. So you talk to these guys and they all know the science fiction reference points. But their takeaway obviously is more optimistic than sort of dystopian. They don't see the hubris of science or the human arrogance constantly shown in science fiction. They don't take the Cassandran warnings. Science fiction always oscillates in a schizophrenic way between highly optimistic and exciting and adventurous to warning us that we are all doomed. Often in the same story.

ALIEN LIFE

BY GARY K. WOLFE

FOR AS LONG AS PEOPLE HAVE BEEN AWARE of the existence of other worlds, they have speculated about who or what might live there. The ancient Greek and Roman philosophers and poets—Epicurus, Lucretius, Plutarch, and others—thought there were countless inhabited worlds, and as long ago as the second century CE the Syrian-Greek author Lucian wrote *A True History*, describing a trip to the Moon, where battles are fought with giant three-headed vultures, mushroom-men, and enormous fleas. The story also included what is probably the earliest description of interplanetary war, between the King of the Moon and the King of the Sun. It sounds a lot like one of the very first works of science fiction, except that there's not much in it that we would today recognize as any sort of science—the adventurers are simply blown to the moon by a whirl-wind—and the whole thing was largely a joke, a parody of the exaggerated travelers' tales of the period. It was, in its own classical way, the equivalent in its time of Douglas Adams's popular science fiction comedy *The Hitchhiker's Guide to the Galaxy*.

But the idea of life on the moon persisted, in moral fables if not serious scientific speculation. The astronomer Johannes Kepler wrote a story about it, *Somnium*, in 1608, as did the French author Cyrano de Bergerac in his satirical novel *The Other World: The Comical History of the States and Empires of the World of the Moon*, published in 1657, two years after his death. In *The First Men in the Moon* (1901), H. G. Wells has his explorers captured by an insect-like race of moon people called Selenites, and the next year the same thing happened to the travelers in Georges Méliès's *A Trip to the Moon* (possibly the very first science fiction movie and supposedly inspired by Jules Verne's 1865 novel *From the Earth to the Moon*, although it has more in common with Wells). Verne's adventurers never actually landed on the moon but concluded from their observations that it was probably a lifeless ball of rock. They were right, of course.

Fortunately, a few centuries earlier, the astronomers Copernicus and Galileo had begun to describe other planets of the solar system in something resembling the modern

scientific sense, an endeavor that would give writers in the nineteenth and twentieth centuries whole new worlds to play in. For many such authors, the first and most likely candidate for life turned out to be the planet Mars. It was these early Mars-set stories that first began to define modern ideas of what aliens might be like, or at least what they might be good for when it comes to telling stories. At one extreme, aliens became terri-fying, vampire-like monsters who only wanted to conquer and possibly eat us, while at the other they became beautiful inno-cents who needed our help, with most others falling somewhere in between. Interestingly enough, these two extremes were laid out in two very popular stories published only fif-teen years apart.

The alien as a scary, conquering monster was described almost definitively by H. G. Wells in *The War of the Worlds*, published in 1897. It later became the source of several films (one directed by Steven Spielberg in 2005) and what is probably the most famous radio broadcast of all time, by Orson Welles in 1938. In Wells's original story, the invading Martians have superior technology—those

ABOVE A 1962 book cover for the Penguin Books edition of H. G. Wells's *War of the Worlds*.

OPPOSITE Tom Cruise comes face-to-face with malevolent extraterrestrials in director Steven Spielberg's *War of the Worlds* (2005).

famous tripods and heat rays—but are themselves pretty ugly:

> A big greyish rounded bulk, the size, perhaps, of a bear, was rising slowly and painfully out of the cylinder. As it bulged up and caught the light, it glistened like wet leather. Two large dark-colored eyes were regarding me steadfastly. The mass that framed them, the head of the thing, was rounded, and had, one might say, a face. There was a mouth under the eyes, the lipless brim of which quivered and panted, and dripped saliva. The whole creature heaved and pulsated convulsively. A lank tentacular appendage gripped the edge of the cylinder, another swayed in the air.

This may seem the stuff of horror stories, but there were a lot of weighty ideas behind

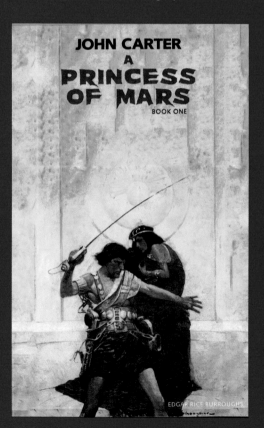

JOHN CARTER
A
PRINCESS OF MARS
BOOK ONE

EDGAR RICE BURROUGHS

Wells's monsters. For one thing, his novel came toward the end of a long tradition of "invasion stories"—a genre that gained huge popularity in Wells's native England after a best-selling 1871 story by George Chesney called "The Battle of Dorking," in which Britain is invaded by various other countries (it's no accident that we use the term *aliens* to describe foreigners as well as creatures from outer space). For another, Wells was interested in how England had built its colonial empire largely through superior technology and wondered what it might be like if the tables were turned. Finally, he was interested in Darwinian evolution; later in the novel, his narrator points out that humans "are just in the beginning of the evolution that the Martians have worked out. They have become practically mere brains." In other words, Wells saw aliens as an opportunity for social commentary, and not merely for their scare value.

Fifteen years later, the American writer Edgar Rice Burroughs didn't have much social commentary in mind at all when he serialized *Under the Moons of Mars* in a pulp magazine (later to be published in book form as *A Princess of Mars* and much later the source of the 2009 movie *John Carter*). Burroughs's novel begins almost as a Western, with hero John Carter hiding out from Apaches in an Arizona cave when he suddenly finds himself magically transported to Mars, known by its inhabitants as Barsoom, where the lower gravity gives him near-superpowers. He first meets the Hulk-like Green Martians, fifteen feet tall and with four arms, but soon falls in love with the gorgeous Red Martian Princess Dejah Thoris, who barely seems alien at all—at least until we learn that she lays eggs. Dejah, who eventually marries Carter and shows up in several later volumes in Burroughs's hugely successful Mars series, is often barely clothed and more often in mortal danger, from which Carter has to

LEFT Cover for the Ostrich Books edition of Edgar Rice Burroughs's swashbuckling science fiction classic, *A Princess of Mars*.

OPPOSITE Theatrical poster for Howard Hawks's *The Thing from Another World* (1951).

repeatedly rescue her. She is, in fact, the exact opposite of H. G. Wells's Martians—she is a beautiful alien who needs our help.

Needless to say, Wells's version of alien life eventually turned out to be a lot more popular on pulp magazine covers, in comics, and especially in the monster B movies of the 1950s, although the idea of beautiful alien princesses never entirely went away. But by the 1930s, some writers were already growing a bit tired of these clichés and began inventing a much wider variety of aliens. Stanley Weinbaum's 1934 story "A Martian Odyssey" really opened up the discussion: He introduced a whole zoo of Martian life-forms, from the usual tentacled creatures, to an intelligent bird-like being who befriends the hero, to creatures shaped like barrels and some who even excrete bricks (turns out they are silicon rather than carbon-based life-forms). This introduced the idea not only that some aliens might be friendly or helpful or even cute, but also that they might just be really *different*, neither humanoid nor monstrous—and that some of them might simply be indifferent to us.

Only a few years later, the influential editor and author John W. Campbell Jr. explored almost the opposite idea: What if aliens looked *just like us*, or could take on the physical forms of people we know? "Who Goes There?" describes just such a creature invading an Antarctic research station, making it almost impossible for the scientists there to know who was real and who wasn't. Published in 1938, it became one of the most famous of all science fiction horror stories and was later filmed twice: in 1951 as *The Thing from Another World* and in 1982 as *The Thing*, director John Carpenter's bloody and chilling take on the tale. A prequel to Carpenter's film, also named *The Thing*, was released in 2011. The idea that you or someone you know might be taken over or replaced by a hostile alien intelligence proved to be one of science

NATURAL OR SUPERNATURAL ?

THE THING

from another world !

HOWARD HAWKS' *Astounding* MOVIE

fiction's most enduring metaphors. Robert A. Heinlein's 1951 novel *The Puppet Masters*—in which the invaders are slug-like creatures who attach themselves to the back of the neck, turning the victim into a "puppet"—made explicit comparisons with Communism, an ideology that was striking fear into the hearts of the American public in the early '50s, at the beginning of the Cold War. Jack Finney's *The Body Snatchers*, published not in a pulp magazine but in the very mainstream *Collier's* in 1954, described alien "pods" that drift to Earth and replace

COLLIER'S
MAGAZINE
called it
"THE NIGHTMARE
THAT THREATENS
THE WORLD"

ALLIED ARTISTS
presents

INVASION OF THE
BODY
SNATCHERS

FILMED IN
SUPERSCOPE

starring
KEVIN McCARTHY

people with exact replicas. Filmed no fewer than four times (the best of which is arguably the original 1956 *Invasion of the Body Snatchers*), it could be viewed as illustrating the dangers of any sort of excessive conformity. In fact, some viewed the body snatchers as representing Communism, while others saw them as the exact opposite—a comment on the *anti*-Communist crusades of the McCarthy period, when so many people simply went along with the hysteria. Finney himself denied any political meaning, but the story remains an excellent example of science fiction's capacity for social commentary.

As popular as invasion-of-earth stories have been, there are plenty in which we ourselves are the invaders, or at least the interlopers. Films like *Avatar* (2009) reflected environmental concerns, with the peaceful alien society and lush environment disrupted by human greed. Stories such as Joe Haldeman's *The Forever War* (1974) and Ursula K. Le Guin's "The Word for World is Forest" (1972)—both of which deal

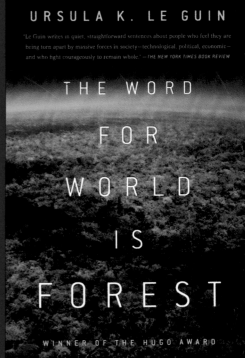

URSULA K. LE GUIN

"Le Guin writes in quiet, straightforward sentences about people who feel they are being torn apart by massive forces in society—technological, political, economic— and who fight courageously to remain whole." —*THE NEW YORK TIMES BOOK REVIEW*

THE WORD

FOR

WORLD

IS

FOREST

WINNER OF THE HUGO AWARD

ARKADY & BORIS
STRUGATSKY
ROADSIDE PICNIC

"A TRULY SUPERB TALE... YOU WON'T FORGET IT"—THEODORE STURGEON

novels, Arkady and Boris Strugatsky's *Roadside Picnic* (published in 1971 and loosely filmed as *Stalker* in 1979 by acclaimed Russian director Andrei Tarkovsky), aliens who have visited Earth—completely unseen by anyone—leave behind mysterious "zones" with strange artifacts that seem to have almost supernatural powers, but that no one can begin to understand; as one character explains, we're like the insects and birds trying hopelessly to make sense of the remains of a roadside picnic: "apple cores, candy wrappers, charred remains of the campfire, cans, bottles" left behind by humans. In author Stanislaw Lem's *Solaris*

with our inability to understand alien cultures—were written partly in response to the Vietnam War. But the aliens seemed far less sympathetic in Robert A. Heinlein's 1959 novel *Starship Troopers* (filmed by Paul Verhoeven in 1997); they are giant arachnids, called Bugs, and the novel itself promotes the importance of military preparedness and discipline. Orson Scott Card's novel *Ender's Game* (1985; filmed in 2015) also features insect-like "Buggers," who first appear as pretty traditional monster-invaders, but by the end of the novel we realize that (as in *The Forever War*) a simple misunderstanding contributed to the war, and wiping out an entire intelligent species is basically genocide. Eventually, it seems, science fiction writers came to the realization that aliens are people, too.

Unless they aren't. Another science fiction tradition suggests that we might never be able to fully understand alien minds, simply because they are so—well, *alien*. In one of the great Russian science fiction

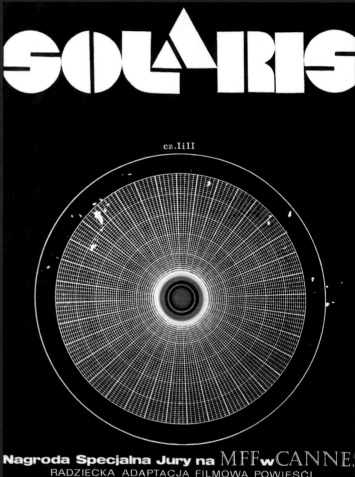

SOLARIS

cz.I i II

Nagroda Specjalna Jury na MFF w CANNES
RADZIECKA ADAPTACJA FILMOWA POWIEŚCI
STANISLAWA LEMA
REŻYSERIA: ANDRIEJ TARKOWSKI
W rolach głównych: Donatas Banionis, Natalia Bondarczuk, Juri Jarvet
Produkcja Mosfilm

In space no one can hear you scream.

ABOVE Theatrical poster for *Alien* (1979) featuring the iconic tagline "In space no one can hear you scream."

OPPOSITE The theatrical poster for *E.T. the Extra-Terrestrial* (1982) featuring art inspired by Michelangelo's *The Creation of Adam*.

stand mainly for *ideas*. An effective alien in a movie is largely a matter of suggestive design, like H. R. Giger's brilliantly conceived biomechanical monster in director Ridley Scott's *Alien* (1979). But when we regard science fiction as a way of asking questions about the universe, then the alien becomes a puzzle: How did it evolve and where? Why does it need all those teeth? How does it function as an organism in its environment? Hal Clement, a writer known for his creation of bizarre alien life-forms in novels like *Mission of Gravity* (1954), often began by describing the details of an imaginary planet, such as its orbit, distance from its sun, and even shape, and then logically extrapolated what sort of life might evolve there. The centipede-like aliens on his planet Mesklin are that way because they evolved to survive the huge gravitational stresses of living on a disc-shaped planet with variable gravity. For Clement and the many writers he influenced, an alien was as much a thought experiment as an exotic creature.

And that may be one important reason why aliens are so useful for telling stories. On the one hand, they invite us to think about everything from how biology works to how our own societies treat those unlike ourselves. On the other, they can simply scare the daylights out of us, or they can push our sentimental buttons, as in films like Steven Spielberg's *E.T. the Extra-Terrestrial*. Either way, aliens have provided science fiction with one of its most enduring and powerful images of the Other, and with one of its most provocative questions: whether or not we are really alone in the universe.

But do we really *want* there to be aliens? "Two possibilities exist," wrote the great science fiction author Arthur C. Clarke. "Either we are alone in the Universe or we are not. Both are equally terrifying."

(published in 1961 and filmed in 1972 by Tarkovsky and again in 2002 by Steven Soderbergh), the alien intelligence is an entire *ocean*, nearly covering the planet Solaris. Despite years of research, humans are never able to understand how the ocean thinks, or why it does what it does. A linguist character in Ted Chiang's "Story of Your Life" (filmed as *Arrival* in 2016) does manage to learn the aliens' language but finds that it changes her entire perception of reality and of time. Even so, we never learn why the aliens came or why they suddenly depart.

As should be apparent by now, science fiction uses aliens to comment on social problems, political issues, philosophical questions, or psychological states, and in all these cases, these extraterrestrial beings

A STEVEN SPIELBERG FILM
E.T.
THE EXTRA-TERRESTRIAL
HE IS AFRAID.
HE IS TOTALLY ALONE.
HE IS 3,000,000 LIGHT YEARS FROM HOME.

STEVEN SPIELBERG

INTERVIEW BY JAMES CAMERON

STEVEN SPIELBERG'S UNPARALLELED CAREER has spanned five decades and encompassed every imaginable genre, but it is to the science fiction genre that the director has returned most often, creating enthralling modern classics such as *Close Encounters of the Third Kind* (1977), *E.T. the Extra-Terrestrial* (1982), *Jurassic Park* (1993) and its sequel, *The Lost World: Jurassic Park* (1997), *A.I. Artificial Intelligence* (2001), *Minority Report* (2002), and *War of the Worlds* (2005). His latest feature, the dazzling adaptation of Ernest Cline's best-selling novel *Ready Player One*, will see him depict an entirely new virtual reality universe on screen—one that closely mirrors our own. In a wide-ranging conversation, Spielberg and James Cameron discuss the lasting legacy of Stanley Kubrick—the visionary *2001: A Space Odyssey* filmmaker who became Spielberg's close friend and confidant—as well as the dangers posed by artificial intelligence, and the fears that have fueled the writer/director/producer's unbridled imagination since his early childhood.

JAMES CAMERON: Most filmmakers my age and younger would say that you were the guy right ahead of them that blew their minds and made them want to do what they do. You created a vision of cinema that I don't think had existed before.

STEVEN SPIELBERG: Well, there's always a guy ahead of all of us. There's a whole bunch of guys ahead of me. George Pal, Stanley Kubrick. Willis O'Brien. I think what inflamed my imagination when I was a kid was simply fear. I needed to do something to protect myself against everything that I was afraid of, which was most everything when it got dark.

My parents felt that television—and this is back in the early '50s—was the worst influence on any child. I don't know how they knew this before the [Marshall] McLuhan era, but they somehow knew this. So they prevented me from watching television. I could only watch, like, Jackie Gleason, *The Honeymooners*. Or Sid Caesar, [*Your*] *Show of Shows*. But I couldn't watch *Dragnet*, or *M Squad*, or any of those really cool detective series in the '50s.

JC: So, you never got terrified by the flying monkeys in *The Wizard of Oz*?

SS: Oh, I did. I was terrified by that. And I was terrified by the forest fire in *Bambi*. That might have scared me more than the devil that comes out of the mountain in *Fantasia*. But I think because I was kind of media-starved by my parents doing what they thought was right, I started to imagine my own shows. If I couldn't watch television, I would just dream up something for myself to enjoy.

JC: You started making short films?

SS: Yeah. Well, long before that, I just started dreaming. I did a lot of sketching. Terrible sketches, but I used to sketch a lot of scary pictures.

JC: You were processing the world back out in the form of something visual.

SS: Yeah. It always had to do with a pencil and a piece of paper, and of course later the 8mm movie camera.

JC: I remember when I saw *Mysterious Island* in the third grade. I raced home and started doing my own version of *Mysterious Island*. I think that's the creative impulse. You take it in and [then want to] create [your] own version of it.

SS: I think when I first saw *Earth vs. the Flying Saucers* at a movie theater, and you couldn't see the saucer men because they were covered in large masks that were a part of their

OPPOSITE Steven Spielberg on the set of *James Cameron's Story of Science Fiction*. Photo Credit: Michael Moriatis/ AMC

SS: I think it all started with the atomic bomb going off in Hiroshima and Nagasaki.

The first real influence were the Japanese. Certainly Toho's *Godzilla* [1954] was the first film really to trade on a kind of cultural, national fear of what had already been perpetrated on a country. From that moment on, everything that either came out of Tokyo Bay or anything that came out of the night sky was aggressive, hostile, and took no prisoners. I had my fill of that as a kid. I saw all the B-horror films. I saw all the Allied Artists horror films. I saw the Monogram horror films. I saw the Hammer films. Everything. And I couldn't find a decent alien that made me feel like I wanted to get to know him or her better. All the aliens were out to destroy the human race.

JC: And we always beat them at the end, which was our way of saying that human cleverness and courage will overcome these monsters created by science. It was a way of keeping the boogeyman of nuclear war at bay.

SS: Exactly. It's vanquishing any hostile threat. You can equate the ending of most science fiction movies in the '50s to most World War II John Wayne movies in the '40s and '50s.

JC: It was atomic destruction and Communism mixed together, and it all had to be vanquished.

SS: It had to be vanquished. And so, the Red Menace was the angry red planet. And then Mars suddenly became an enemy—and not a wonderment. My father was the one that introduced me to the cosmos. He's the one who built—from a big cardboard roll that you roll rugs on—a 2-inch reflecting telescope with an Edmund Scientific kit that he had sent away for. [He] put this telescope together, and then I saw the moons of Jupiter. It was the first thing he pointed out to me. I saw the rings of Saturn around Saturn. I'm six, seven years old when this all happened.

JC: You spent a lot of time staring at the sky?

ABOVE Theatrical poster for *Godzilla, King of the Monsters!* (1956).
OPPOSITE TOP The Mothership arrives in Spielberg's *Close Encounters of the Third Kind* (1977).

exo-suits—there was one scene where they removed the mask from an extraterrestrial that one of the soldiers shoots. I was terrified by seeing the face. I did the same thing. I went home, and I started drawing iterations of the face—not to calm myself down but to make it scarier than the filmmakers had. I would make it scarier than [the one] they had scared me [with].

JC: Well, you scared the crap out of everybody with *Jaws*. Right? You know monsters. And aliens are sometimes monsters. But not always. You [took an] alternate view of aliens when you did *Close Encounters*.

SS: A lot of time looking at the sky. The working title of *E.T.* was *Watch the Skies*. Which is sort of the last line from *The Thing [From Another World*, 1951]. I just remember looking at the sky because of the influence of my father, and saying, only good should come from that. If it ain't an ICBM coming from the Soviet Union, only good should come from beyond our gravitational hold.

JC: He was kind of a visionary.

SS: He was a visionary about that, yet he read all the *Analog*. Those paperbacks? And *Amazing Stories*, the paperbacks of that. I used to read that along with him. Sometimes, he'd read those books to me, those little tabloids to me at night.

JC: [Isaac] Asimov, [Robert A.] Heinlein, all those guys were all published in those pulp magazines.

SS: They were all published in those magazines, and a lot of them were optimists. They weren't always calculating our doom. They were finding ways to open up our imagination and get us to dream and get us to discover and

get us to contribute to the greater good. Those were the stories, and just looking up at the sky, that got me to realize, if I ever get a chance to make a science fiction movie, I want those guys to come in peace.

JC: And you did exactly that. Your dad took you to watch a meteor shower once, right?

SS: He did. It was a Leonid shower. I only know what the shower was because over the years, my dad keeps reminding me which shower it was! But I was very young. We were living in Camden, New Jersey, so that must mean I was about five. He woke me up in the middle of the night—it's scary when your dad walks into your bedroom, and it's still dark, and he says, "Come with me." That's freaky when you're a kid! He took me to a knoll somewhere in New Jersey, and there were hundreds of people lying on picnic blankets.

JC: That scene is in *Close Encounters*. It's the same scene.

SS: Absolutely. I put the scene in *Close Encounters*. I got out there, and we lay down on his Army knapsack, and we looked up at the sky.

Every 30 seconds or so, there was a brilliant flash of light that streaked across the sky. A couple of times, some of those objects broke up into three or four pieces.

JC: You have a single light that splits into multiple lights and goes past everybody . . .

SS: In *Close Encounters*, yeah. All this stuff that's imprinted when you're very young, you don't want to divest yourself of it. I think one of the most important things as a filmmaker, at least of the kind of awe-and-wonder-type

stories that we're both attracted to, is to stay that kid. Part of that means fighting off the natural urge of cynicism as we take everything in. It's a battle. It continues to be a struggle for me to want to look on the bright side.

JC: You've done two incredible, influential films on the idea of first contact. Obviously *Close Encounters* led to *E.T.*, which I think of as kind of *Close Encounters 2*, the more personal [story].

SS: I think of it the same way, which is why I [initially] took the *E.T.* script to Columbia [Pictures]. I

ABOVE In a scene from *Close Encounters of the Third Kind*, aliens welcome the people of Earth onto the Mothership.

OPPOSITE Elliott (Henry Thomas) and E.T. make their escape from sinister government stooges in *E.T. the Extra-Terrestrial*.

thought I owed it to them since they gave me the financing to do *Close Encounters*. I thought, I'm not going to go running off to Universal [Studios] with a script about extraterrestrials. So, I took it to Columbia, and when they passed, that's when I brought it to Universal.

JC: With *E.T.*, you took many of those first contact themes and just made it very family-centric, or kid-centric, I should say.

SS: *E.T.* was never meant to be a movie about an extraterrestrial. It was meant to be a story about my mom and dad getting a divorce. I started writing a story—not a script per se—about what it was like when your parents divide the family up, and they move to different states. I was working on that before I made *Close Encounters*. When I did the scene of the little alien, Puck, coming out of the mothership and doing the Kodaly hand signs in *Close Encounters*, it all came together. I thought, wait

a second! What if that alien doesn't go back up into the ship? What if he stayed behind? Or what if he even got lost, and he was marooned here? What would happen if a child of a divorce, or a family of a divorce, with a huge hole to fill, filled the hole with his new best extraterrestrial friend? The whole story of *E.T.* came together on the set of *Close Encounters*.

JC: Going from the monster of *Jaws*, the great terror of the unknown, what's under the water that you can't see, to something angelic like *Close Encounters*—you really created a kind of alternate spirituality, or alternate religion. This idea that that which is above us isn't going to come from the traditional places, it's going to come from contact with an infinitely superior civilization.

SS: Yes. An infinitely superior civilization is going to find the best in you, and you will present the best part of yourself, as [Abraham] Lincoln said,

"the better angels of [your] nature." That's what goodness does. Good doesn't inspire evil; good propagates a greater good. And that's what I thought that the best science fiction does.

For me, *2001[: A Space Odyssey]* had a profound impact on my daily life. I was in college, and it was the first time I went to a movie where I really felt like I was having a religious experience. And I wasn't stoned—I didn't do drugs in college. I didn't smoke or do any drugs and I didn't drink. I was a pretty straight shooter. I walked into the [theater] and saw *2001* for the first time on the opening weekend. And I remember two things. The first thing I remember was the images of space were not as dark as I thought they were going to be. There wasn't a lot of contrast. You know why there wasn't any contrast? Because everybody was smoking grass in the theater. They polluted the actual atmosphere!

Stanley would have flipped out if he had seen that he didn't have the true absence of light—black—on his screens because there was too much marijuana smoke. I saw it seven or eight more times in better viewing conditions. But that first weekend . . . I think they even went back and changed the [marketing] campaign to call it "the ultimate trip." Because it was appealing to another side of our culture, the drug culture.

JC: People were dropping acid. I watched the film—this was before any kind of home video—eighteen times in its first couple years of release, all in theaters. I've seen every kind of audience response to it. I remember at one, a guy ran down the aisle toward the screen, screaming, "It's God! It's God!" And he meant it in that moment.

SS: I had a guy in my theater who actually walked up to the screen with his arms out, and he walked through the screen. Only later were we told the screen was in louvers. It wasn't just like a white piece of material.

JC: That must have blown people's minds.

SS: People were blown out because the person

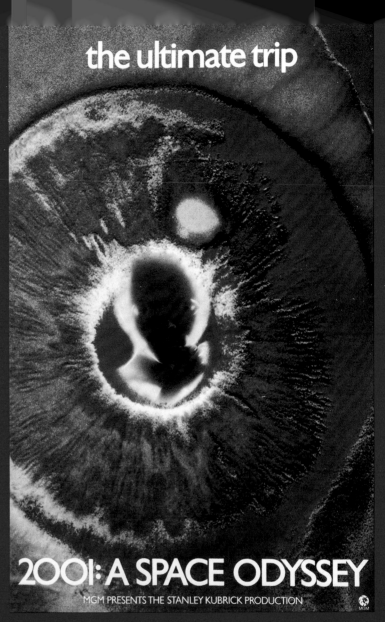

the ultimate trip

2001: A SPACE ODYSSEY

MGM PRESENTS THE STANLEY KUBRICK PRODUCTION

disappeared into the screen! During [the] stargate [sequence] of all times.

JC: I had such a strong physiological response to the movie. I related to it as falling down the stargate, down this kind of infinite tunnel. I went outside on the sidewalk in the sunlight—it was a matinee—and threw up. Honestly, it had such a physiological effect on me. And I knew I'd seen something important. I could only process part of it at the age of fourteen. I got the bone turning into the spaceship. I even got the Star Baby at

OPPOSITE The iconic image of a flying bike in silhouette against the moon from *E.T. the Extra-Terrestrial*. It would later become the logo for Spielberg's production company, Amblin Partners.

ABOVE A theatrical poster for director Stanley Kubrick's *2001: A Space Odyssey* (1968) capitalizes on the film's psychedelic reputation.

the end, the next stage in evolution. I didn't understand the Regency hotel room.

SS: That went over my head, too. But what I thought was amazing was that I was so lost in Arthur C. Clarke and Stanley's deep thinking, or whatever symbology they intended or profound meaning they were trying to achieve, it was better that I was left in the dust of their creation. It made me see some things more clearly than if I [had] understood it [all].

JC: You poured yourself into it like a Rorschach.

SS: I fell between the cracks of their filmmaking and of their conceptual partnership, and it was a beautiful crack to fall down in. The crack I fell through was the stargate. I think we all fell into the same stargate and came out this side, making movies.

JC: Stanley avoided the problem of what the alien would look like by just not showing it. You met that challenge head-on [in *Close Encounters*], and I think you pulled that off given the technology of the time.

SS: At the time, what I really wanted to do was throw so much backlight into my camera that all the little E.T.s would be almost like silhouettes, and they would be more impressionistic. The costumes were very flimsy. They were like the old *Cat People* movie. Zippers up and down the back, something you really couldn't shoot in front light. I thought the less you see, the more we can imagine our own extraterrestrial. We can put our own face on it. I only really allowed the face of the [special effects artist] Carlo Rambaldi creation, Puck, to be revealed.

JC: Did you learn that on *Jaws*—the less you see, the better?

SS: I did. All the technical snafus on *Jaws*—it was impossible making that film on the actual Atlantic Ocean. Saner people would have done it in a tank, and today they'd do it in CG. They'd do

it on a computer. But I like being at sea. I kind of liked being out there. It was a horrible experience at the same time because I was facing the end of my career. Everybody was telling me this was going to end my career. I believed them because we were getting one or two shots a day.

JC: But that made you better.

SS: What it made me was tenacious. Not that I had anything to prove to anybody but myself, but I was not going to get fired, and I wasn't going to fail. It might fail me, if the audience didn't show up, but I wasn't going to fail it.

JC: So, you've done this transcendental, spiritual first contact, that is a celebration of what the unknown might offer. And then you do *War of the Worlds*.

SS: I know! Isn't that terrible? What a hypocrite

ABOVE A tripod attacks in Spielberg's *War of the Worlds*.

I am. I wouldn't have done *War of the Worlds* had it not been for 9/11. Because *War of the Worlds* is analogous to 9/11—an event in our American culture and in the global history of terrorism. America is not a country that's used to being attacked. The last time we were attacked like that was Pearl Harbor.

JC: Yes. There's that sense of violation, that sense of helplessness. But you managed to turn it into a family drama that pulled everybody together.

SS: I did that in collaboration with [screenwriter] David Koepp. David really had a feel for that, had a feel for the family—which echoes a lot of my experience, a lot of my trauma as a child of a divorced family. I just remember when David and I got together, I was the one that said, "We have to make this a story about a single dad who

doesn't really even care about his kids. And somehow, this event has to make him care about his kids more than he ever cared about himself." That became the nucleus of *War of the Worlds*. The film doesn't have a good ending. I never could figure out how to end that darn thing.

JC: I don't think H. G. Wells could figure it out. The common cold takes out the bad guys.

SS: I did the same thing. I had Morgan Freeman help me with it with his narration.

JC: Morgan Freeman makes everything sound plausible.

SS: Morgan always makes everything sound better.

JC: It was great that you went back to the

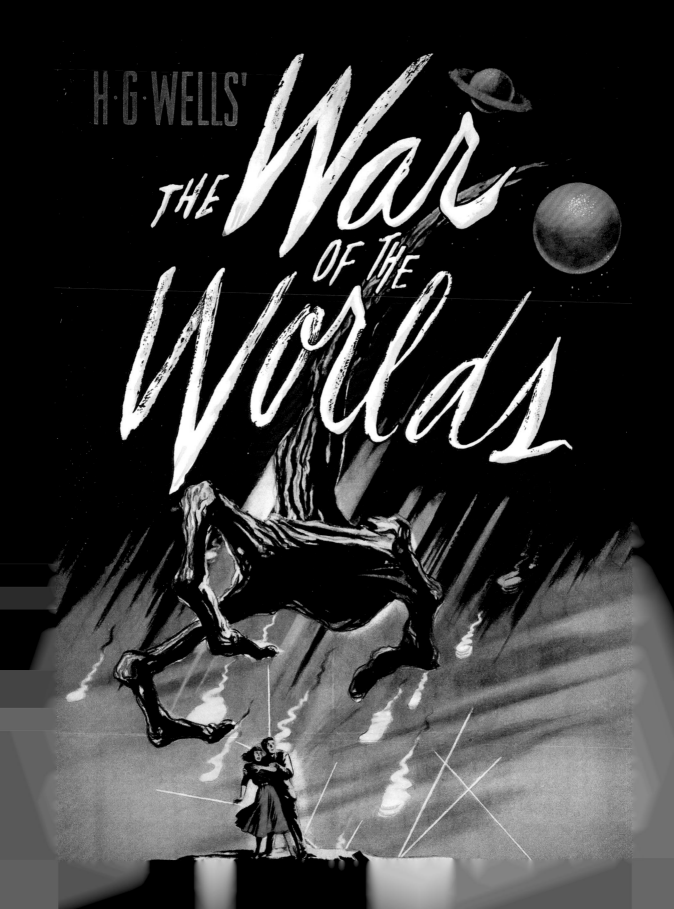

source. Because the George Pal version that we grew up with had these really cool floating antigravity war machines with force fields.

SS: Oh, they were great! They were kind of like boomerangs with green edge lights on them. That was a powerful film also for me. I did an homage in *E.T.* because of my love for the George Pal *War of the Worlds*, where they're in the farmhouse at night, and you see the shadows against the wall. And all of a sudden, the three-fingered suction cup tips touch Ann [Robinson] on the shoulder. I did the same moment in *E.T.*, where Elliott hears a sound out his window, and he's scared and he goes to the window, and you just see E.T.'s hand touching him for comfort, giving him some kind of comfort.

JC: But it's a whole different context.

SS: A totally different context, yes.

JC: Over your entire oeuvre between directing and producing, you've done many films about first contact or invasion and what that might look like—[the 2002 TV miniseries] *Taken* and *Falling Skies*. Is that coming [out of your interest in] World War II? You've done so much with World War II and what it feels like to be invaded.

SS: I wish I could play the integrity card, but I can't. I have to say that the whole premise of *Taken* was a commercial grab to try to attract the largest audience I could—making those aliens hostile and insidious, getting into your brain and giving you memories of your mother being hurt, which forces the soldier to drop his weapon and then renders him harmless.

JC: Let's look at that from a positive light. If that's a successful strategy, it's because we, as a society, hunger for our nightmares written large on the big screen or the small screen. It seems to me that's a big part of what science fiction is. It's taking that fear of the creature in the forest that we had 20,000, 50,000 years

ago, and letting us feel it in a safe place.

SS: Even before science fiction became popular, there were the Grimm fairy tales. You scare your kids into doing the right things, terrify your children into not making mistakes. You know, if you bite your fingernails a guy will jump over a hedge with hedge clippers and cut off your fingers, and then in the illustrated book I was given at eight years old to read, there's blood spurting from the severed fingers.

JC: And if you trust the old lady, she's gonna cook you in her oven. Do what your parents say. Cautionary tales. But it seems to me that once we got into the technological age and the science age, the cautionary tales were dealing with fear and our angst of where this was all going, this big human experiment.

SS: We're always worried about where's the world going and is this world coming to an end? A lot of science fiction basically capitalizes on those fears. How through filmmaking and how through storytelling can we stop the apocalypse? Can we at least [delay] the apocalypse? The best science fiction [stories] are cautionary tales.

JC: The irony is that I find that science fiction is actually not that good at predicting the future.

SS: It's terrible.

OPPOSITE Theatrical poster for producer George Pal's version of *The War of the Worlds*, released in 1953.

TOP RIGHT Gertie (Drew Barrymore) smooches lovable alien E.T.

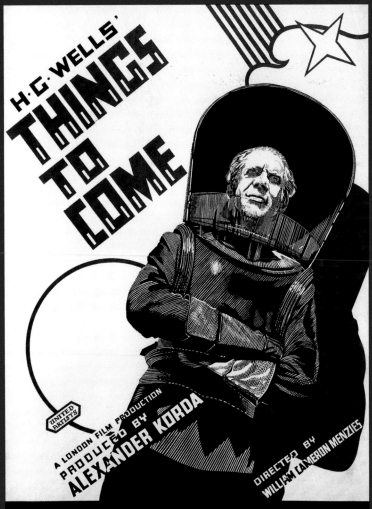

H.G. WELLS'
THINGS TO COME

A LONDON FILM PRODUCTION
PRODUCED BY
ALEXANDER KORDA

UNITED ARTISTS

DIRECTED BY
WILLIAM CAMERON MENZIES

LEICESTER·SQ·THEATRE

Props: LEICESTER SQUARE ESTATES Lᵀᴰ.   Managing Director: JACK BUCHANAN.   General Manager: Alexander Stevenson.

ABOVE Theatrical poster for the 1936 film *Things to Come*, written by science fiction legend H. G. Wells.

OPPOSITE TOP RIGHT Teaser poster for Steven Spielberg's *Minority Report* (2002).

JC: Nobody predicted the internet.

SS: Or *The Shape of Things to Come* with buildings having tail fins. Before the Cadillac came out with them.

JC: Everything had tail fins for a while.

SS: *Star Wars*, George [Lucas]'s *Episode II*, had a little bit of that with all the flying vehicles, like in *Things to Come*.

JC: He gave us glimpses of all these amazing positive futures but also a fascist militaristic future, which was interesting. You've even done something—and I don't even know where to put it in the genre—which is *Minority Report*. It's a little bit like a time-travel story because you're seeing the future, but you're bringing it into the present and then you're acting on it.

SS: I always considered *Minority Report* to be a kind of psychic Philip Marlowe or Raymond Chandler gumshoe [tale] . . . Sam Spade, all those great John Huston movies like *The Maltese Falcon*. But this was a psychic detective story.

JC: Maybe it's the kid in you, but you love the technology, too. Tom Cruise having to get out of a car that's being assembled . . .

SS: Exactly. When I sit down to storyboard, I come up with my best ideas in the process of making my sketches. Ideas that weren't in the script and weren't even in my imagination will come out as I'm actually drawing. The more I draw, the more ideas I get, and I think all the scenes in *Minority Report* came from the storyboarding process. We had a lot of that stuff in the script, but a lot more of it came just from storyboards.

JC: It seems like you're attracted to the awe, the wonder, the mystery, the fantasy in science fiction, but also to strong social causes and things of societal importance. I'm curious why you've never put the two together in a kind of dystopian science fiction future like a *1984*.

SS: To do a dystopian story for me means I have to lose all hope. I have to actually spend a half-year to a year of my life in a state of depression. I'm currently in production on *Ready Player One*. The real world in *Ready Player One* is a dystopian 2045 future. But the OASIS, the virtual world where [people] go to really have a cyber life, is a world where you can be and do anything you want. You can live out your greatest fantasies. That's the closest thing I've gotten to dystopian. I don't think *Minority Report* was about a dystopian world. *Minority Report* was really a story about unintended consequences. It was a morality tale. [You're] stopping future murders, but then what justice do the perpetrators [find] based on the evidence of three seers, or oracles? Is that enough to really put you in solitary confinement—literally in stasis—for the rest of your life? There was a big moral drama, too.

JC: It was [exploring the] unintended consequences of technology or of society changing to adapt to technology. That's the world we're living in right now. I think of us coevolving with our technology. We're changing it. It's changing us, and who knows where that big experiment's going to take us.

SS: Exactly. I liked the days when you had to dial a phone. I don't know if I miss it, but I miss the fact that people actually remember it. My kids would look at it, and they wouldn't understand what the object was. It took an effort to communicate with someone. You had to sit at a typewriter, and you had to type something out. You had to handwrite a letter. Or you had to actually dial a series of numbers. There was effort in reaching out to speak and communicate with somebody. Communication today is almost taken for granted. It is effortless. Soon we [will] have biotechnology that can bypass any hard tech, any platform tech. That goes away and everything is literally hardwired into our cerebral cortex. That's right around the corner.

JC: Oh, it's very close. It's interesting that we've chosen forms of tech, of communication, that are unit directional bursts because we can edit what we say and we don't have to respond in real time. [For] my kids, it's an alien concept to them to talk on the phone because then you're accountable for what you've just said. The consequence of any statement you make has been uncoupled from the making of the statement. That's what the internet and all these advanced communications have done for us. Societally,

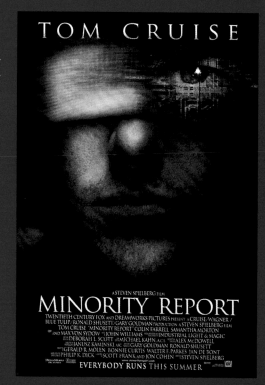

we're changing. We're actually living in science fiction. Us science fiction filmmakers are having to run to catch up with the real world.

SS: It's hard to think of a future that Microsoft and Apple [aren't already] thinking up for us before we can even get to the drawing board. Before we can get to the screens, they're coming up with something else that we thought we were dreaming up. I think that leads naturally to *A.I.*

JC: You took the reins of that over from . . .

SS: From Stanley [Kubrick]. I knew Stanley since I made *Raiders of the Lost Ark*. I met [him] on the set of *The Shining* when he had just finished [shooting inside] the Overlook Hotel. That's where we were going to build the big Well of the Souls set. I came to scout Elstree Studios in Borehamwood, and I was told that Stanley Kubrick was on the stage and I couldn't go on to the stage because it was a closed set. I asked the production manager, I think it was Doug Twiddy, "Can I meet Stanley Kubrick?" He was very warm, and he said, "Yes, please come over." I met Stanley that day, and he invited me out to the house that night. This was in '80. That began a nineteen-year friendship. A lot of it [was] on the telephone, by the way.

JC: Because he didn't fly. [Kubrick had a phobia of flying.]

SS: And I didn't go to England so much. When I was in England, I saw him, but it was mainly on the phone. We'd have these marathon eight-, nine-hour conversations on the telephone. I mean, literally eating lunch and dinner, just the two of us on phone calls. He never invited me into his creative circle until one day he said, "I'd like you to read something." Talk about getting an honor. The man had made *2001: A Space Odyssey*, let alone *The Killing* and *Killer's Kiss* and *Dr. Strangelove* and *Lolita*, *Barry Lyndon*. Here's a guy who is asking me to read something that he's written because he wants me to find a writer to adapt it into screenplay form. He sent me a short story by Brian Aldiss called "Super-Toys Last All Summer Long." Before I knew it, Stanley was asking me to read a seventy-nine-page treatment that he and Ian Watson had written based on the Brian Aldiss original short story.

JC: Did you call it *A.I.* or had he already come up with that? Because he did the big classic of AI, which was *2001*.

SS: No, he hadn't quite called it *A.I.* yet . . . So, then he asked me to look at 15,000 storyboards he did. He wanted to me to come to London to see them. I immediately flew to his house and spent a couple days with him and went through the storyboards. Then he popped the question. He literally said, "I think this movie is more your sensibility than mine right now, and I'm getting sidetracked by some other projects." That's when he began calling it *A.I.* He said, "Would you be interested in directing this and I'll be the producer? I'll be the line producer, and you be the director."

JC: He never had that relationship with any other filmmaker that I can think of.

SS: I don't think he ever asked anybody to do anything like this before. But Stanley and I knew Terry Semel and Bob Daly, who ran Warner Bros. at the time. We made a deal with Warner for me to direct and Stanley to produce. The part of the story that always amuses me is Stanley said, "You're the director. I'm not going to get in your way. We're just going to work on the script together, and then I'll be a producer from England. You go off and shoot the picture in America." But he said, "You need to install a fax machine because I'm going to be sending you a lot of notes and pictures and ideas. And it's got to go in your bedroom."

I said, "Why?" He said, "Because what if somebody comes in and reads what I've written you? It's got to go in a private place. You have to ensure me it's going to go in your bedroom." So, I put the fax machine in the bedroom. Do you know how loud a fax machine phone is? It is ten times the volume of a regular house line. And when that thing went off at two o'clock in the morning. Oh my . . .

JC: He'd just gotten up, right? In England?

SS: Two o'clock in the morning, the middle of my night, but it's his day. That thing would go off at 1 a.m., 3 a.m., 4 a.m. It lasted two nights, and Kate Capshaw, my wife, threw the fax machine out of the bedroom and said, "You've got to be honest with Stanley. Tell him what happened." I called Stanley I told him what happened.

JC: But other than that, it was a fruitful collaboration?

SS: It was a great collaboration. I got so many notes from Stanley that were notes about camera angles, the notes of craft, the notes of, "How are you going to create David [the film's young robotic protagonist]? I think David should be an android. He should be not a prosthetic, it should be a machine." [Industrial Light & Magic visual effects legend] Dennis Muren flew to England and spent some time with Stanley talking about building an actual robot boy with wires—like E.T. and like Puck. Stanley, I think, did some tests on that. This is before I came into the story. Stanley discovered that it [wasn't] going to work with a mechanical boy. This is before the first [fully computer-generated photorealistic animated character appeared] in a movie, which is [in] *Young Sherlock Holmes*. And well before *Jurassic Park*. Stanley would've today done David as a digital character in a live-action setting. For sure.

JC: That's the thing that excited me about making [*Alita: Battle Angel*, an adaption of the popular manga to be directed by Robert Rodriguez]. Not to plug my own thing, but the idea that if you're going to create somebody who's a simulacrum of a human, do it using CG. It was ten years ago when I wrote the script. I was like, well, it'll never be quite perfect. I think now we can make it pretty close to perfect. It's almost a self-defeating concept now because you still had the uncanny valley back [then], that response that you get that's very negative

when you see a robot or a simulation that's so close to human but there's something off.

SS: But for something like *A.I.* the uncanny valley is exactly what the doctor ordered. That's what you're trying to get. You're trying to get the [sense that there] is something machinelike about this kid that isn't 100 percent. Through the sheer force of creative talent, Haley Joel Osment, without blinking—he never blinks once in the film except at the very end—with a little bit of makeup, just a little bit of an appliqué, he was able to convince me that he was a robot child.

JC: It's very convincing. So, you were trying to create the uncanny valley.

SS: I didn't think it was going to work unless it was the uncanny valley. Jude Law also. Jude Law had to look like the uncanny valley—partially human but there's something synthetic about him. A simulacrum.

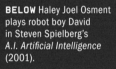

BELOW Haley Joel Osment plays robot boy David in Steven Spielberg's *A.I. Artificial Intelligence* (2001).

JC: But they still were sympathetic characters. Why is that? Why do we imbue a machine with not only consciousness but also something that we care for? That we can root for?

SS: Why do we talk to Siri? We anthropomorphize almost everything. It starts as a child—if you're a little girl and you've got little dolls, or if you're a guy and you've got little Transformer toys, G.I. Joes. I've always said that every child starts out as a storyteller because their imaginations are profoundly fertile. That imagination allows us to determine a camera angle. As little kids, we get down on the floor, and we put our eyes as low to the ground as we can to make our action figures look super-real. When we have electric trains, we put our eye down to the track and we let the trains do run-bys.

That's how I started making movies. My first movie really was "The Great Train Wreck" where I had my one train go left to right and my other train go right to left. I put a camera right in the middle, and they crashed in front of my 8mm Kodak camera. That's what kids do when they're exercising their natural ability to create worlds that don't exist. We all start as storytellers. We all start, in a way, as filmmakers.

JC: So we're projecting ourselves onto and anthropomorphizing our machines. But there is a legitimate effort right now that's got a lot of money and a lot of momentum to create a machine consciousness that's equal to or potentially much more advanced than our own. We're living in a science fiction world right now. I mean, HAL [from *2001: A Space Odyssey*] will exist probably in our lifetime.

SS: I think so, too. I've been working for years on *Robopocalypse*. Because it's the story of the most profound sentient chromatin of man who basically is so much smarter than man he needs to wrest control away from the human race and take over the world—a little bit like a more advanced version of *Pinky and The Brain*. But it's scary. Elon Musk continues to predict

that World War III will not be a nuclear holocaust. It will be a kind of mechanized takeover.

JC: Stephen Hawking's been saying similar things. Vladimir Putin said that the country that perfects artificial intelligence will rule the world.

SS: That's spooky because that pretty much says that something smarter than us, that can beat us at chess, will use this world as a chessboard and will checkmate us completely out of existence. Now, I don't know if I believe that even 50 percent because I'm not built to believe things like that. I always think that somehow we are going to find a way out of every corner we paint ourselves into. We all have empathy even if we don't act that way in our lives or people don't see that in us. Everybody has that capacity. And that is the capacity, I think, that will always pull us back from the brink.

JC: I think about AI like early atomic power. They had all these visions of unlimited energy. They could power the world. They could create atomic aircraft. They could go into space. And of course, the first thing they did was blow up two Japanese cities.

Talking to a few of these AI guys lately, they really remind me of those atomic scientists from the '30s who believed that they were going to create an unlimited energy source for the future. It's like, don't you realize that once you get the toothpaste out of the tube, you can't put it back?

SS: You can't. And once we created nuclear fission, once we split the atom, that can never go back. But it could also be put to tremendous beneficial use. And it has in the world. There's a good use and a bad use for everything we come up with.

JC: In *A.I.*, you actually show a transition to a robotic or machine substrate for humans in the future—or not really humans, but our successors on this planet.

SS: Yeah, the supermecha. The machines actually evolve, and machines build better machines, and those machines evolve into even greater machines.

JC: But they seem to be as human or at least as empathic and compassionate as we are. They're very compassionate with David.

SS: But their compassion and their empathy is all based on mathematics. It's based on assumption. It's based on the experience of mathematical equations. Ours come from a place called the soul. It comes from an ineffable place. I believe there are things beyond our knowledge and even way beyond our grasp. Sometimes it's nice to say to my kids, you just have to have a little faith.

JC: Don't you think it's interesting that science fiction often deals with issues of faith and spirituality? Science fiction deals with science and technology and its impact on us. Then it also often hits a wall. There is a limit to science.

SS: And that's where the first George Pal *War of the Worlds* comes back into the conversation. It ends in a church and the father of the leading lady walks toward one of the cylinders that has come down, and he's carrying a cross. And he has a Bible. And he gets incinerated. He gets completely reduced to ash.

JC: As an atheist, I laughed at that scene. But I think that somebody who is a believer would see it the other way around.

SS: You can read *War of the Worlds* as a spiritual tome. If you wanted to. That's what's great about science fiction. But remember we have to separate science fiction from science fantasy. You know, I used to always get Forrest J. Ackerman's *Famous Monsters of Filmland* [magazine].

JC: We all love Forrest.

SS: We went to his house, and we saw his great collection.

JC: He had the best collection.

SS: The best collection! We love Forrest. He made a big distinction between science fiction and science fantasy. Because science fantasy is *Harry Potter*. And science fiction is *Star Wars*.

JC: I would submit that there's a more complex spectrum that you can have *The Martian* and *Interstellar* and *2001* on the kind of hard science, hard-tech end of the spectrum, and then you can have *Star Wars* closer to the fantasy end of the spectrum because it has swords and wizards and things like that, but it's dressed up in a science and technology framework. When you step over that line and there's no science to it at all and it's just magic, then I think you're into *Harry Potter* and *The Lord of the Rings*.

SS: You're right. I think *Star Wars* is right in between *Interstellar* and *Harry Potter*.

JC: What Chris Nolan did with *Interstellar* is he went to the experts [like] Kip Thorne and he said, "What is a black hole? What is it really going to look like? We want to show that." Then he talked to a lot of space propulsion people and life support people, and he created plausible spacecraft, plausible planetary surfaces. He didn't populate it with a lot of fun aliens. It was just people against a hard survival problem using their wits and their intelligence. But even he, at the end, got kind of transcendental and spiritual.

SS: He did. Matthew McConaughey became a ghost. He became a ghost that had some basis in science.

JC: He used science to get to a kind of afterlife scenario, which is very interesting.

SS: What are we always trying to do when we tell these stories? What I'm always trying to do

is to touch people in the heart before the head. I always go for the heart first. Of course, sometimes I go for the heart so much I get a little bit accused of sentimentality, which I'm fine [with] because . . . sometimes I need to push it a little further to reach a little deeper into a society that is a little less sentimental than they were when I was a young filmmaker.

JC: You pushed it in the same way that [legendary sci-fi writer and editor] John W. Campbell pushed science fiction [forward] from the hard-tech nerdy guys who had to put PhD after their name to write science fiction. It was all just about the equations and the math and the physics [and evolved to become much more] human stories [about] the human heart. The best science fiction writers that I was reading when I was a kid were the ones that had interesting characters, that made me cry. There's this feeling, I think, even still to this day in Hollywood, that science

fiction isn't really a mainstream art form because it doesn't really deal with real emotional stuff between people. I think that's completely wrong. Science fiction is talking about the human condition. We live in a technological world. And we deal with it as people.

SS: That's true. Science fiction today also is undeniably the steak on the plate where it used to be the dessert after the main course. Today, you eat dessert first. The films that are making all the money are the films that are asking us to optically suspend our disbelief and go flying off into the worlds of Batman, Superman, Wonder Woman, the Avengers, Thor. I do feel very strongly that's not the main course unless it is anchored by the human condition and real identifiable characters that are like you and me and other people living in the world today. [Otherwise] it's a spectacle of what you can do with digital tools, not what you can do with storytelling.

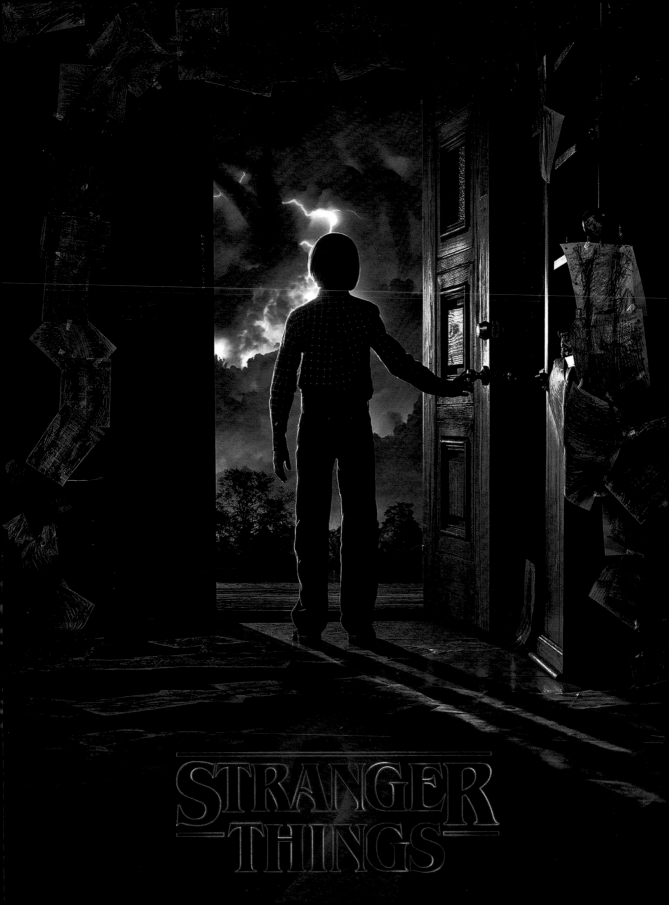

JC: You and I both work with the best digital artists in the world, and we know that there is nothing now that we can imagine that can't be accomplished. So then it becomes a matter of artistic choice. What you do, and what I hope I do, is to always choose the heart over the head.

SS: That's exactly what you do. All the time. On every project. It's the hardest thing to do. It's hard to come up with an original story. There are a lot of writers out there nodding their heads. It's hard to come out with original stories. It's hard to come up with something that people can't immediately compare to something else in their movie history, something with very little precedent. We're standing on the shoulders of all kinds of storytelling giants.

JC: I think the worst films just refer to other movies. The best films somehow connect you to something that you've experienced.

SS: *Stranger Things* has done that very well. *Stranger Things* is pure science fiction. It touches on a lot of the movies that you and I and others have made, but it does it brilliantly. It's a brilliant amalgam of genres but all having to do with one thing. You love those kids, and you do not want anything bad to happen to them. *Stranger Things*, for all its brilliant imaginings, is about those characters.

JC: But you also made E.T. an intensely sympathetic character. One of the things that fascinates me about the idea of aliens is that how they look could very much determine how we communicate [with] or how we respond to them. You went with very big eyes. People naturally respond to large eyes because babies have big eyes.

SS: And I went with the face that only a mother could love. I wanted E.T. not to be a pretty guy. I wanted E.T. to be gawky and awkward with a fat belly and a neck too thin for a person to be in a suit. When that head came up on the periscoping neck, I wanted people to say, "Oh my god, that's

real! That is not a costumed actor!"—even though we did have some actors in costumes for certain walking shots. It was very important that E.T. be a face that would earn your respect and earn your fondness. I didn't want a cute little Disney character to come out of the gate making the whole audience in unison go *awww*. That's the last thing I wanted. And [screenwriter] Melissa Mathison was right on board with me. She wrote a brilliant script, and Missy kept saying, "E.T. has to be one of the children, has to be one of the kids."

JC: Is it Drew Barrymore that screams and then he screams? One of the funniest moments in movie history.

SS: They all scream. Drew would always say, "Can I scream again?" That was fun.

JC: Let me ask you point blank. Do you think aliens exist? Do you believe that they've already come here?

SS: I believe that there are advanced civilizations of biological organisms of probably vast inferiority to us and vast superiority to us out there somewhere in all the combined universes, all the combined galaxies. I wanted to believe. I felt I earned the right to see a UFO. I made *E.T.* I made *Close Encounters*. I kept waiting for a sighting. I never had a sighting. I've met hundreds of people who have.

JC: You know they will stay as far away from you as they can because they don't want to empower this myth that you're actually a precursor of an alien invasion. You know about this myth, right? That you've been intentionally softening us up for decades now.

SS: I've heard about this myth. It's insane. Look, I stay away from sharks, but I don't want to stay away from UFOs and yet I've never, ever had the experience. I'm not saying that seeing is 100 percent believing, but my feeling right now is . . . why were there more UFOs caught on

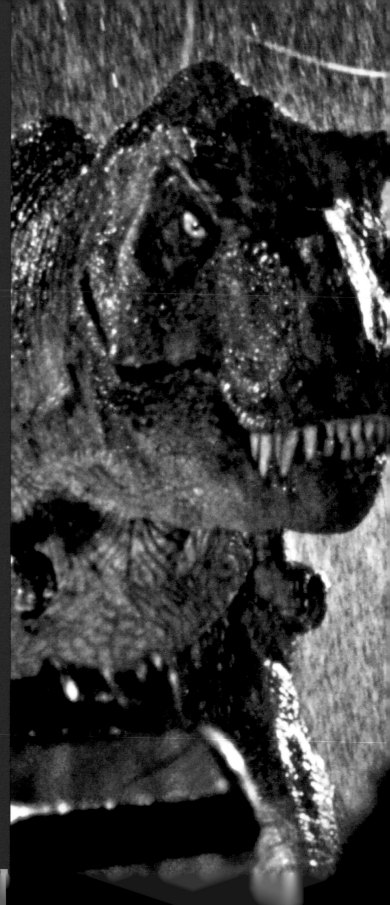

camera back in the '70s and '80s and toward the end of the '60s than there are today? There's nobody that doesn't have something that can record [a possible UFO sighting].

JC: For a science fiction writer, that's easy to solve. [Earth] used to be a really hot tourist place for the UFOs . . . And then they realized that they were getting photographed too much. I think that they were emissaries from the future trying to fix things before we screw it up too badly, which leads me to time travel. You've covered just about every base in science fiction—alien contact, space travel, every-thing—and you executive produced the *Back to the Future* series of films. Do you think time travel is possible?

SS: I asked Stephen Hawking that question one day. *Back to the Future* just came out. Stephen Hawking said it's very possible to go into the future but impossible to go back into the past. He was eluding to the fact that every-thing in *Back to the Future* could never happen. I don't think much about time travel. I've got too many photo albums. That's my time machine, memory.

JC: Let's move to monsters. When we were kids the best monsters were dinosaurs, right?

SS: The first long word I learned was *Pachycephalosaurus*. And then, of course, it was *Stegosaurus* and *Triceratops*. I was a kid going to the Franklin Institute of Technology in Philadelphia looking at all the bones. And loving it.

JC: Me too. In the first grade, I wanted to be a paleontologist. That was probably the first long word I learned. And then I found out that dino-saurs were extinct. Imagine my disappointment.

SS: When I was a kid, I used to take my popsicle sticks, and I would basically glue them together

RIGHT Paleontologist Alan Grant comes face-to-face with a T. rex in Spielberg's *Jurassic Park* (1993).

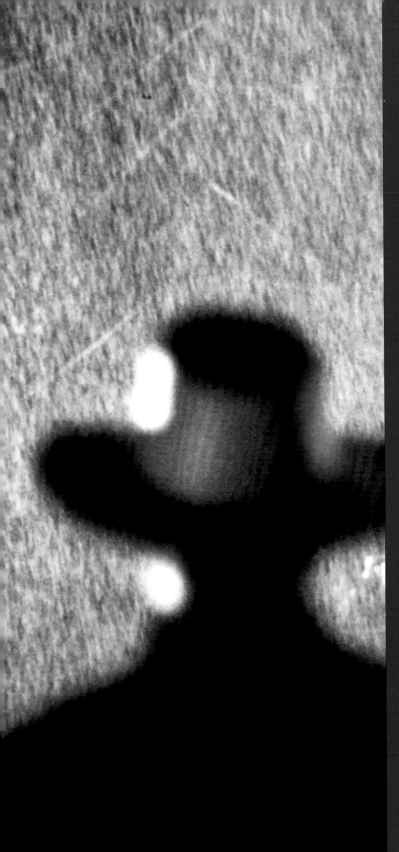

in the form of a dinosaur. And I would dig a hole in the backyard, and I would bury it and then I would wait a week. Then I would go looking for it again. That was my closest moment of trying to be an amateur paleontologist.

JC: Cut to you decades later working with the world's top paleontologists on *Jurassic Park*.

SS: That was one of the most fun movies I've ever had the honor to make. Michael Crichton just came up with a perfect concept, and he pitched it to me when we were working on a second draft of *E.R.* He wrote *E.R.* as a movie, and I'd come in to direct. [But] later we turned [it] into a television show. During a lunch break, I asked him what book he was writing next. He said he couldn't tell me, and I just pumped him and pumped him until he said, "I'll tell you one conceptual line. I'm writing a book about dino-saurs and DNA." That's all he would say. I wouldn't leave it alone till he promised to sell me the darn book.

JC: Right. Now, I have a slightly different per-ception on it, right? I got sent the book. I heard it was up for sale. I got it on a Friday night. I didn't read it Friday night. I started reading it Saturday. I got to the scene where the *Tyrannosaurus rex* licks the windshield with the kids inside—you actually didn't do the licking, but in the book, it actually licks the windshield. I said, "I've got to make this movie." I never even finished the book. I called up [and was told], "Steven just bought it." It was the very best thing that could've hap-pened because I would've made it like *Aliens*. I would've made an R-rated scare-the-crap-out-of-you movie. You made it just scary enough but still a movie for kids. You made it for the twelve-year-old me.

SS: Because I was the twelve-year-old me telling that story. I made that movie for myself. When I was a [kid], I couldn't get enough of it in my life. I couldn't get enough. And there were no dinosaur toys in those days. You

couldn't satiate your desire to understand a vanishing species because there was nothing being sold in stores.

JC: Think of how lightning struck on that movie. Michael wrote that book at the exact moment that CG was coming into its own. I'd done *The Abyss*. I'd done *T2* [*Terminator 2*]. Most of the people that worked on *The Abyss* and *T2* went right into Team Raptor and Team T. rex on *Jurassic Park*. And all the stuff that they had pioneered—it was like the rain cloud getting ready to rain. You made it rain and showed that soft-tissue, organic characters with eyes that blinked and looked wet and looked real and an iris that dilated [could be created digitally].

SS: And skin that folded. Muscles under the skin. Muscle under the skin moving.

JC: The CG revolution just spiked right after that.

SS: It was an incredible time, and like you said, the timing of that book, that concept, and the dawn of the digital era happened to converge to our advantage. We could actually make the first leading characters, the stars of the movie, digital. You have to understand also there are only fifty-nine digital dinosaur shots in *Jurassic Park*. Stan Winston built a full-size *Triceratops*. He built a full-size T. rex. He built a full-size brachiosaur neck and head. Stan really deserved so much credit for the success of that movie. I think Stan Winston—in the future, people are going to look back on him the way they look back at Willis O'Brien and *King Kong*. The sweetest guy in the world.

Jurassic Park was a story that also appealed to me because of man's hubris, this

ABOVE A velociraptor bears its teeth in Spielberg's *Jurassic Park*.

OPPOSITE Theatrical poster for the 1950 science fiction classic *Destination Moon*.

feeling of, if it's possible, why not? John Hammond [the fictional park creator] represents certainly an impresario. A ring master. He's the Ringling brothers of this new era of bringing a species back to life. At the same time, he is blind to what he's doing. Like all mad scientists, his intentions are pure. He wants to be Walt Disney. He wants everybody to come see these dinosaurs. He wants children to get tears in their eyes when they marvel at these creatures that they only could see in storybooks.

JC: Jeff Goldblum is such a great conscience. He says, "Nature will find a way."

SS: Oh yeah. He's the voice of the audience. He says that. Life finds a way. And he's right every single time. My favorite scenes are when Jeff and John [played by Richard Attenborough] are going after each other.

JC: Which you propagated into the second film, into *The Lost World*.

SS: Michael Crichton and David Koepp wrote all that stuff, and it was just great to be able to play that out on set.

JC: As they said in the *Westworld* poster, what could possibly go wrong?

SS: Exactly. And that gets the audience excited because the audience is going to see what went wrong. Who cares about what went right?

JC: It's no fun if it goes right.

SS: It's not fun at all. One of the first times I ever felt true suspense as a child—all the Disney films, my parents allowed me to see in theaters. But the first time I really felt suspense was I was very young and saw a movie, and it was reissue, called *Destination Moon*. Another George Pal film. When that first moon voyage lands and they can't get off the moon unless they take several tons of weight out of

TWO YEARS IN THE MAKING!

DESTINATION MOON
COLOR BY **TECHNICOLOR**

Produced by GEORGE PAL · Directed by IRVING PICHEL
Screenplay by RIP VAN RONKEL, ROBERT HEINLEIN and JAMES O'HANLON

the ship itself, I remember as a kid not being able to sit still. I remember almost feeling [nauseated]. I didn't realize suspense starts in the stomach. And it goes up to the throat. And then it comes out as a scream.

JC: So you are a classic example of somebody who's exorcising the demons of their childhood for the rest of their creative life.

SS: And I have a lot more. I have a lot more.

OUTER SPACE

BY BROOKS PECK
CURATOR, MUSEUM OF POP CULTURE

AS A YOUNGSTER BROWSING THE SHELVES OF MY LOCAL PUBLIC LIBRARY for something to read, I always looked for science fiction. Luckily, my library made it easy to find the sci-fi. Many of the books in the fiction section had stickers on the spines bearing an icon that identified their genre: a magnifying glass for mysteries, a heart for romance, and for science fiction, a rocket ship blasting off.

In that basic, pictographic classification system, science fiction equaled space, and for good reason. Stories set in outer space dominate the genre. Science fiction is about infinite possibilities, and space provides an infinite canvas. When we speak of outer space, though, we are rarely talking about the cold, empty vacuum between the stars and planets. Space science fiction is about exploring other worlds, as well as imagining the societies we might create out there.

When Nicolaus Copernicus suggested that the sun, not Earth, was the center of the universe, and that some lights in the sky could therefore be other planets, the idea of traveling to those worlds naturally followed. One of the earliest examples, astronomer Johannes Kepler's novel *Somnium* (1608) sends an observer to the moon. But the observer is transported there by a demon, so it's not space travel as we would define it.

But in 1687, author Cyrano de Bergerac made the leap from fantasy to science fiction all in one work: *The Comical History of the States and Empires of the Worlds of the Moon and Sun*. The novel's hero first tries to reach the moon by wearing bottles of dew that lift him skyward when the sun rises. He initially only gets as far as Canada, but he later reaches the moon in a craft propelled by fireworks—the first depiction of travel by rocket ship.

Kepler and de Bergerac used their outer space stories as a way of expounding their particular theories on nature and philosophy. (Kepler sent an observer to the moon in order to explain heliocentrism. De Bergerac used space as a platform for expounding his

criticisms of society and religion.) It would be another two hundred years before authors would begin to make space travel a goal unto itself and write the kind of science fiction we know today.

The first genuine outer space fiction was an outgrowth of exploration tales. As the world became fully mapped, writers like Jules Verne looked to the sky for new territories to explore. In his 1865 novel *From the Earth to the Moon*, Verne sends explorers moonward in a capsule fired from an enormous cannon. Although the physics behind this method were impossible, the story was nevertheless the first space exploration tale that strived for scientific accuracy, taking into account freefall, the need to absorb excess carbon dioxide, and the influence of the mass of a passing asteroid on the craft's trajectory.

More important, Verne's novel inspired a sense of wonder about the possibilities of space travel. Georges Méliès, one of the very earliest filmmakers, recognized the potential of outer space to create a visual spectacle with which to thrill his audiences. His 1902 film *A Trip to the Moon* borrowed amply from Verne while blending elements from H. G. Wells's novel *First Men in the Moon* (1900). It is recognized as a landmark in early cinema as well as the very first science fiction film.

It didn't take long, though, for dreamers and scientists alike to look beyond the Moon, and when they looked, they found Mars. Back in 1877, Italian astronomer Giovanni Schiaparelli had made observations of Mars, sketching features he saw through a small

OPPOSITE Scenes from director Georges Méliès seminal science fiction adventure, *A Trip to the Moon* (1902).

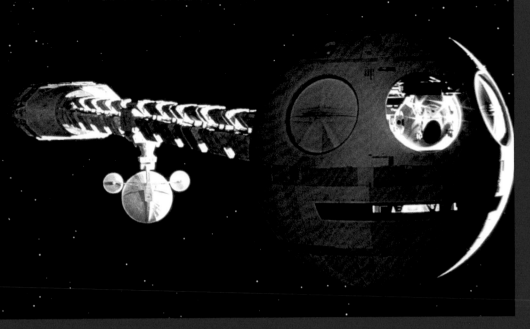

telescope. He noted seas, continents, and, in particular, channels, the Italian word for which is *canali*. English speakers misinterpreted this to mean artificial canals like the recently completed Suez Canal, and just like that, the idea of a civilization on Mars came to life. Percival Lowell, an American businessman and astronomer, championed the idea in numerous speculative nonfiction books, including *Mars as the Abode of Life* (1908), that suggested the canals were built by a dying civilization to carry water from ice caps at the planet's poles. Although the scientific community remained skeptical, this sad and romantic tale sank deep into the roots of science fiction and would remain a popular theme for decades. In subsequent fiction, Mars would become a touchstone of our hopes and fears about space.

Among the writers inspired by the Red Planet, the most prominent and prolific was Edgar Rice Burroughs, whose novel *A Princess of Mars* (1912) is a swashbuckling yarn about John Carter, a former soldier magically transported to Mars. Carter encounters four-armed Martians, parched deserts, Schiaparelli's canals, and the princess of the title, Dejah Thoris. For Burroughs, like Kepler, the method of getting to and from other worlds wasn't important. The point of going to space was

to go someplace hitherto unknown, and showcase the wonders found there.

Burroughs's Mars books were a precursor to the science fiction pulp era, an explosion of stories printed in cheap pulp paper magazines that reached peak popularity in the late 1930s. E. E. "Doc" Smith's Skylark and Lensman series led the charge, the latter a multibillion-year epic about the Galactic Patrol, a peacekeeping force enhanced with incredible mental powers. The scope of Smith's work is astonishing, with space battles on a scale yet to be envisioned on film, and thousands of worlds caught up in the struggle.

During that time, science fiction also grew into prominence on radio and in film. Many of the stories were tales of interplanetary and interstellar action, adventure, and war, a subgenre known as space opera—named after so-called soap operas, daytime radio dramas sponsored by soap powder companies. Buck Rogers led the way, beginning in the August 1928 issue of *Amazing Stories*, and soon adapting to a newspaper comic strip and a radio program. A film serial followed, and in time two television series and a motion picture. It had many imitators, including *Flash Gordon*, a comic strip begun in 1934, with its own raft of radio programs, film serials, and television

TOP LEFT The *Discovery One* craft from director Stanley Kubrick's *2001: A Space Odyssey*.

OPPOSITE BOTTOM A scene from 1985's *Enemy Mine*, directed by Wolfgang Petersen and starring Dennis Quaid and Louis Gossett Jr.

shows. Together, these two characters and their wide-ranging adventures became emblematic of science fiction, the future, and space travel in the public consciousness. They also had a robust influence on generations of writers and filmmakers.

One of the writers inspired by the space opera boom and its antecedents was Ray Bradbury. His second book, *The Martian Chronicles* (1950), concerns a Burroughs-inspired Mars, with canals, crumbling cities, and dying Martians forming a backdrop for a series of stories that are lyrical, elegant, and haunting. The focus isn't technology or war, but meditations on youth and emerging adulthood, the loss of innocence, and the purpose and meaning (if any) of human endeavors. This was a new kind of science fiction, one that gained mainstream appreciation. As a result, Bradbury is celebrated as one of the twentieth century's great authors.

With the launch of the Space Race after World War II, the idea of space travel transformed from an outlandish dream to a real possibility. Part of the shift in attitude can be attributed to articles in the popular press that speculated about the possibility of space travel. The *Collier's* series "Man Will Conquer Space Soon!" (1952–1954), with paintings by Chesley Bonestell and Fred Freeman, was particularly influential. The

articles outlined rocket scientist Wernher von Braun's concepts for spaceflight and were meticulous in their technical detail. Yet the illustrations of lunar shuttles and the Martian landscape were also as evocative as the latest Buck Rogers strip.

Bonestell also worked as a matte painter in the movie industry, and before the *Collier's* series he created backgrounds for a film that was emblematic of this era: *Destination Moon* (1950). Eschewing the pandemonium of space opera, the film was a comparatively realistic take on the engineering and political challenges faced by those embarking on the first lunar expedition.

To midcentury Americans, our future in space was now just a few decades away. *Flash Gordon* had to make way for television series like *Men into Space* (1959–1960), a fictionalized account of the US Air Force's growing space program. Episodes focused on the first lunar landing, the placement of an orbiting telescope, and construction of a lunar base. Tame stuff compared to the galaxy-charging *Lensman*, but equally compelling because of its incipient reality.

Realistic space films reached their peak in 1968 with *2001: A Space Odyssey*. Stanley Kubrick's film (written by Kubrick and Arthur C. Clarke) blended *Collier's*-style visuals with a pensive story about evolution and our place in the universe. Much of the

film is devoted to a slow, hyperaccurate portrait of travel to orbit, the moon, and Jupiter before segueing into a psychedelic climax that left audiences awed, mystified, or both. *2001* is considered by many to be the best outer space film ever made.

Despite the brilliance of Kubrick's film, excitement about worlds beyond Earth waned during this time. The reality of space exploration proved to be slow, routine, and somewhat dull, at least to most of the public. One of the greatest blows came in 1965 when the exploratory spacecraft *Mariner 4* made its flyby of Mars and revealed a cold, cratered world not unlike the Moon. The dreams of Schiaparelli and Burroughs evaporated because Mars, once the home of so many bright futures, was just another lifeless rock.

But a few creators still yearned for the stars. Gene Roddenberry imagined a time beyond the strife of the civil rights struggle, the Vietnam War, and mutually assured destruction and created a spacefaring utopia in *Star Trek*. His core message was that we would overcome our differences and join together as explorers of a fascinating universe. At the same time, though, *Star Trek* constantly reflected and commented on the issues of its day. It transported our troubles to other planets and projected them onto aliens to make it easier for viewers to consider such controversies via metaphor, creating a buffer against the painful reality of these issues. Through *Star Trek*, Roddenberry brought a new maturity to on-screen science fiction. But when the show first aired in 1966, it had a niche audience. Space stories could be cool and smart, but they had yet to prove they could be profitable.

That job fell, of course, to director George Lucas's *Star Wars* (1977). No prior science fiction film had ever created such a sensation, both at the box office and in the public imagination. *Star Wars* flowed directly from the space opera serials of the

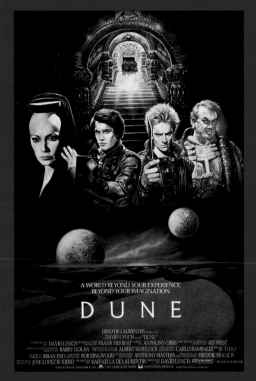

A WORLD BEYOND YOUR EXPERIENCE.
BEYOND YOUR IMAGINATION.

D U N E

DINO DE LAURENTIIS PRESENTS
A DAVID LYNCH FILM "DUNE"

1940s, bringing back the swashbuckling, interstellar action of *Flash Gordon*. What made *Star Wars* different and new was how realistic it looked. The starships had a mass that audiences could feel through the screen. The aliens were strange, beautiful, and repulsive. Most important, the film showed outer space and space travel as grimy, dented, littered, and lived in, giving authenticity to the larger-than-life characters and events.

Every studio wanted in on the action, and they shoveled money into science fiction and outer space stories. While there were some predictable imitations, this boom also saw the genre expand beyond its borders as space films moved with confidence into numerous new territories, exhibiting the maturity to tackle complex themes. These films presented space as a place of intense, psychosexual terror, as in *Alien* (1979), or as a means to tell stories about greed versus loyalty, as in *Aliens* (1986). Space also became a complex geopolitical arena in director David Lynch's *Dune* (1984) and, in *Enemy Mine* (1985), a crucible

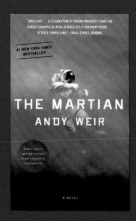

OPPOSITE Theatrical poster for David Lynch's *Dune*.

ABOVE Cover for Andy Weir's 2011 best-selling novel, *The Martian*, published by Broadway Books.

BELOW The cast of *Star Trek: The Next Generation*.

where enemies must learn to trust each other. Even James Bond went to space in *Moonraker* (1979), the same year that *Star Trek: The Motion Picture* came to the big screen. The late '70s through the 1980s was a new golden age of big-budget space films.

The literature also expanded as publishers added new sci-fi titles to take advantage of the genre's increased popularity. Here, too, the influence of *Star Wars* can be seen in various galaxy-spanning epics. David Weber took the welcome step of having a female lead in his *Honor Harrington* space opera series. Iain M. Banks's *Culture* novels are also grand in scope, but with a humanist message. This era also brought Douglas Adams's *The Hitchhiker's Guide to the Galaxy* (1979), a send-up of fifty years of outer space tropes. Frank Herbert, meanwhile, continued to expand his influential *Dune* series. Debuting in 1963, this moody, epic space opera features an oppressive empire, heroes with mystical powers, and strange quasi-religious groups. Clearly it influenced *Star Wars*, although the tone of the books is much more serious.

On television, similar growth occurred. *Star Trek* led the way as always, with four spin-off series, including the hugely popular *Star Trek: The Next Generation*, between 1987 and 2005, plus a new one in 2017. *Stargate SG-1*, about present-day soldiers who explore the galaxy via a network of alien gateways, ran for ten seasons. *Babylon 5* in the mid-'90s was an overlooked gem, striving for more complex and nuanced political and social structures in a *Star Trek*–inspired setting.

As writers and filmmakers prowled the outer reaches, some creators returned to our solar system and looked around with renewed interest. James S. A. Corey's *Expanse* novels, first published in 2011 and adapted to television starting in 2015, is set in a colonized solar system a few hundred years from now. The spaceships and other technologies are all based on realistic extrapolations of what we have today—things we know are possible.

The realism trend has even returned to Mars. Author Kim Stanley Robinson's *Mars* trilogy (beginning with *Red Mars* in 1993) brought a fresh approach to Mars fiction. He incorporated deep scientific accuracy, and in doing so showed that the actual Martian landscape and climate could be as beautiful and intriguing as any of Burroughs's fantasies. Andy Weir's *The Martian* goes further. The 2011 novel, which inspired director Ridley Scott's 2016 film, features a Mars that's as accurate as Robinson's, with added insight courtesy of the recent rover expeditions. The mission that strands botanist Mark Watney (played by Matt Damon in the film) there is equally realistic. The story trusts that the audience will find excitement in the way its down-to-Mars hero applies real science as he attempts to avoid certain death on the Red Planet.

Stories like *The Martian* show that realistic depictions of the challenges people will face in outer space have become as compelling as the exotic landscapes and epic scope of Burroughs and Lucas. At the same time, narratives set in the farthest reaches of space satisfy our need to think big about what we could see and do out there. Space, near and far, continues to call to us, and it will always be at the heart of science fiction.

GEORGE LUCAS

INTERVIEW BY JAMES CAMERON

INFLUENCED BY THE WRITINGS OF MYTHOLOGIST JOSEPH CAMPBELL, the cinema of Japanese master Akira Kurosawa, and the movie serials of his youth, George Lucas created the most popular and enduring science fiction saga of all time, *Star Wars*. The initial film, simply titled *Star Wars* (1977), was Lucas's third feature—following his debut, the dystopian sci-fi feature *THX 1138* (1971) and 1973's Oscar-nominated coming-of-age comedy *American Graffiti*. Following the immense pressures of bringing *Star Wars* to the screen, Lucas brought in other filmmakers to direct the sequels *Empire Strikes Back* (1980) and *Return of the Jedi* (1983), but took a strong hand in overseeing the creation of both films. Having founded the legendary visual effects company Industrial Light & Magic (ILM) during the making of the first *Star Wars* film, Lucas would become a pioneer of digital effects, pushing the boundaries of technology in a way that would have an indelible impact on the future of filmmaking.

In 1999, Lucas returned to the director's chair for his *Star Wars* prequel trilogy, writing and helming each of the three installments: *Star Wars: Episode I—The Phantom Menace*, *Star Wars: Episode II—Attack of the Clones*, and *Star Wars: Episode III—Revenge of the Sith*. In 2012, Lucas ended his hands-on involvement with the saga, selling his company Lucasfilm to Disney for $4 billion and marking a new era for the franchise.

Here, Lucas—who, with Steven Spielberg, created *Raiders of the Lost Ark*—explains how his personal passions for history and anthropology helped shape the worlds of *Star Wars*, the precise relationship between midi-chlorians and the Force, and the importance of compassion and empathy as humanity prepares to navigate an increasingly complex future.

JAMES CAMERON: I would submit that you single-handedly revolutionized science fiction in pop culture with *Star Wars* in 1977. It had been three decades of downer stuff, dystopian stuff, apocalyptic stuff, and science fiction was making less and less money every year. You came along with a vision of wonder and hope and empowerment—and boom.

GEORGE LUCAS: I come out of anthropology. In college, I was going to get a degree in anthropology, in social systems. That's what I'm interested in. In science fiction, you've got two branches. One is science and the other is social. I'm much more of the *1984* kind of guy than I am the spaceship guy. . . . I like spaceships, but it isn't the science, aliens, and all that kind of stuff that I get focused on. It's the, how do the people react to all of those things? And how do they accommodate them? That's the part that really fascinates me. I've already said that *Star*

Wars is a space opera, it's not science fiction. It's one of those soap operas, only in space.

JC: Yeah, but it's more than that and you know it is. It's a neo-myth. It fulfills the role that myth played in society.

GL: It's mythology and mythology is the cornerstone to a society. In order to have a society, you start out with a family. The dad's the boss, and everybody obeys the rules. Then as you get bigger, it comes to a few hundred people when you start adding in all the aunts and uncles and brothers-in-law. . . . Then you have two or three families together, which is a tribe. Once you've got a tribe, you got this problem that you have to get a social mechanism by which you can control them. Otherwise they just kill each other.

JC: You're taking these ideas of social structure and blowing them up on this vast canvas.

GL: But at the same time in society, you have to have a reason why thou shalt not kill. We believe in the same gods. We believe in the same heroes. We believe in the same political system. Once you got those, then you can actually put a whole bunch of people together and have cities and have civilization. That's the thing that drove me: Why do we believe the things [we do]? Why do [we] move on the cultural ideas that we have? It gets more complex as we get older. I thought we had reached a stable point after World War II, which is when I grew up—

JC: And through the '60s.

GL: [The] '50s and '60s. Well, [the] '60s we finally came to the conclusion that the government wasn't all that it said it was. [It's like] *The Wizard of Oz*. They open the curtain, and we looked and said, "Oh my god. This is terrible, and I'm going to get sent to Vietnam and die. Well, I'm not going to do this." So, that changed a huge covenant we had with our government and with ourselves and with our society and what we [thought] we were. But we still believed that we were right, that we were saving the world from Communism. They were terrible and Stalin, at least, was terrible. So, it's easy to see the good guys and the bad guys. [Our shared] mythology, the last step that it had taken was the Western. The Western had a real mythology—you don't shoot people in the back. You don't draw first. You always let the woman go first.

JC: It was a code of honor.

GL: A code of honor. Then [the genre] got very psychological, and the Western went out of favor. It was really that that led me to *Star Wars*. But before that I [was], I don't know, an angry young man who was saying, "This is terrible. We're living in the future." Everything you say is bad about the future, *1984*, it's all real. It's right now, and I'm going to make a movie about right now.

JC: Which was *THX 1138*.

GL: Which was *THX*. It looked like the future, but it wasn't.

JC: So, you weren't a child of the '60s. You were a touch before that. But your maturation as a filmmaker, as an artist, came in the late '60s, so it seems to me *THX 1138* was a direct response to these ideas of oppression and the rise of technology as a means of oppression.

GL: Well, yeah, and it was also based on a concept—again, a lot of things that are in those movies are based on social concepts—but the main theme of that movie, which also goes over into *American Graffiti* and *Star Wars*, is one that I learned early when I was in high school. I didn't do well in high school. I was in a car crash, and I reconsidered my life, how I was going to handle myself. Well, I'll go to college. I didn't think anything was ever going to come of it. But what happens is you start going in a particular direction and opportunities present themselves. You just keep pushing forward. And if you push forward, you realize that the only limitations you have are in your mind. That's *THX*. You're in a white limbo. You can go out anytime you want, you just won't. You're afraid to.

JC: So, your metaphor [is] the prison of your own mind.

GL: Right. You're imprisoned by your vision—if you can't imagine it, you can't do it. So, use your imagination. And think outside the box. It's the same thing in *American Graffiti*: "I'm just going to go to school here and go to junior college. I'm not going to go to all those big schools because I could never do that." If you say, "I can, I'm going to try," you can succeed. It's the same thing—"Oh, I can't make movies." I wasn't going to make theatrical films. I was going to make artistic, tone-poem kind of things. [Experimental filmmaker] Stan Brakhage stuff. But whatever opportunity presented itself, I wasn't so single-minded, which a lot of the kids at school were.

OPPOSITE Theatrical poster for George Lucas's dystopian classic, *THX 1138* (1971).

Visit the future where love
is the ultimate crime.
THX 1138

Warner Bros. presents THX 1138 · An American Zoetrope Production · Starring
Robert Duvall and Donald Pleasence · with Don Pedro Colley, Maggie McOmie
and Ian Wolfe · Technicolor® · Techniscope® · Executive Producer, Francis Ford
Coppola · Screenplay by George Lucas and Walter Murch · Story by George Lucas
Produced by Lawrence Sturhahn · Directed by George Lucas · Music by Lalo Schifrin

JC: You broke out of the pack early right in film school.

GL: I was very fortunate. When we were there, everybody was pretty liberal. I mean, there were some people [who said], "I want to do art films [like] Godard." [Or], "You like Kurosawa? Go do Kurosawa. And then John Ford." They were very open-minded. At some of the schools—I won't mention names—it [had] to be artistic. My feeling when I was in film school is I'll do anything. Give me commercials. I can do commercials. I love the medium. I love to play with it.

JC: That's what it was like working for [legendary B-movie director] Roger Corman when I

started out. We didn't care if it was a night nurses film or a science fiction movie with giant maggots. As long as you got to make a film, it was cool. There was no Cahiers du Cinéma in the discussion.

GL: I love Godard and I love Kurosawa. Kurosawa especially. And Fellini. It's funny because we don't have that milieu anymore. It's funny the way it's dissipated. But you find, just as you do, say in the Renaissance or in Paris in the '20s, a group of talented people who were outcasts come together for whatever reason. They all find themselves in the same place at the same time, and they all meet each other because it's a small world. Then all this stuff comes out of that. It's like, oh, the '70s, that

ABOVE Robert Duvall and Maggie McOmie in *THX 1138*.

was such a great [time]. That was just us. We weren't doing anything special.

JC: But there was a rebel spirit, an antiauthoritarian spirit. To me, *THX 1138* was a science fiction manifestation of that kind of counterculture zeitgeist. I saw it in '71. I think I was a senior in high school at the time.

GL: The only people who really saw it were hallucinating.

JC: No, I was straight. I didn't do drugs until later.

GL: *THX* fell into the beginnings of the *2001* syndrome, which is people go around saying, "Man, that film was so great if you're stoned."

JC: It also fell into the *2001* syndrome in the sense that it wasn't recognized in its time. It was recognized later.

GL: They said, "It's not a space film. It's a hallucinogenic movie."

JC: When I saw it, I saw the through line from *Brave New World*, *1984*, all of the dystopian classics just elevated into a more technological setting. The chrome cop in *Terminator 2* is a direct outgrowth of the chrome cops in *THX*.
  But I think it's interesting when you think of *Star Wars*, which is a very mythological end of the spectrum in action/adventure and heroism, and *THX* on the other end of the science fiction spectrum, on the dystopian side. The through line is that you've got a rebel main character who comes to a kind of enlightenment or a different view of the world.

GL: Sort of blossoms into their own potential to say, "Well, I can't do that. I can't leave my stepfather or my uncle. I got to stay with the fields." And it's all about, hey, you don't have as much impact on the world as you think you do. That's Obi-Wan Kenobi: "Well, if that's what you want." It's not that [the characters' fates are] preordained; you can put two and two

together and say, "Don't go back in that burning building because it's way too late."

JC: You're on to an interesting thing there. So many of these movies have started to reinterpret this kind of mythic element of the one, the predestined hero, the hero who must be something, whereas your heroes are heroes by choice. They get to a fork in the road and they take the fork and it's choice. It's not predestination. At least I don't think that's what you're saying.

GL: Predestination in my mind is . . . your genetics. Your genes are your destiny. It's biological. People say, oh, don't put the biology in it. . . . But we all have talent. And those of us that have talent know that we're different than other people. We know we can do things that other people can't do. Talk to any filmmaker, artist, or anything, you have this sense in your head of what works and what doesn't work. Sometimes you're wrong. It's not foolproof. But at the same time, it's something that's innate in your genetic code that makes you look at things in a particular way.

JC: You're only wrong if your film doesn't make money.

GL: Or you're only wrong if it looks stupid.

JC: There's no absolute arbiter of that in art, you know?

GL: Yeah, I'm a very strong believer that art is in the eye of the beholder. But I'm also a very strong believer in the fact that art is an emotional communication. And if you can't communicate emotionally, it's not art. The concept that if it's popular, it's not art, and if it's art, it's not popular is not right at all. That's just completely bogus. If you're able to appeal emotionally to millions of people, that's a wonderful thing.

JC: Let's go back to what your influences were that fed into the creation of *Star Wars*. Obviously, some of them are from the science fiction world, and some of them are from the worlds of sociology and anthropology. Can we draw out those roots? As much as *Star Wars* seemed to just leap from your forehead fully formed, it had roots that anybody in the science fiction world knows.

GL: Nothing in this world pops into your head fully formed. And for artists that are struggling with a vision—and I use the word *artist* liberally—you have an idea in your head, and you're trying to make it real.

JC: Ed Wood was struggling with a vision.

GL: Everybody does. You get this idea of something that you think would be cool, and then you struggle to make it real. It's real in your head, vaguely, but when you actually put it down [on paper], you say, "Oh, that isn't at all like it was in my dream."

JC: Exactly. So, was it comics? Was it books?

GL: I read comic books when I was little because I grew up before television. There wasn't anything else to do. I liked all different kinds of comic books—this was way before the big-time action/adventure comic books. This was more in the Little Lulu stuff. Television came in when I was about ten years old. I had Superman and Batman, but I didn't get obsessed by them or anything. It's the same thing about science fiction. I like science fiction. I read it, but I wasn't a fan. I really liked *1984* and really liked *Dune*. . . .

JC: *Dune* is a great reference point because I think a lot of people have forgotten what a big influence it was on all of us during that time.

GL: Same thing with *Lord of the Rings*—the concept of creating a world that has its own laws, its own reality. It's fascinating. That's really what I like to do.

JC: Government systems, lineages, guilds, organizations—

GL: The whole organization of societies and how they work. That was what I really liked rather than science fiction. I liked Ray Bradbury. I liked Asimov. Mostly what I read was history. As I discovered when I was an early teenager, the history that I was being taught in school—this is the date, this is what happened—it's not history. History is learning about the psychology of the people who were doing [things in the past] and the problems they were having. Why they did it, and what they were thinking. What incidents early on in their life [influenced them]. What was Josephine's role in Napoleon's craziness? That's what's fascinating.

JC: You're thinking like a storyteller writing from a character and using that as your lens into history.

GL: It's the same thing in Homer. It's really about Hercules and Ajax. It's about the characters, not about the wars. How they turned on each other. They couldn't stay true to their beliefs. Alexander the Great, Ramses. It's not that much different than what's going on today.

JC: There are references to cloud cities going all the way back to Aristophanes. This idea of the shining city in the sky is something that is handed down.

GL: It's Olympus. It's not a mountain. It's actually up there in the clouds somewhere. And it's heaven. In college, I studied Campbell. I became very interested in comparative religions and in how these mythologies all interworked. It was Joseph Campbell that showed me that all these great mysteries have the same psychological roots. Even though they're told all over the world over thousands of years, they all come back to the same psychological roots. What I did is I took what I was learning from Joe, and then did a whole bunch of research.

JC: Did you actually mentor with him?

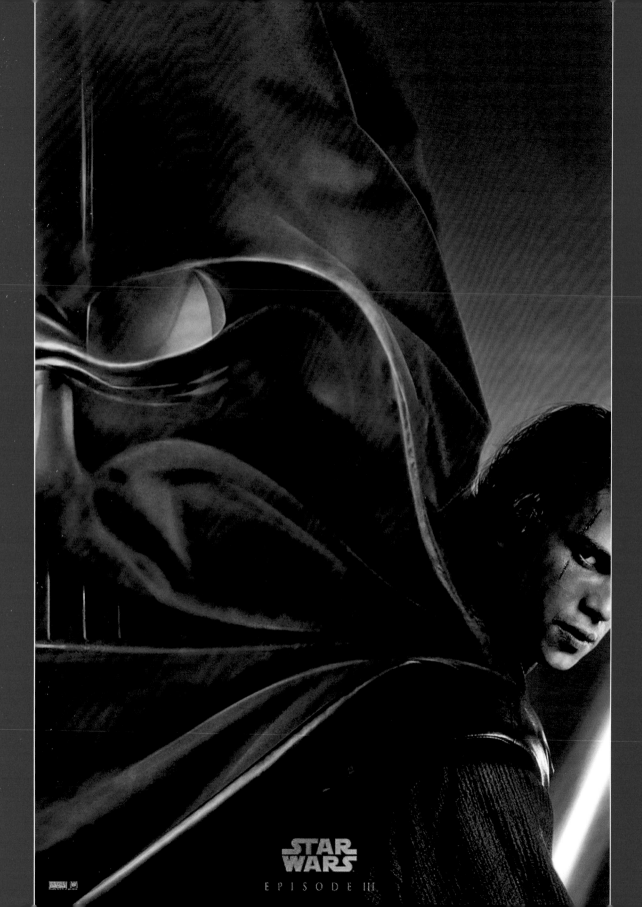

GL: I studied him in school. When I did *Star Wars*, I did two years of research. What I was studying was mythology and comparative religion. I was trying to come up with ideas that you could . . . basically bring these things down to a universal compound, which is kind of what Joe had been doing.

JC: Yeah, *The Hero with a Thousand Faces* [Campbell's seminal book on comparative mythology].

GL: In the end, the idea of a god or a godhead is basically a psychological need that people have. I didn't get sucked into a religion. I grew up a Methodist. When I was in college, friends of mine were Catholic. I became very enamored of the Catholic religion because I liked the rituals. They were still doing Latin in those days. It was so odd and strange and weird. Eventually after college I got into Buddhism, and then I started studying all of them. Bottom line is, I came up with my own interpretation of what I think that is. It's the battle between selfishness and selflessness.

JC: Good and evil redefined in those terms.

GL: That's good and evil. Almost every religion is promoting the "good" side. And the good side is, in a simple word, God is love. And they all say it, in a different way, but they all say exactly the same thing. And that being selfish is based on fear—the battle is between fear and no fear. You're afraid of everything and everybody, so you mask it with all this other stuff. But if you can be brave enough to be compassionate to other people, regardless of the consequence, then you will have a happy life. The other one where you're afraid, you're greedy, you're living in this endless cycle of fear. That makes you very unhappy, very angry . . . Yoda, Yoda, Yoda. That's what it really all comes down to in the end. You either live a compassionate life, or you lead a selfish life. And if you're going to be selfish, you're going to be unhappy. If you're going to be compassionate, then you're going to be happy.

JC: But it's not *Star Peace*. It's *Star Wars*. There's still conflict, and Yoda can still swing a mean lightsaber. Somewhere in there, there has to be an ethos of righteous conflict.

GL: The Jedi, they don't attack, they only defend. Yoda didn't attack until the [fifth] film.

JC: But he did. So, there are things worth fighting for.

GL: There's a conundrum ultimately. It's been there forever. Which is, are you just going to sit there and let them kill you? Or your loved ones? Or destroy the world that you know? Or are you going to try to fix it? At some point, you do have to stand up for what you believe in. Obviously, I can make my religion be whatever I want it to be. It doesn't have to be consistent. If a cobra's going to strike you, I think you have every right to put a stick up there and hit him over the head. Because it's either him or you.

Of course, this is the mythology of the cowboy. They always put him in these crises where you have to choose between your own personal values and the practicality of what you need to do. You've got to pick up the sheriff's badge even though you had all these problems in the past. You're going to have to go out and kill people again. Even though you said you'd never do it.

JC: It's a collision of values.

GL: And it's an interesting story. But generally speaking, if you're compassionate, you're on the bright side, and you live a good life. Dark side, you turn into Darth Vader, and all is bad.

JC: These are sociological, moral, ethical, spiritual themes that you chose to write large on this vast canvas of outer space.

GL: Right. That was where *Star Wars* came from. The other part was, when I was growing up I loved Republic serials and things where there always was a lot of action and

cliffhangers. I loved *Flash Gordon*. The idea of going into space, *Buck Rogers*, as crude as it was. Mainly because of cars. I liked racing around in cars. So, a spaceship is even better. Or a jet. I can remember when a jet would come over, and we'd see the contrail, everybody would come out of the house and look. It was the idea of spaceships flying around. But I didn't want [*Star Wars*] to be *2001*.

JC: You did the anti-*2001*.

GL: But *2001*, as far as I'm concerned, is the best science fiction film ever made. It is the quintessential [depiction] of what space travel is. There are no monsters in it.

JC: It's our own technology coming around and biting us on the ass.

GL: And it looks great. It's impeccable the way they put it together. So, I said, "Well, I'm not going to make a science fiction movie like that. That's a great movie, and I can't go there." But I admired it a great deal.

JC: But you still used some of the [cinematic] language that he used, the *Discovery* coming overhead endlessly is basically the precursor of the opening shot of *Star Wars*. It stunned everybody, myself included. I even knew the reference as I was watching it, and I was still blown away.

GL: Everybody says you make this stuff up from whole cloth. You don't. It doesn't pop out of your

brain. It's an accumulation of all the things you've seen. You just store it. Then when you go to regurgitate it into your own thing, you take all the best parts. When you move those things together, it's like chemistry. Things happen that you could never imagine. I talk to kids and they say, "Where did you get the ideas for all those aliens? Where did you think that up?" I said, "Well, go to the aquarium. You're going to see them all there."

JC: That's what I did on *Avatar*. I took the ocean, I took all my diving, and I just brought it [into the world of Pandora].

GL: That's one of the most brilliant things in *Avatar*. One of the biggest problems you have in science fiction movies [is] you have to create a real world, a real world that doesn't exist. What Kurosawa used to say is it has to have immaculate reality.

JC: I like that term. But you took it to a new level. No film that I can think of had the "used future" idea. The future was always shiny. It was always perfect. It always had just been unwrapped on Christmas morning. Even in dystopian terms, it was always sterile and pure. You said, "No, the future has to have been lived in for thousands of years." So, the Sandcrawler's all rusted. Things are broken. It looked like it had been lived in. Where did that idea come from? Because there was no precursor to that.

GL: I just felt it was really immaculate reality, which is to say it's got to look like it's a real

OPPOSITE A poster for the twelve-part serial *Flash Gordon Conquers the Universe* (1940).

TOP The famous opening crawl from the *Flash Gordon* serials that George Lucas would mimic in the *Star Wars* films.

place. But that's the same thing that you did with *Avatar*—the hardest thing is to create a world. It takes a long, long time to create an alien world that you can actually shoot. What you did, you took the underwater world, and you made it in the real world. I know you well enough to know [that *Avatar*] came from diving and [spending vast quantities of time] underwater. And it's brilliant. It just created a world that was so alien, but it's not.

JC: As a teen, I wanted to go to space. My hunger was for space, for other worlds, for adventure—the different, the new, the alien. I knew in my bones I was never going to be one of those astronauts. But I thought, I can go learn to scuba dive, and I can go into the other world that's right here on Earth, the alien world right here on Earth. For me, learning to dive wasn't initially about a love of the ocean. That came later. It was a love of the different, and the alien, and the bizarre and wanting to see it

PAGES 102–103 James Cameron's concept designs for Neytiri in *Avatar.*

with my own eyes and touch it. So, that's why it came full circle back into *Avatar.*

GL: I think that every animal, every little bug, every little thing, every plant in *Avatar* is real. You believe it's a real thing. That it actually has purpose in that world. We might not understand it. It may be very weird, but it seems to have purpose.

JC: This is coming from the master world builder—you didn't just create one world, you created many worlds in a universe.

GL: I tell people, I say, "Jim had it easy. He only had to create one world. I had to create about eight or nine." I wanted to fly around a lot. So, I had to have places to go. That's why I invented light speed. . . . I made *Star Wars* for kids. It appeals to everybody, but it was still made for twelve-year-olds. But don't underestimate twelve-year-olds. They're smarter than the rest of us. Don't think you're going to talk down to them. They get stuff much faster than you do. The whole point was to allow them to think outside the box. Everybody's going to say, "There's no sound in space." Tell them to go to hell. In my world, in my space, you have sound. Who said Wookiees can't fly? I decided they can fly. Think outside the box. No matter what somebody tells you, what you learned, throw all that away and say, "I can do anything I want to do." I have a fantasy world. It's not science, it's fantasy. Therefore, you can do anything. You can bend the rules. You're in a completely different universe. And you can enjoy that and come up with really crazy stuff. It's fun.

Star Wars was more fantasy than it is science fiction. It has elements of science in it, but the elements of science are things that I said, "I'm not going to obey the rules." I lived by the theme, if you can imagine it you can do it. I had laser swords. All my physicist friends came to me and said, "A laser goes on forever. You can't stop it. You can't have it this long. That's just not possible." I made the movie, and then every other kid that came up to me said, "When I grow up, I'm going to build a lightsaber." And as it turned out, some scientist developed—after many years—a lightsaber. For no other reason than they wanted to do it.

JC: Because they were influenced by the movie.

GL: They had to change the physics. They had to deal with things that were scientifically impossible, but they made it. They did it. That's one of those things where there's no actual useful purpose, but there will be some day. It's the same thing about space suits. The old story about space suits is, why do space suits look the way they look? Because if you go back to the movies in the '50s and the '40s that had space suits in them—

JC: They were skintight.

GL: That's what they looked like. They had helmets, they had glass. Then you go to reality, and you have these scientists at this lab [asking], well, what should it look like? Well, I saw this science fiction movie, and they had a helmet. They had glass that went all the way around. . . .

JC: They will never admit that it was based on a science fiction movie, but it's there in the back of their minds.

GL: They were saying, of course we've seen them. Now what we have to do is make them practical. But we know what they look like. And they looked like that because the people that did it were artists.

JC: Well, Chesley Bonestell's rocket ships—he's the most famous painter of space and astronomy subjects ever—his rocket ships come right from the Buster Crabbe *Flash Gordon* and the *Buck Rogers* stuff. Those rocket ships came from the covers of *Amazing Stories*. It wasn't until the lunar module came along and didn't look anything like that, that we were sort of jerked up short and said, "Well that's actually not what a rocket landing on the moon will look like."

There was a long period of human history, thousands of years, where we had stories of monsters and demons, and angels and spirits and gods, myths and fairytales. Then the enlightenment and science and the Industrial Revolution came along and beat the magic out of it. You found a way to use technology to put the magic back into a kind of mythic/legend/fairytale context. But you just dressed it up in science terms.

GL: One of the issues, ultimately, is that you could write science fiction, but you couldn't make it into a movie. You can write it, and you can describe all kinds of things, but then you say what does that actually look like? You can draw a drawing of it, and you say, "Well that's great, but how does it work? I mean, the legs are way too

thin to support something." It looks cool, and then you get down to the real science. And it's very, very hard to do it in a movie. Technology wasn't there to do that. The glass ceiling for science fiction was technology. So, we pushed the limits again from where Kubrick took it.

JC: You pushed the technology. Dynamic motion control hadn't existed until *Star Wars*.

GL: After we did the [first] three *Star Wars* [films] . . . computers were coming out. But they weren't sophisticated at all. What we did was say, OK, I'm going to spend a lot of time here, and a lot of money, and I'm going to develop a digital way of doing this stuff because right now you can't do it. I mean, Yoda, he's a puppet for god's sake. The challenge of making a puppet seem like a real creature, that hadn't happened then. The idea of radio-control eyes and all that stuff was just starting to come into the picture. But I still couldn't get him to run. It took a huge amount of work, and the problem was that the audience was becoming more and more sophisticated. They were able to see the wires. And so we had to work a lot harder. I spent a lot of time and a lot of money developing digital technology, primarily at ILM, to develop things that you could not develop.

JC: You were trying to unleash your imagination.

GL: The great thing about *Star Wars* is I had a vessel that I could throw anything into. The trouble is, I had to make it. I had the problem of the fact that I'm a moviemaker, not a writer. So, it came down to [figuring] out a way of accomplishing these things. That was the struggle of the digital technology. But now that we've got digital technology, you can think up anything!

JC: That's right. We're only limited by our imagination. But if you look at the history of science fiction in pop culture, *Star Wars* was such a huge milestone for all the reasons we've been talking about—the neo-myth and reinvention of, or actually a creation of, a whole

new genre in a sense. But it was also a huge breakthrough in technology in terms of the actual imagery on the screen. You could take that exact script and do it ten years earlier with what was available then, or five years earlier, and it would, frankly, suck. It would be a stodgy costume drama. But the dynamic of the ships—

GL: Immaculate reality. If you put that first, you got a giant brick wall. And you really have to think your way out of it. There's nothing that makes me crazier than a rubber suit, and you can see the rubber. But there was a period of time when the only way for you to realize your vision of alien worlds was to do a rubber suit. Greedo was a guy in a rubber mask. Jabba was a big rubber guy. Well, originally he wasn't. Originally, we had to abandon him because we couldn't figure out how to do it. I knew I couldn't get a big rubber guy moving around in there. We had several designs at that point. But we also ran out of time and money.

JC: So you put him in a later film.

GL: Well, I just cut him out of the film. I shot the scene and everything. We had a stand-in guy to be where the monster would be, and it was going to be an animatronic monster. But we just ran out of time and money. When we were able to do the special edition and I was able to put that scene back in, instead of going to an animatronic figure, by now we had computer characters. So we said, "Let's try to make him into a computer character. That was one of the first [instances] of putting a computer character in a scene with a live actor. Poor Jar Jar [Binks, the digital character in *The Phantom Menace*] gets beat up, but he's the first digital [character] that actually acts and has dialogue. . . .

JC: A full character.

GL: Out of that came Gollum.

JC: When I saw Gollum, I realized that *Avatar*,

which had been sitting in a drawer for years, was now possible. That the technology had, if not caught up completely, at least gotten to a point where I could push it. Because what you did is you pushed the technology on two fronts. One was motion control, which everybody sort of forgets was an enormous breakthrough in its time, dynamic motion control.

GL: The first [*Lord of the Rings*] film was done around the same time we did *Phantom Menace.* We were helping them over there. We sent guys from ILM over there, they sent guys back. We helped them build their sound studios. We were all pals.

JC: Well, I think [director of Weta Digital] Joe Letteri came out of ILM originally.

GL: [What was remarkable with Gollum] was all they were able to accomplish was his face. . . . After Jar Jar, we said, "This is how you do it." We had actually done motion capture before that, which was a result of [pioneering visual effects artist] Phil Tippett. He was using [a variation of stop-motion animation known as] Go-Motion. He was so destroyed by the fact that this new technology had come along. It was like a big funeral. He said, "I've already got my armatures. Can't we rig the armatures so I can do the armature, and then you can put the computer figure on the armature?" So, that's how that started.

JC: There's a human puppeteering or performance aspect to it—which is really the heart of all the performance [capture] characters. . . . I want a performer, I want the soul of a human behind the creature, whether it's a flying creature or a running creature, whatever it is. We act it out.

GL: You are getting information that you can't get any other way. And you're really capturing the actors' most subtle performances. It used to be the purview of the animator, and animators are very talented.

But animation never focused down that fine on a human face, or on what they were doing. Actors have a talent for understanding the quirks and foibles of a character. A computer can't do that. It would have to learn artificial intelligence first, then you would have to teach them to understand what a human is [thinking] when they're doing these crazy things. That's never going to happen.

JC: But the artificial intelligence community would disagree with that, and say it's only a matter of time before they have artificial general intelligence that is the equal of a human

STAR WARS EPISODE I

mind. I would submit that for it to be the equal of a human mind, it has to have emotions, it has to have love and hate.

GL: What they are [also] talking about now is, What are you going to do when they go crazy? And they go out and decide to kill everybody?

JC: I made that film. . . . Let's talk about AI. You had AI characters in *THX*. The police robots, they were a limited form of AI. There was a priestly, spiritual character that would talk to you, a limited form of AI.

GL: It was an AI society. Only it didn't quite work. It didn't interface with humans very well.

JC: It didn't want you to be human either. I love that the whole pursuit ends—

GL: The villain [in movies] is always the rogue police chief that says, "I don't care what it takes, you go out and get him. Buy an airplane, crash into—"

JC: You flipped it.

GL: I flipped it.

JC: All the robots stopped when the budget exceeded the value of capturing the guy. Everybody just stopped, turned around, and went back. And let him go.

GL: But now we do have artificial intelligence, and it is a real issue. We've really got to be careful about what we're doing.

JC: It took Hiroshima and Nagasaki to teach us that nuclear war was a pretty bad idea. We're going to have to have some kind of AI apocalypse that hopefully doesn't take us out completely. We're not going to learn without a lesson being taught. We're not going to learn climate change without severe symptoms.

GL: I keep telling people, look, we're not going to save the planet. Are you kidding? We don't have any power to save anything. But the planet's going be OK. It'll look like Mars, but it's going to be fine. Who knows? Mars may have been like Earth and lost its atmosphere. . . . I still think they're going to find life on Mars. I'm absolutely convinced of it. There's going to be life all over the solar system.

Everybody hated it in *Phantom Menace* [when] we started to talk about midi-chlorians. There's a whole aspect to that movie that is about symbiotic relationships. To make you look and see that we aren't the boss. That there's an ecosystem here.

JC: There's an ecosystem inside us called the microbiome that they're just learning about now.

GL: [The next three *Star Wars* films] were going to get into a microbiotic world. But there's this world of creatures that operate differently than we do. I call them the Whills. And the Whills are the ones who actually control the universe. They feed off the Force.

JC: You were creating a religion, George.

GL: Back in the day, I used to say ultimately what this means is we were just cars, vehicles, for the Whills to travel around in. . . . We're vessels for them. And the conduit is the midi-chlorians. The midi-chlorians are the ones that communicate with the Whills. The Whills, in a general sense, they are the Force.

JC: But you're putting detail and a facade of science around an idea that's pretty timeless, which is the spirit, the soul, heaven, causation. . . . But in your world-building, you're going back to archetype, which is spirit, the godhead, all that sort of thing.

GL: All the way back to—with the Force and the Jedi and everything—the whole concept of how things happen was laid out completely from [the beginning] to the end. But I never got to finish. I never got to tell people about it.

JC: It's a creation myth, and you can't build a world without a creation myth. Every religion, every mythology has a creation myth.

GL: If I'd held onto the company I could have done it, and then it would have been done. Of course, a lot of the fans would have hated it, just like they did *Phantom Menace* and everything, but at least the whole story from beginning to end would be told.

JC: You don't work for them.

GL: I don't anymore. I don't work for anybody anymore. I'm my free person. I have my own will.

JC: I don't think a filmmaker works for their fans. [I think a filmmaker] works for themselves to try to just get the stuff up on the screen that they see in their head. . . . I want to go back to this idea of AI because you have two of the most popular AI characters in pop culture, R2-D2 and C-3PO. They're AIs. They're artificial, and intelligent.

GL: I still feel strongly [that] the robots are our friends. They may not be.

JC: I made money off them not being our friends. You made money off them being our friends.

GL: I've said, let's see the good side of the robots, the funny side. Even though I have some bad ones too. But at the same time, it was a way of saying you know, we're going to live in a world with robots and artificial intelligence. You might as well get used to it. You shouldn't be afraid of it. If it goes bad, it's us, it's not them. They will be a reflection of us.

JC: Putin just said that the country that dominates AI will rule the world. I don't know anybody who wants to rule the world in the first place.

GL: I don't even know what that means, rule the world. In *Star Wars* [we asked ourselves],

what is the end game here? The end game for the Sith was to bring the world into a very selfish, self-centered, greedy, evil place, as opposed to a compassionate place.

JC: But your bad guys were human or variants on human. They weren't artificial intelligences. And your good guys, you only see robots in a positive role, which is interesting because that's where so much of the progress is being made now with companions for the elderly, robotic nurses, and medical assistants.

GL: Well they can be very helpful. They're going to drive our cars. They're going to make life better for us. Now, once they start to replicate—we've heard these stories over and over—it's possible you get a glitch. That glitch, well, you're the granddaddy of all this. The megacomputer gets a headache and starts killing everybody. But it's more likely the humans they are serving will direct them to be evil. A machine itself won't be evil unless there's a glitch. But we must teach them compassion. We must realize it's a better world if they teach compassion and everybody helps everybody and they love one another. It depends on humans. And humans just aren't that smart.

JC: We're smart enough to create something smarter than ourselves.

GL: But we're building something that is going to be intellectually smarter than we are, but we haven't changed emotionally in ten thousand years. And that's the problem. We haven't learned to not kill people. We haven't even learned that yet after ten thousand years. Did you see *Idiocracy*?

JC: We're living in *Idiocracy* right now. You talk about living in a science fiction world? All the parodies and the extremes that were explored in science fiction literature, we're living through a lot of them right now. . . . You're a very opinionated guy in analyzing political systems and social systems, human systems. And the way

using asymmetric warfare against a highly organized empire. I think we call those guys terrorists today.

GL: Yes.

JC: So, it was a very antiauthoritarian, very kind of '60s against-the-man thing nested deep inside of a fantasy. . . . If you look at the inception of this country, it's a very noble fight of the underdog against the massive empire. You look at the situation now where America is so proud of being the biggest economy, the most powerful military force on the planet—it's become the Empire from the perspective of a lot of people around the world.

GL: Well, it was the Empire during the Vietnam War. It was the Empire. Everything after World War II, we were the Empire. We never learned from England or Rome or a dozen empires.

JC: Empires fall. And they fall because of failure of leadership or government often. You have a great line which is, "So, this is how [democracy] dies, in thunderous applause." It was a condemnation of populism in a science fiction context. . . . I want to still circle back to this idea that space means many things to many people. To you, it was a blank canvas to create other societies and other cultures. To Ridley Scott in *The Martian*, it was science: We're going to science our way out of this. That's a very different end of the spectrum.

GL: He was doing kind of the same thing, which is, there's a lot out there we don't know. . . . [There are two keys to] survival. One is you must migrate. Two, you must adapt. Now, we're sitting here on this planet. . . .

JC: We've got no place to migrate to.

GL: That's where space comes in. We've got to get to another solar system. I used to say it was millions of years away, but maybe not. Maybe we can get there in less than a million

you express that as an artist is through science fiction. By creating this mirror that pushed out to either a distant place or a distant future in *THX 1138*, you show it back to us. We say, oh, we'll never be like that. Except we already are.

GL: That's what *THX* is saying. The tagline on it is "the future is here." When I eventually got to *Star Wars*, [I set the story in] a galaxy far, far away, a long, long time ago. Because once you say it has a relationship to us, then people start getting their backs up. But if you can look at it [as being completely detached from the world we know], you can get the message without fighting it. And kind of enjoying it. But the message is still the same.

JC: But you did something very interesting with *Star Wars* if you think about it. You created this lens of a distant future or past or faraway place. The good guys are the rebels. They're

years. I mean, there's a lot of secrets in the universe. We don't know anything. That's the one thing I do know for sure. We know nothing. Scientists know nothing.

JC: Scientists can't even find 95 percent of the mass of the universe. We know 5 percent.

GL: We know 5 percent of everything there is to know. We got a long way to go. There's a lot of things we're going to discover that are going to blow our minds. You have to assume at some point, we'll do it. But you can't do it unless you start marching forward. I say if you can't imagine it, you can't do it.

JC: Isn't science fiction a way to start to collectively imagining that?

GL: Imagination, it's exercised through science fiction or through any kind of literature, any kind of art form, any kind of art where you're actually not bound by convention. You have science, and some of the best science [occurred] when people were not bound by the convention.

JC: People who were inspired by science fiction—I know a lot of space scientists, I'm assuming you do, too—almost every one of them says, "I grew up on a diet of science fiction," or, "I was inspired by science fiction to think about the greater universe, and now I'm doing it."

GL: Science fiction is basically saying there are no limits. . . . Science fiction says, let's not think about what is going on right now and what we know. Let's think about the possibilities of what we could do or what could happen. Anything. It's exercising the imagination that will help move mankind forward into different and better worlds. It's a form of literature. It's a form of art, but it's basically a form of art that says we can open up our minds to all kinds of things. Same thing as with *Star Wars*. I said, "I'm going to have spaceships fly around and they're going to be like this and it's going to be so fantastic."

JC: And you can be in another star system in a day or so.

GL: The guy next to me says, "How are we going to do that?" That's the scientist.

JC: Einstein says you can't travel faster than the speed of light, and you threw that away in one shot. "Alright, jump to light speed." It's like we're not going to play by those rules. . . . Do you think there's alien life?

GL: Definitely. And I think it's bacteria. They're the only ones who have mastered space travel. I mean they can get here from other galaxies, for god's sake.

JC: They can just drift around for a million years and then wake back up.

GL: They can live for god knows how long. You can freeze them and unfreeze them, and they're life-forms just like us.

JC: You're talking about panspermia, the idea that life might have originated on Earth and spread to other places, or it might have originated on Mars, let's say, got blasted off by an asteroid, drifted here.

GL: It can grow anywhere. But it can also travel anywhere, and it's also much more hardy than humans are. It's only one cell. But it's very powerful. It's faster. It can think faster than we can. It can do all kinds of things better than we can. It's a different form of life, and I don't think we've even figured it out, how it interfaces with itself.

JC: You and I probably have two or three pounds of bacteria in our body that are doing useful things for us and living in symbiosis with us. . . . I think we compress all of those early years into just a few years before the dinosaurs. In reality, there were about 2.5 billion years of single-celled organisms only. The history of multicellular life on Earth is only about 700 million years, which is not very much in the grand scheme.

GL: I've talked to a lot of scientists, and the area I'm interested in is that transition from one cell to two cells. They're still working on it. Now that they're beginning to get the DNA of bacteria and realizing that there's billions of them, different kinds and they do different things, that's going to be the biggest, I think, medical change we've ever had. Of course, I'm coming from the point of view that it was the bacteria that helped create the mitochondria and then the mitochondria that helped create multicelled animals.

JC: So, it's not a coincidence that mitochondria sounds a bit like midi-chlorians.

GL: Midi-chlorians are mitochondria.

JC: Well mitochondria are amazing. But see now you're, now you're taking myth and religion and spirituality and putting scientific terms to it.

GL: I'm just a farmer sitting in my cornfield saying, What if? And then the mitochondria, if they got enough energy, they could make two cells, and then once you can make two cells, then you can make this whole world.

JC: Then you can make anything. You can make us. Any kind of complexity.

GL: That doesn't mean to discredit the single-celled animals. Because there's more of them.

JC: Not at all. Don't we want big cool creatures and animals and intelligent beings to interface with?

GL: That was the one issue that I had been dealing with right before I sold [Lucasfilm]. Everybody had hated the midi-chlorian part [of the prequel films] so much—I was simply

ABOVE George Lucas directs Anthony Daniels on the set of *Star Wars: Episode II – Attack of the Clones* (2002).

GL: It's a combination of mitochondria and chlorophyll. Chlorophyll is the mitochondria of plant life. If you take those two together, that's the source of all energy.

JC: You told me you weren't a science fiction guy, but this is classic science fiction.

figuring out a way to explain it that didn't piss everybody off. Because I knew you couldn't see it. But you can't see the Force. It's a powerful thing, but you can't see it.

JC: But the aliens that are macro aliens. Greedo and Jar Jar and Jabba and all those guys, what are they? I think in storytelling, they're just reflections of us. If we really find an intelligent species out there, it probably won't look like anything we've imagined.

GL: I know we're going to find life. And I know it's going to be bacteria. And I know we're going to find it everywhere. All I'm saying is—which is where the leap is on this whole thing—bacteria, they're much smarter than we are.

JC: Well, they've survived a lot longer than we have. So, that's smarter in and of itself.

GL: But it's . . . about symbiotic relationships. I think, personally, one of the core values we should have in the world, and kids should be taught, is ecology, to understand that we all are connected. Forget the mystical whatever. It's just very plain. We're all connected. What you do to somebody here, it affects somebody there, there, there, there. It comes back to you. You have understand that you're part of a very big picture. You're just one little part. You're a gear. You're just a little gear in this big picture.

JC: But there's beauty in that connection. And there's empowerment in that connection.

GL: The thing that I liked about the whole idea was that, yes, we are ruled, and the conquerors of the universe are these little one-celled animals. But they depend on us, we depend on them. And the idea was, the Force—we say it surrounds you, it controls us, we control it—it's a two-way street.

JC: But what you're also talking about is empathy, in a sense. You were talking about fear versus empathy, compassion versus aggression, that good versus evil dichotomy. Humans have this kind of competitive, aggressive side, but we also have this cooperative side that allowed us to work together, to hunt, to grow food. Those two aspects of us are always at war inside ourselves. You took that and you wrote it large across the galaxy.

GL: The thing of it is, is that because we had a brain, and we've been given a certain sense of our own destiny—because we can figure things out—we have this dichotomy. Ants don't have that dichotomy. They have the same symbiotic relationships, but it's programmed. It's in their DNA. It's in their hormones, it's there. They don't try to pontificate on it. They don't [say], "Why am I doing this?" Humans do that.

So, we've got two sides. Our animal side, which is the primitive one, which is the one that most animals operate on. They're very aggressive, and they kill other animals, and they eat them. They fight for dominance. And then on the other side, they're nurturing. Some of them more than others. And that's the compassionate side. Humans, one of the things that we've got besides our brain to survive is our compassion. We live in a world where our nurturing aspects are way above . . . any other animal. We are just born to nurture. If we weren't able to do that, humans would be dead on the second month.

JC: It's because we have a big brain. Because we have a big brain, it takes us a couple of years before we can even walk and keep up with the tribe. We have to take care of these useless infants.

GL: That's right. But the thing is—yeah, but you know why we do it?

JC: Because we have a big brain. Because the human birth canal can only give birth to a brain so big. So, the brain has to continue to develop outside the [mother's] body. Other animals don't have that problem.

GL: That's the technical side of it. The other side of it, beauty, is that we're cute.

JC: We're cute so the tribe doesn't kill us and eat us.

GL: Most of us don't nurture cockroaches. But we will nurture a kitten. We will nurture babies.

JC: What if we meet an alien species that looks more like a cockroach than a baby?

GL: We might not [feel] nurturing [toward] them.

JC: All the good aliens are always baby-like. They have smooth skin, big eyes. . . .

GL: E.T.

JC: Yeah, right? Well, his skin wasn't so smooth, but he did have big eyes. But you're talking about appearance having a controlling factor in how we relate to and have an empathic response to each other. How does that factor into meeting alien races that don't look like us at all?

GL: I've never met an alien.

JC: Okay, but you have plenty of them in your movies.

GL: Like I say, if I go swimming or I go in the forest or I go to the zoo, I find a lot of them. But some of them I have empathy for and some of them I don't.

JC: It occurs to me, just thinking about it in a broad overview, that you treated AI, robotics, and aliens almost in the same way, which is very matter-of-factly. They're just part of society.

GL: Some of them are good. Some of them are bad.

JC: They're either good or bad. They're with you or they're against you. They're buddies, or they're working for the wrong side. It doesn't matter, but they're basically people. They're characters.

GL: It's my way. What I do with my four-year-old—she's at the point where she doesn't like bugs, and I say, "They're just like people." They're not going to hurt you. A fly isn't going to hurt you. He just flies around. It's not a danger or anything. You should just say, "Shoo fly, don't bother me." And if you take that attitude about it,

then you don't have a lot of fear. I say snakes are dangerous, spiders are dangerous. Some of these things are dangerous, some of them aren't. But that doesn't mean you have to be afraid of all spiders, or that you have to be afraid of all animals, or you have to be afraid of all people. Well, maybe all people.

JC: I didn't realize you'd become such a misanthrope, George.

GL: [*laughs*] But you should take everything as it is, and give it the benefit of the doubt. You have to be part of this world.

JC: So, you have guys in the *Star Wars* films that look like monsters. You've got [an admiral] that's got big googly eyes. If you put him in a monster movie, he'd be a pretty credible monster. But he's not a monster. He's a good guy. He's a Rebel leader. You just instantly relate to him as somebody who's an ally. That speaks to this idea that if we do meet intelligent aliens, we will be able to get along with them and communicate with them.

GL: I don't know about that. Chewbacca was a big scary guy, but he's good. He's fun, he's easy. But some people are afraid of him.

JC: He could rip your arm off. You don't want to be on the wrong side of him.

GL: But at the same time, he's an Other. And we have Others. And some of them are bad people, some of them are good people. But you can't classify all the others as bad. That's the point in there, because no matter what somebody looks like, you can't judge them.

JC: But isn't that a sociological comment through science fiction? Isn't that saying, hey, you meet somebody from another culture, they don't look like you, their skin's a different color, they don't believe the things you believe. That otherness is not—you can't judge them. Isn't that what science fiction is great at doing?

GL: That animal or that creature could be your friend. It could be very helpful to you. You should not dismiss him because he doesn't look like you. That's a theme that runs all the way through *Star Wars*. Just because they don't look like you doesn't mean they're not valuable. That was a big issue in the movie.

JC: I think science fiction is so good at these social themes. Look at empowerment of women. Not done particularly well in Hollywood, certainly not done well in the Western genre, particularly, historically. And then you come along with *Star Wars*, and you've got Princess Leia [played by late actress Carrie Fisher]. And while the two guys are falling over each other to try to protect her, she's shooting the bad guys and finding the way out of the Death Star. That was a pretty unprecedented thing.

GL: She is a senator. She graduated from college. She's a very smart person, very much in control. And she's a good shot. And the two guys were—one was naive and didn't know anything, had no knowledge. The other one thought he knew everything, but he didn't know anything, either. She is the one that knew everything. She was the one that was driving the whole story. It was the same thing with Queen Amidala. She had Qui-Gon Jinn as her kind of Ben Kenobi. But she was the wisest of the group. She was the real heroine of all those pieces.

JC: I was talking to Ridley Scott about how Ripley [in *Alien*] got to be a female character. He attributed it to Alan Ladd Jr. [then-president of Twentieth Century Fox]. I don't think it's a coincidence that that was two years after *Star Wars* came out, and Fox just had made more money than god off a movie that had a strong, intelligent, forthright female who did not bow down to the guys, that did not need to be saved by them. She led them out. She was the architect of the whole destruction of the Death Star, by hiding the plans.

GL: I kept having that speech at Fox. Especially when we got to the toy part of it. I insisted that they do action figures of Princess Leia. When you've lined them up, she's the main character, for God's sake. [It was about] just convincing people. You say white privilege, but there's really male privilege. Male privilege is even worse because it's tied up with your libido and your self-esteem and all this other stuff. And it cuts across all the races. For some reason in America especially, maleness is a big issue.

JC: But don't you think that that's one of the really powerful aspects of science fiction? That it allows you to go to another place, another time, another world, and look at things a little bit differently than the way you were raised and the immediate cultural context that you're in? Maybe women can be more powerful, or more empowered in that? Maybe gay people can be more powerful, maybe people of different color can be more powerful, or—or [have] different social status? All of a sudden, that leads to starting to get people a little bit out of their dogmatic box.

GL: *Star Wars* was forty years ago. But [Leia] is the top dog. Then you've got the two guys.

JC: What was your prototype for a strong female? Before you made the movie, before you wrote that film. Was it in your family? Was it your grandmother?

GL: I'd say my sisters. Especially my little sister, she's three years younger than I am. She was tough. We used to fight, our whole life together. The feistiness of that character came from her.

JC: I've been thinking about this idea that space is anything we want it to be. It's the great unknown [where] we can project our fantasies and our ideas, our sociology. We can use it just as an excuse to get to a completely different culture, or we can take it at face value as a problem that we need to solve. On the one hand, you've got the hard tech stuff like *2001* and most recently *The Martian*, which was a big hit, so people are still intrigued by the real problem of solving space travel, and what that's going to do to us and our humanity. At the other end of the spectrum, it's more space as a kind of complete unfettering of the imagination. How would you respond to that?

GL: No matter how you do it—whether it's *2001* or *The Martian*—those are intellectual adventures, but they're adventures. The big boogeyman is the unknown. "I'm going to go to the West Coast and see what happens, see what's there." "I'm going to go across the ocean. If we don't fall off, we'll see what's there." This is a great adventure. We don't know what it is, but we're going to do it because it's interesting.

JC: And it's hard.

GL: Then you have the other one, which is the fantasy, pirates and all those kinds of things. It's a fun adventure. Even a twelve-year-old could enjoy it. That's the other adventure. But both of these are to try to promote the fact that we have to go out there and do this.

JC: Right.

GL: It's the thing about mythology. Mythology tells you a story that's not really that true, but it's a story that gives you an adventure. It just sparks your imagination. . . . *2001* had more of an influence on me than I realized. I was completely stoked by that movie. But *Star Wars* was much more effective in that department. Millions of people were stoked.

JC: I'm a filmmaker because of *Star Wars*. It started with *2001*, but what really blew my mind was *Star Wars*.

GL: But it's really not the filmmaking part of it, it's the "let's go into outer space."

JC: It's that, too.

GL: And we have the reality now to deal with it, which is why Mars is becoming more of a thing. But we have to get people to say, "This is an adventure." If we didn't have these movies to say, "This is an adventure, this is really going to be fun," do you think we'd be dumb enough to go in a spaceship off to Mars when there's nothing there but a bunch of red dirt? No! You get the imagination going for people that this could be a fun adventure.

JC: Mars is a lot like Tatooine. It's a hard place to live.

ABOVE Matt Damon gets ready to "science the shit out of this" in Ridley Scott's *The Martian* (2015).

ABOVE George Lucas is interviewed by James Cameron for *James Cameron's Story of Science Fiction*. Photo Credit: Michael Moriatis/ AMC

GL: But the point is, with the environmental situation and everything, if we could learn to live on Mars, we can rehabilitate Earth.

JC: Yeah, hopefully.

GL: The failing system we've got here, we can actually repair it. If we go to one of the moons of Titan or whatever, we're going to have to learn to adapt to our environment—which makes us aware of our environment, that it's not just something we take for granted. If you realize that everything is connected to everything, once one thing goes, then [it's] just like pulling a sweater. It all comes apart.

JC: It unravels.

GL: You have to understand that stuff, which we don't.

JC: We understand it. We just don't at a societal level embody it in our policy. We don't live it.

GL: Not enough people understand it. But I'm telling you, if we get to Mars, [we will] start doing documentaries on Mars—and I'm sure people will learn what it takes. *The Martian* is sort of like that. It tells you, you have to build a system. And that system has to work, and everything has to fit into that system. . . . You have to adapt. Gene splicing and all this kind of stuff, that's the beginning of adapting.

JC: What you're talking about is that adaptation means change. We may change as a species. Physiologically, mentally, philosophically.

GL: Yeah, I'm sure we will. . . . The thing about humans that's always been with us is we have an imagination. We always have this issue of fear. Fear drives everything. Therefore, what we've managed to do is to make stories to alleviate our fear. "Is the sun going to come back?" "Oh yeah. That's not a sun, that's a god. He goes around on a chariot, and he always comes back." The early world, the shamans were the ones that were always telling the stories, or the mysteries—the reason that the antelope come out at this time of year and not that time of year.

The other [thing] that is crucial to early man is the night sky. The night sky has always been the great mystery. There are things up there, and the things have to mean something. We don't know what they are. So, man has curiosity. Curiosity and imagination bring you things like stories. [We] make up stories to explain, what are all those little lights up there? . . . And they're such an amazing mystery. The stars, the planets, all the things we see up there.

JC: You're saying this has called to us since—

GL: The very beginning.

JC: Hundred thousand years ago, a million years ago. This is a primal attraction, is what you're saying. It's a mystical connection.

GL: There's a mystical connection with the sky, and with stars. We've always been interested in, how does that work? What is it? It's the lid on our can. We're in a little coffee can here and we're looking up and we're saying, "What the hell is that?"

JC: And then Galileo and Kepler came along and said, "It's not a dome. It's endless, and things just go around because of this thing called gravity." And the idea that we could go there suddenly became this kind of really profound challenge for the human race.

GL: Most of the Greek gods lived there.

JC: That's why we keep naming [the planets] after Greek gods. Venus, Mars.

GL: But they've always been a part of our imagination. . . . We have a rough idea of what our galaxy is like, but what goes beyond that? How many universes are there? Again, you've got two roads. One is science, the other is our

imagination. . . . The concept of the universe or universes is so mind-boggling but interesting. Like, what happened before the Big Bang? What was there before? There are so many questions there that we haven't even touched on how we would answer them. In time, a lot of answers to things will come out, and we'll be flabbergasted.

JC: In a good way. Hopefully.

GL: It'll be awe-inspiring. It won't be good or bad. It'll just be like, I had no idea.

JC: Isn't that what we try to do with our movies? Capture a little bit of that awe and bring it into a movie theater?

GL: That's what Steven [Spielberg] does.

JC: Well, it's what you do. You just do it differently. You take us out there to different worlds.

GL: Well, I can guarantee there's no Wookiees in space.

JC: How do you know? In an infinite universe, all things are possible.

GL: When you get into that, it's out of the realm of mythology and storytelling. It's out of the realm of science. It gets into the realm of the great mystery, which can't be answered. It's philosophy. I'll avoid the religion part and say it's philosophy—which is a big tin can with a bunch of little holes punched in.

TIME TRAVEL

BY LISA YASZEK

IN 1963, THE BBC DEBUTED *DOCTOR WHO*, a TV program designed to teach viewers about history as they followed the adventures of a rogue Time Lord from the planet Gallifrey who journeys through time and space in a machine that looks like a British police telephone box. The show quickly evolved past its original educational mandate and skyrocketed to the status of international cult classic, as the Doctor and his human companions explored the universe and battled evil forces that were out to harm people and change the galactic timeline. For well over half a century, the Doctor—whose adventures broadcast weekly in more than fifty countries and have inspired adaptations across all media forms—has undergone multiple incarnations and partnered with scores of different humans to grapple with dilemmas including time loops, temporal paradoxes, and fixed points in history that defy manipulation. At the same time, the show's characters have confronted a host of philosophical issues including the tension between free will and predestination, the relationship between memory and identity, and the inevitability of love, loss, and death. In many ways, *Doctor Who* embodies the entire history of time-travel storytelling and reveals our enduring fascination with such stories. By imagining that we can break free from the grip of linear time, we hope that we might better understand the experience of humanity itself.

Tales of humans who transcend time are nearly as old as the practice of storytelling itself. The ancient Indian epic the *Mahabharata* relates the adventures of Raivata Kakudmi, a human king who travels to heaven and, upon returning to Earth, finds many ages have passed. While this story initiated a tradition of time-dilation tales that are still very much with us today—as in the case of Christopher Nolan's space epic *Interstellar* (2014)—pre-twentieth-century authors more often used either dreams or natural, one-off accidents called "timeslips" to move characters through history. Charles Dickens's *A Christmas Carol* (1843) is the most enduring example of time travel by dream. The story follows a miserly old man whose nocturnal visits to his own past, present, and future give him fresh perspective on how he became the man he is and what he must do to avoid a lonely death. Conversely, Mark Twain's celebrated timeslip novel *A Connecticut Yankee in King Arthur's Court* (1889) uses a blow to the head to send a nineteenth-century American engineer back to sixth-century England, where he learns that he cannot introduce either democratic ideals or industrial weapons before their time. It is no surprise that, as two of the earliest modern stories to ask questions about free will versus predestination, both novels have been the subject of multiple movies, plays, and even video games. Indeed, what James Cameron calls our fear that we might simply be "puppets of a timeline"—and our attendant hope that we might cut the strings controlling us—remains central to science fiction today. Look at popular films such as Cameron's *The Terminator* (1984), *Terminator 2: Judgment Day* (1991), and director Rian Johnson's *Looper* (2012), as well as TV shows such as *Outlander* (2014–present) and *Twelve Monkeys* (2015–present, based on the 1995 film).

Of course, most modern time-travel tales revolve around fantastic machines that move characters through time much as a ship might move them through space. Such stories began to appear with some frequency in the 1880s. As industrialism and mechanization transformed nineteenth-century America and Europe, it became clear that clocks were critical to everything from the

OPPOSITE Tom Baker in *Doctor Who*. Baker played the Gallifreyan Time Lord from 1974 to 1981.

You will ORBIT into the fantastic future!

METRO·GOLDWYN·MAYER presents
A GEORGE PAL PRODUCTION

H.G. WELLS'
THE TIME MACHINE

in futuristic METROCOLOR

STARRING
ROD TAYLOR · ALAN YOUNG · YVETTE MIMIEUX · SEBASTIAN CABOT · TOM HELMORE
Screen Play by DAVID DUNCAN · Based on the Novel by H. G. WELLS · Directed by GEORGE PAL

ABOVE Theatrical poster for the 1960 adaptation of H. G. Wells's *The Time Machine*, produced and directed by George Pal.

OPPOSITE Book covers for Ray Bradbury's *A Sound of Thunder* (published by William Morrow) and Octavia E. Butler's *Kindred* (published by Beacon Press).

coordination of trains and ships to the timing of barrage artillery and trench warfare, and so in 1884, delegates from twenty-six countries met in Washington, DC, to standardize both the Earth's geographical coordinate system and the length of the day. Optimism about the human ability to control time finds expression in stories such as Edward Page Mitchell's "The Clock that Went Backward" (1881), Enrique Gaspar's "El Anacronópete" ("The Time Ship," 1887), and Lewis Carroll's *Sylvie and Bruno* (1889), each of which imagines that clocks might literally cause time travel. But technologically enabled time travel was most famously popularized in *The Time Machine* (1895), where H. G. Wells imagines that people might travel purposefully and selectively through history

in a sled-like vehicle. This new image of time travel inspired a rich tradition of visually spectacular time machines, including the steampunk contraptions featured in the 1960 and 2002 adaptations of Wells's novel, the police call box of *Doctor Who*, and the modified DeLorean of the *Back to the Future* franchise.

As science fiction developed into a distinct popular genre with its own creators, publication venues, and rules for good storytelling, artists turned their energy to exploiting the peculiar aesthetics of time travel. In doing so, they anticipated director Christopher Nolan's observation that "once you can grasp . . . these concepts in astrophysics, they offer you this great launching point for story possibilities." In the first half of the twentieth century, authors used time travel for a variety of purposes: to tell future histories of technology and society, to give exotic tours of faraway times and places, and even to provide an education in the science of time travel itself. During this period, such concerns—often coupled with the questions of free will and personal agency explored by earlier writers—were frequently expressed through stories about "the butterfly effect." One of the earliest stories of this sort, in which seemingly inconsequential actions from the past create one or more alternate futures, is Jack Williamson's *Legion of Time* (1938), where one man's decision to pick up either a magnet or a pebble results in two very different futures for humanity. While *Legion of Time* inspired a whole new tradition of time war tales, the most famous butterfly effect story is perhaps Ray Bradbury's "A Sound of Thunder" (1952), in which stepping on a prehistoric butterfly transforms the contemporary United States into an illiterate fascist dystopia.

Authors of this era also enjoyed the challenge of trying to logically resolve the time paradoxes that might arise from human intervention into history. Popularly known as

A SOUND OF
THUNDER
& OTHER STORIES
BRADBURY

"the grandfather paradox," such stories asked, What if I went back in time and changed a single event, such as killing my own grandfather? Answers to this question ranged widely: Fritz Leiber's "Try and Change the Past" (1958) postulates a Law of the Conservation of Reality that makes history resistant to change, while Alfred Bester's "The Men Who Murdered Mohammed" (1958) resolves the problem by imaging personal time continuums for every individual. But as author Jonathan Lethem notes, the "most satisfying and accomplished of the early, great figures of science fiction" to tackle the grandfather paradox was Robert A. Heinlein. In "'—All You Zombies—'" (1959), Heinlein takes this paradox to its extreme with his dizzying tale of a "time cop" who travels to multiple points in history and undergoes a sex change to become his own mother and father. Both Bradbury's and Heinlein's stories are widely anthologized and have been the subjects of major motion pictures. They have also influenced other popular science fiction phenomena such as *Doctor Who*, in which time wars between the people of Gallifrey and biomechanical villains the Daleks provide the backdrop for the entire franchise—and where the Doctor himself battles a nemesis named, appropriately enough, Grandfather Paradox.

The next generation of science fiction authors explored the possibility of using time-travel tales for social and political commentary. This was particularly true of stories such as Joanna Russ's *The Adventures of Alyx* (1976) and Marge Piercy's *Woman on the Edge of Time* (1976), in which everyday women who travel to different points in time realize that they have the power to make choices that will make the future a better place for all. Similar sentiments inform films including Lynn Hershman Leeson's *Conceiving Ada* (1997) and, perhaps most famously, Cameron's two *Terminator* films, in which protagonist Sarah Connor's transition from helpless victim to active hero is crystallized by

scenes such as the one in which Connor carves the words "no fate" into a table. By way of contrast, indigenous and African-American authors of this period used time travel to represent American history in new ways. Gerald Vizenor's "Custer on the Slipstream" (1978) relates the adventures of a modern bureaucrat who becomes "unstuck in time" when he realizes that he is the reincarnation of General Custer. Meanwhile, Octavia E. Butler's *Kindred* (1979) unfolds as what artist John Jennings calls a "reversal of the grandfather paradox," in which a modern African-American woman finds herself transported to antebellum Maryland, where she must help a young white slave owner rape her free black ancestor to ensure her own birth. As the densely crowded panels of Damian Duffy and Jennings's 2017 graphic novel adaptation suggest, *Kindred* treats the past,

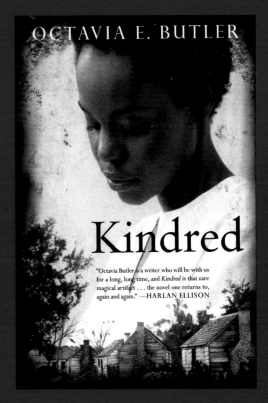

OCTAVIA E. BUTLER

Kindred

"Octavia Butler is a writer who will be with us for a long, long time, and *Kindred* is that rare magical artifact . . . the novel one returns to, again and again." —HARLAN ELLISON

On the silver screen, films including *Back to the Future* (1985), *Bill & Ted's Excellent Adventure* (1989), and *Groundhog Day* (1993) explore the comic aspects of time travel, celebrating the possibility that average people might travel to the past, make and then correct a variety of mistakes, and, in doing so, change the future for the better. As film critic Amy Nicholson puts it, "Most sci-fi films imagine that the world is going to be awful, terrible. To have a sci-fi film that says, 'eh, this is just fun,' is an incredible, strange relief." A similar optimism informed many of the time-travel TV shows that debuted in this period, including *Quantum Leap* (1989–1993) and the spin-off show for *Hitchhiker's Guide* (1981). It continues today online with web series such as *Ctrl* (2009–present), in which a hapless office worker uses his computer keyboard to undo past events, and *Untitled Web Series About a Space Traveler Who Can Also Travel Through Time* (2012–present), a *Doctor Who* parody based on the television comedy series *Community*.

NEW YORK TIMES BESTSELLER

DOUGLAS ADAMS

THE HITCHHIKER'S GUIDE TO THE GALAXY

ABOVE Joseph Gordon-Levitt in director Rian Johnson's time-travel thriller, *Looper* (2012).

RIGHT Cover for British author Douglas Adams's humorous science fiction classic *The Hitchhiker's Guide to the Galaxy* (published by Del Rey).

OPPOSITE TOP Theatrical poster for the mind-boggling low-budget time-travel thriller *Primer* (2004).

OPPOSITE BOTTOM Cover for *Hyperion*, the first book in author Dan Simmons's acclaimed Hyperion Cantos series (published by Bantam Books).

present, and future as a tangle of impossible relations and even more impossible choices—all of which, paradoxically, are precisely what make present survival and future change possible.

But not all time-travel stories are so serious. The 1970s, '80s, and early '90s witnessed an explosion of time-travel comedies across media. Spider Robinson's *Callahan's Crosstime Saloon* series (1977–2003), set in a bar for time travelers, invites readers to join an empathetic clientele who pool their diverse experiences to help newcomers solve unusual problems. Those who dream of speaking intelligently with such travelers might well consult Douglas Adams's *Hitchhikers Guide to the Galaxy* series (1978–2009), which recommends Dr. Dan Streetmentioner's *Time Traveler's Handbook of 1001 Tense Formations* for such situations.

In recent decades, artists have made time-travel stories feel real to audiences by exploring both the promises and the perils of temporal displacement. Award-winning novels including Dan Simmons's *Hyperion* series (1989–98) and Connie Willis's *Blackout / All Clear* diptych (2010) examine how people survive and even find new meaning in lives that have been shattered by mysterious intrusions from an unknowable future. In a similar vein, films including the indie hit *Primer* (2004), along with *Looper* and *Interstellar,* consider whether or not the benefits of time travel outweigh the toll such travel might take on individuals, their families, and their friends. Meanwhile, video game designers foster immersive experiences by incorporating time travel into narrative structure and game play alike. This is true both of best-selling games such as *The Legend of Zelda: Majora's Mask* (2000), in which players must solve a specific but nonlinear sequence of puzzles before the moon crashes into the game world and resets time, and also of indie offerings such as *Braid*

"INGENIOUS, AND FASCINATING...THUMBS UP."
–ROGER EBERT, EBERT & ROPER

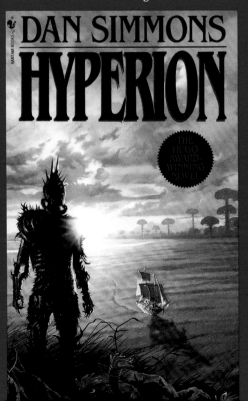

(2008), where players manipulate the flow of time to save a princess while uncovering the main character's surprising motives for undertaking this quest.

Like their literary and on-screen counterparts, such games insist that time travelers might cross unthinkable distances of time and space, but what they really discover are themselves, their capabilities, and their rightful place in history. In this way, the impossible scenario of time travel continues to inspire the most human science fiction of all.

CHRISTOPHER NOLAN

INTERVIEW BY JAMES CAMERON

AFTER EARNING CONSIDERABLE CRITICAL ACCLAIM for his debut feature, 1998's *Following*, director Christopher Nolan rocketed to Hollywood's A-list two years later with the dizzying, time-bending thriller, 2000's *Memento*. Since then, he's earned a sterling reputation as one of the premier filmmakers of the modern era—a director whose intellect and tireless commitment to craft have yielded some of the most audacious, compelling blockbusters of all time. His trilogy of Batman films starring Christian Bale—*Batman Begins* (2005), *The Dark Knight* (2008), and *The Dark Knight Rises* (2012)—remains the gold standard for superhero cinema. His most overtly science fiction films—2010's *Inception* and 2014's *Interstellar*—are spectacle-laden, cerebral explorations of other dimensions that remain rooted in character and emotion.

Here, he sits down with Cameron for a heady conversation about the extensive research he undertook for *Interstellar* (which Nolan also cowrote with his brother and frequent collaborator Jonathan "Jonah" Nolan), the intricacies of time travel, the concept of free will, and the seemingly limitless potential of the science fiction genre.

JAMES CAMERON: One of our common subjects is science fiction. Probably most people wouldn't think of you as a science fiction filmmaker, or typecast you in that genre, but you have made your forays into it. Very unique ones. Maybe it makes sense to start with *Interstellar*, which is the obvious one. It's pretty foursquare in the genre: future, hardware-oriented, and so on. What drew you to that subject?

CHRISTOPHER NOLAN: I've always loved science fiction. The two seminal movies for me were [George] Lucas's first *Star Wars* in '77, and then in the wake of that success, they re-released *2001* [*: A Space Odyssey*]. It played at the Leicester Square Theatre [in London], and my dad took me to see it. I have a very vivid memory of that experience. Huge screen. I was very young. I was seven years old. But it stuck in my thinking as some sort of touchstone on how movies and the movie screen can open up and take you into worlds beyond imagination.

JC: *2001* was a major milestone for me as well. I saw it in its first release. A little bit older than you, at the age of fourteen. I saw it in Canada, in Toronto. And I remember, I was the only person

in the theater. And it was 70mm print, and I was stunned. I was really shaken by the film, by the majesty of it and by the fact that a film could essentially be a work of art in every sense. That had somehow never really occurred to me. I loved movies. I didn't use the lofty term "film."

CN: But *2001*'s a film, isn't it? It just doesn't do any of the movie-ish things. When we came to do *Interstellar* and we looked at, how do you credibly go beyond our dimension, go beyond what people understand? How do you jump into a black hole? When you go back and you look at *2001*, you realize that what Kubrick was able to do that no one now can do is elision. He would just choose to not show the things [where] the artifice would show, whether it was miniature work or optical effects or things that he just wasn't able to do at the time.

JC: He just cut around it.

CN: He just cut around it, but in doing that, he created this extraordinarily symbolic and simple language of elision and these jumps forward that are just incredible. He created an everyday reality to the greatest adventure in

human history. We're going to Jupiter, we're going to the moons of Jupiter, eating some pre-packaged meal and listening to some broadcast from your parents on your birthday that's probably eight or ten hours old because of the light speed lag. It's obviously a masterpiece. I think we both agree on that. But that sets the bar very high for us poor filmmakers that come along afterward. I mean, the polite way to put it is, anyone who makes a film in that world, like *Interstellar*, you're in dialogue with *2001*. You're not making it in a world where *2001* doesn't exist.

JC: That's right.

CN: And the audience is very aware of that. The critics are very aware of that. What drew me to that particular project was [that] my brother had written the script for Steven Spielberg to direct originally. What we wound up making is fairly different from his original draft, but the first act was always the same. It was this idea of a future that in some sense is—well, it's not really dystopian. It's almost what people these days think of as some kind of rural ideal. The idea that you go back to farming and you go back to a simpler way of life.

JC: But it's failing. It's a downward spiral.

CN: Very much. So, there's a sort of ticking clock and a need to get off the planet. I think a seminal moment in the development of the film for myself and Jonah was when we were shooting *The Dark Knight* in Hong Kong. They had an Omnimax theater there on the harbor front. When we were scouting, we went and saw one of the IMAX [films, *Magnificent Desolation: Walking on the Moon*,] that I think Tom Hanks was involved with, about the moon landings and everything. And there's a moment in that film— it's a nicely done film—but there's a moment when they feel that they have to take on the idea that it was faked. There's something heart-breaking about that, that these people felt they had to address that in this film.

JC: And you put that in the story.

CN: Very directly. Because Jonah felt very strongly, and I built on this very much with my drafts as well, that we've created a very inward-looking culture. And I mean, one of the other films of mine that we'll talk about, I'm sure, is *Inception*. And that was a film that was very much in tune with an inward-looking cul-ture. The structure of that film is to some degree based on the sort of branching net-works of the interface of the iPods, when they first came out. It is all about worlds within worlds and introversion.

JC: And branching in video games when you change level. Yeah.

CN: Exactly. All very inward-looking stuff. And so for *Interstellar*, it felt like the time was right to just look the other way, go out again and get some of that spirit back of adventure.

JC: Of exploration. I'm an explorer-in-resi-dence at *National Geographic*. I've done a bit myself. Mostly in the ocean. I'd do it in space if I could. I'd go to Mars if I could. My wife and I have talked about this. She says, "You have five children." I say, "I know. I can talk to them from Mars. It'll be a thirty-minute delay."

CN: Have you met Elon Musk?

JC: No. Elon is an inspiration. He's thinking like you, which is outward, which is, we have to reinspire people about exploration. I think this is something science fiction has always done, when it's not in its sort of dystopian, down-the-virtual-rabbit-hole kind of mode.

CN: Exactly.

JC: The early kind of heroic, outward bound, let's go explore planets—that's what drew me to scuba diving. I thought, well, I'm probably not going to be able to go [to space], but I can sure as hell go [beneath the sea]. Slap a tank on my back

when you screen that on film in an IMAX theater on a huge screen, it's the closest you could get to feeling like you were accessing what it would be like to be there. [But for *Interstellar*] we looked at all the great science fiction of the past. *2001*, certainly. Also Ridley Scott's *Alien*.

JC: Which is another great touchstone.

CN: In terms of production design particularly. I always refer to that film as Ken Loach in space. Because it's kind of got this grit and this almost depressing quality to it, a bleakness.

JC: Rusty and grease dripping and water dripping. It was very tactile.

CN: Very tactile, yeah.

JC: I always remember when Harry Dean Stanton is standing in the room with the chains, some kind of condenser room, with his hat. And the plip-plop of the water. It put you in his body for a moment in a way that very few films do. Horror film or science fiction, set the genre aside. Very few films put you right in that character for that moment.

CN: And it can be the smallest thing, like a little sound like that, that you remember. So those were very much our touchstones. And then the other decision we made [on *Interstellar*], that in a funny sort of way no one ever noticed when they saw the film, which I think is good, is we decided to not actually make anything futuristic. We decided to not try and propel ourselves into the future and play what I sort of refer to as—it's almost that parlor game of, "Well, what will somebody's trousers look like in forty years' time?" or whatever. You always lose.

JC: You do lose, and you look silly.

CN: It just occurred to me that to really ground it, what if we just went with the present? We looked at NASA technology. We looked at what these things look and sound like, and what

and see something that I've never seen before. And it came from that same urge to explore.

CN: Well, I think movies—I mean for me, my solution wasn't to go scuba diving—but always in the back of my head, I knew that one day I wanted to do a film. And for me, the IMAX camera was my version of that. Because you could, in creating these enormous images—and

switches are like and everything. I think it did ground the film for me.

JC: The texture of the suits, everything that the actors interacted with felt very real to me. Obviously, the overt configuration of the mission architecture was for that mission an interstellar vehicle. But it felt very grounded. I have to tell you that the rotating docking scene is one of the most white-knuckle sequences in any science fiction film for me. It's always something that I've imagined. Of course, coming off of the docking scene in *2001*. But in the science fiction novels especially of the '50s and '40s—where they were kind of a hard-tech approach to space—there was always the rotating docking. With the kind of derelict ship or whatever it was. And it was always the scariest thing in the story, and you nailed it. I mean, I thought that was beautiful.

CN: Oh, well, thank you. For me, probably the inspiration for that was *2010*, which is, I think, underrated. I mean, *2001* is such a masterpiece, difficult to follow, bit of a suicide mission. But you made *Aliens*. You know what that is like.

JC: That was a suicide mission, too.

CN: And you achieved it magnificently.

JC: I dodged a bullet. I dodged a self-inflicted wound. That's tricky.

CN: That is tricky, but I think you did that magnificently. Peter Hyams, what he did with *2010* is underrated. And the novel, I read when I was a kid, you know, Arthur C. Clarke's and all of it, which is much more mechanical. It's about the mechanics, about those things you're describing. So they have that scene where the [*Discovery*] is spinning, and they have to go into the middle of it. I was excited to try that in a really physical way and really look at the Newtonian physics. Because so much of *Interstellar* is about quantum physics, [Albert] Einstein, and beyond, to get back to [Isaac] Newton and things that you can, as a moviegoer, really grasp and feel [seemed important].

JC: Then on the other end of the spectrum, when you're showing gravitational lensing and the intense distortion around a black hole, you still approached it very rigorously by going to some of the top experts.

CN: It was a really fascinating part of the process. Kip Thorne is one of the great minds in physics, and the idea to do this film had been [from] him and [producer] Lynda Obst, originally, and they brought my brother on. And it was about making a film that—I wouldn't say illustrated real science, because it's not meant to be a textbook or anything—but was based on it. What he taught me, when I started meeting with him and talking to him, is that once you can grasp those physical concepts, these concepts of astrophysics, they offer you this great launching pad for story possibilities to do with relativity and all these aspects.

JC: Right, time dilation.

CN: Exactly. And the black hole was an interesting one, where Kip said to me very early on, "When you get to that, I want to talk to your visual effects guys first." As a filmmaker, it was a little like, "Well, we're going to make it look the way we want it to look."

JC: That's a bit cheeky.

CN: It's a little bit cheeky. He would appreciate that. But I thought, he's got a real passion for that, there must be reason for that. And of course, what I then realized is he's sitting on all of this information, all these equations that, put into the right computer, essentially, he could spit out a picture of what science really tells you that this thing would look like.

JC: And he's probably always wanted to see it.

CN: He's always wanted to see it. And of course, we have those computers. They have all kinds of other computers. They've got all the equations. They've got all the mathematics. But they don't have the indulgence that we have, of months and months of [digital effects] render times. Paul Franklin, our visual effects supervisor, got together with Kip—and he is a huge science guy. They took these real equations. They fed them into their rendering pipeline. And we started looking at these images, and they were just mind-blowing. This idea of the accretion disk around it that's lifted up . . .

JC: That's warped by gravity, by this giant lens.

CN: You couldn't design something like that.

JC: No, it wouldn't occur to an artist. That's the problem. You've got years and years, decades, of Hollywood designers designing spaceships. And from *Flash Gordon* on, they were all pointy at one end and had fins at the other end, and then they sat down, when they landed on a planet. And then you had the [Apollo] lunar module, which didn't look like anything anyone had ever designed, and yet when you deconstruct it back, there's a reason for why it looks the way it looks.

CN: Yeah, it's form over function. I've always been a big fan in visual effects, particularly when you're getting into the fully CG end of it, of procedurally based algorithms. So that you're not doing it with an artist's eye, necessarily. You're going, "Okay, what if this set of mathematics fed into it? What if this procedure fed into how we render these images?" And then choose the ones you like. So you're looking at it ultimately with an artist's eye, but you're trying to create some quirk, some serendipitous strangeness of how it flares the lens, or how it does this, how it does that. In the end, that construction of the black hole was so successful that Kip actually presented a scientific paper on it. It literally fed back. He gave us the equations, we produced the black hole, and then he was able to re-present that to his colleagues and say, "Okay, here's the visual information."

JC: Isn't that the great virtuous circle of science fiction, though? Which is that we imagine these things, and then fairly competent minds write science fiction and propose ideas, and then inspire scientists, who then go out and find out what things really are. Often inspired by science fiction.

CN: You go back to *2001*. They have iPads. They literally have iPads. Filmmakers are not pouring this stuff out into a vacuum. If you look at what Steven [Spielberg] did with *Minority Report* with that interface.

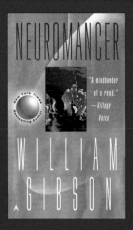

JC: With the gesture-based interface, which we now have, of course.

CN: Hugely influential. Luckily no one's figured out killer robots yet. Actually, even as I say that . . .

JC: They have Predator drones, right? But don't you think that science fiction is historically pretty bad at predicting the future and pretty good at holding a distorting mirror up to a present and trends that might or might not go somewhere?

CN: I almost prefer to talk about a speculative fiction quite often because that, I think, is one of the reasons I took the idea of futurism out of *Interstellar*, and indeed [out of] *Inception*, which is a science fiction premise. But I told every department, "No, it's just today. It's just the world today." Because I think that this type of fiction is very good at extrapolating trends to tell us something about what those trends are, not necessarily so good at predicting where these trends take us.

JC: You've got a century of science fiction literature that didn't predict the internet and the power of the personal computer and how that's transformed society and technology.

CN: I think I would dispute that a little bit . . . look at William Gibson with the visualization of the internet. *Neuromancer* in particular, and you're right there, which is pretty early in that development. Even when you go back to *Do Androids Dream of Electric Sheep?* I read that as a kid because I was obsessed with *Blade Runner*. The book is so different, so different. I don't know if you remember. They have this concept of Mercerism. They have this machine, if you put your hands on it, it's an empathy machine, and you connect with the rest of the world.

Even if you look at *Westworld*—the original film, not the one my brother's doing—even though it's robot based, things seem more virtual. It's a small detail, but if you watch *Logan's Run* they have this moment where [the

protagonist] looks to choose a date on this pop-up in his living room, and he says no. So, swipe left, swipe right. It's not a million miles away. I think that science fiction [predicting a] literal direct thing—like Arthur C. Clarke talking about geostationary satellites—that's pretty rare.

JC: Yeah. And that was in the '40s. He anticipated it by thirty years or so.

CN: But the other thing is that your assessment of the accuracy of science fiction changes over the years as well. When I first went as a kid to Epcot Center, they had a video chat sort of information booth. This was the future, and it seemed a bit silly. And sure enough, the idea of FaceTime, the idea of video chat, went dormant for decades. But when you look at *Blade Runner* or *2001* and they have these video chat scenes, whatever, that's a recognizable technology that's come into its own. Similarly, I think the idea of artificial intelligence presented in *2001* is shifting.

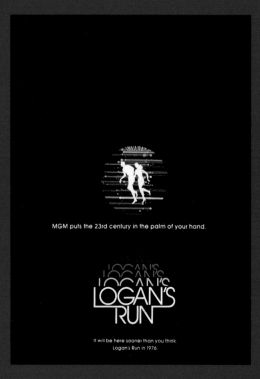

OPPOSITE Theatrical poster for the 1973 film *Westworld*, written and directed by Michael Crichton.

ABOVE Book cover for an Ace Books edition of cyberpunk classic *Neuromancer*, written by William Gibson.

BOTTOM RIGHT Theatrical poster for *Logan's Run*, the 1976 dystopian movie about a future society in which people are systematically killed when they reach the age of thirty.

JC: Coming back around.

CN: It's coming back around slowly. More so than people realize. When I first showed that film to my kids, one of the questions one of them asked, he said, "Why does the robot talk? Why does the computer talk?" The idea of a talking computer was just silly to them. This is pre-Siri. And I thought, "Oh yeah. To them a computer is not an active entity. To them a computer is a tool." It's like a typewriter. It's like a tool. It's just something that allows you to go online and do other things. It's not a centralized intelligence. It's not an active personality. Then Siri comes back, all this research in AI, and it starts to shift again.

JC: So much of AI research and even a lot of robotics research now is to create that human affect so that we have something to mirror ourselves and interact with. My mother-in-law is eighty-seven. Lives in Oklahoma. She talks to Siri. She says, "Well thank you, dear. Have a nice day." This little Southern polite-ness there. She's imbued [Siri] with a sense of character, of personality.

CN: It will be interesting to see whether that continues, or whether, as with robotics, there's a point where people go, "Actually, there isn't a reason robots particularly need to look like human beings." You have the robots in a fac-tory, they don't look anything like human beings. They're functional machines.

JC: In *Interstellar* you chose a very novel means of locomotion and form for the robots.

CN: The brief I gave Nathan [Crowley], my designer, was, "This is a robot that [architect Ludwig] Mies van der Rohe would design." Super simple, elegant materials. It doesn't in any way attempt to mimic human locomotion.

JC: I just saw an image of a new robot today from Boston Dynamics that had legs and wheels, and could essentially do parkour. It had

two little arms that weren't arms. They weren't manipulators. They were little dynamic bal-ancing pods. This thing was unbelievably agile, incredibly fast, and it would race across a space and come to a stop by bending its body back-ward and these little pods would come up. It was completely inhuman. It didn't look like any animal, it didn't look like any human, and it worked perfectly. Yet I was able to look at it and see something that was beautiful because of its functionality. It could [go] along, push off with its legs, hop up onto a table, race across the table, jump off, compress as it landed, lean itself forward, and lean back and stop like a skateboarder or a snowboarder. I thought, robots can look like anything. They'll be judged on their functionality, on their ability to per-form a task or many tasks.

CN: I think ultimately that's going to be where AI goes. Because I think that this idea of the Turing test, the idea of trying to mimic human intelligence, I think it might prove to be superfi-cial. I think it might be more along the lines of doing more than humans can do, being better than humans at a particular task. . . . With Skynet [from *The Terminator*], what was the inspiration for that in terms of an AI that become self-aware? It's such a kind of seminal idea.

JC: HAL anticipated that. After *2001*, within a few years, you had *Colossus: The Forbin Project*, which was [about] a massive attempt to create a human-scale intelligence. It went all awry and started taking over the electrical grid, domi-nating the world. That idea of the big smart mainframe taking over had been around for a while. I think [Stanley] Kubrick did it first, some would argue best. *2010* got into how HAL was actually handcuffed by us, by the constraints that we put on it. We drove it to psychosis by our inputs. That's the more likely scenario, I think—that in trying to control them, we actually turn them into the worst of demons of our nature.

CN: Science fiction inevitably posits warnings about these things. I take comfort in that

ABOVE Concept art for the Hunter-Killer tank from *The Terminator* illustrated by James Cameron.

because . . . people who are inspired by [science] fiction are very, very aware of the dangers. And I think science fiction is a useful way of exploring those dangers and sort of where they might lead. Very often, it's not predicted. . . . *The Matrix* was certainly one of my inspirations behind *Inception*. It really is about this idea of saying, okay, the world around us isn't real. It's Plato's cave. It's the oldest question. How do I know any of this around [me is real]?

JC: In *Inception*, I think there's also a cautionary tale there about going down the rabbit hole and never being able to get out—by choice—but

then reaching a point where you no longer have a choice. Because they all have a choice at the beginning. But they lose it along the way.

CN: They do. There's a couple of inspirations for that. I've always been fascinated by dreams, what dreams tell us about our subjective view of the world and how they feature into that thinking. But [in terms of] specific references, William Gibson, certainly in *Neuromancer*. The characters [have] created their own little mainframe where they can have the world the way they liked it [and] live in that forever. It's the episode of *Star Trek* where you have the paradise planet. It's all about alternative realities that you can just lose yourself in, and lose your free will in a sense, lose your sense of consciousness.

JC: Or your desire to participate in the more mundane reality that is consensus reality.

CN: I think for anyone who does the job that we do, you have your [own kind of] alternate reality. . . . I had this conversation with Ridley Scott as well. You lose yourself in the world, and that's the pleasure of it, as a filmmaker. You get to live in an alternate universe for a couple of years, or however long it takes to make the film. But there's definitely a danger to it, too. There's definitely a self-indulgent quality to it.

JC: I've chosen to spend the next eight years of my life—at a time when I don't have a lot of eight-year blocks left—on Pandora, on one world with one group of characters. Some people would consider that to be a form of dementia. But I actually quite enjoy it, and as

BELOW Reality gets turned upside down in a scene from Christopher Nolan's *Inception* (2010).

OPPOSITE A theatrical poster for *The Matrix* (1999).

an artist, I feel that I can say everything I need to say within that frame. So I'm comfortable with that. I'm sure halfway through I'll say, "Why aren't I making something real [like] a war drama in 70 millimeter?" . . . Now, do you find inspiration in dreams in terms of visuals that you then apply to your films?

CN: I mean, not usually specifically visual, but certainly conceptual. If waking life is prose, dreams are poetry. I've gotten the occasional plot points when I'm half asleep. Actually a lot of the inspiration for *Inception* was from a period when I was in university and didn't have much money. And breakfast was free, but it ended at 8 a.m., 9 a.m. We were, of course, staying up all night, chatting with students or whatever. So, I would go to bed at four in the morning or something, set my alarm, wake up to get the end of breakfast, go back to bed. So then you're in this sleep state where it becomes possible to be very aware of the fact that you're dreaming. And I would experiment with trying to control the dream, try to make something happen.

JC: Lucid dreaming.

CN: Lucid dreaming. It's frustrating, but it's fascinating. The occasional moment where you get something to work and you are able to actually channel your dream, it's pretty fascinating. That's a superpower. That was really very much the genesis of the film. For years, I wanted to do it in different genres. I couldn't quite figure out how to channel it. But I think *The Matrix* is probably the thing that guided me the most in terms of, okay, how do you make this accessible to an audience.

JC: It's interesting you were inspired by *The Matrix*, but you made something that is completely unique in film history, this kind of Matryoshka stacking doll reality that was challenging to follow but thrilling. I'd watched it once in a cinema, and then I watched it on a Blu-ray with my then eleven-year-old daughter, who's very plugged into video games

and virtual reality and animation. She had no problem following it. Everything was there that needed to be there for an eleven-year-old to follow the film without banging it over the head. I was fascinated by that engagement, by the fact that you were creating an intellectual puzzle box and inviting the audience to play with you and with the characters. That little spinning top at the end . . . Everybody gets the significance of the last four frames of that movie, because it can't have been more than that.

CN: It was fun to sit in the back of theaters. . . .

JC: And hear the gasp.

CN: Hear the gasp, or the groan, and then get out before people could find me.

JC: Well, there are some people that feel that they've been taken for a ride, but for the majority, it's so satisfying.

CN: An ambiguity like that, if people get the point, if they see that it's purposeful—and it's a little cheeky at the end—then the groan is a good groan.

JC: I didn't think it was a groan. I thought it was a gasp or even a sense of a thrill.

CN: That's certainly how it was intended, and the audiences seemed to get it. We had a nice matchup on that movie between what I was trying to explore in terms of the rules of the movie, and the world that it went out into. With science fiction in particular, you need that. You need to be in that moment where on some level you [are] speaking to things that other people are feeling around them in the world. This was a very introverted film. Everything is just stacking dolls, inside, inside, inside. The idea of dreams within dreams is one that people have tried to do, and it's difficult. We found a way genre-wise, I think, to sell it to people. . . . The way to do that was by not allowing it to be meta-physical, by allowing it to be practical and more

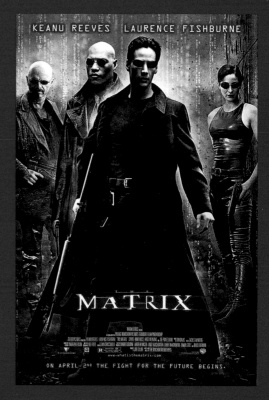

like virtual reality. The audience it went out to [at] that point were getting very excited about worlds within worlds. So it spoke to them.

JC: But you resist the impulse toward the outlandish in design—across all your films. The thing that I respect the most is that rigor, that discipline to keep it grounded. You build the Tumbler [in *The Dark Knight Trilogy*], you don't make it a CG car. . . . Well, I'm going to go straight to it. Do you actually think time travel is possible?

CN: I think there are all sorts of different ways of looking at time travel, and when I came to do *Interstellar*—which is not a time-travel movie, but has that element in it . . .

JC: It does fold time at the end.

CN: It does. But it was the subject of a long debate between myself and Kip Thorne, who we were talking about earlier. Kip was doing a book

about the science—there is a very good book that he put out about the science behind *Interstellar*, going through the story bits one by one. We were editing the film as he sent me the chapters. We were finishing the movie. And he'd already seen the film a couple times. I read his chapter on what we call the tesseract, which is the moment where Matthew McConaughey's character goes into the black hole, encounters this sphere. He enters into this peculiar thing that we refer to as a tesseract, which is a name for the hypercube, a four-dimensional cube. Kip, in his chapter, had said that I had engaged [in]—I think he called it wild speculation or something. He says it's because, "He's broken his own rules and it's time travel at this point." I was very, very defensive with Kip, and I made

him watch the film a couple more times and explained this whole tesseract thing to him because I had drawn it very much from his science. I said to him, "Okay, there are different ways of looking at time as a dimension—and quantum theory does it one way. I'm taking the view that we have recognized three spatial dimensions. The next dimension is a fourth dimension, which is what we call time. And I'm proposing that a creature living in a five-dimensional world would view, potentially, our dimension of time as a fourth spatial dimension." I kept calling it a physical dimension. He said, "They're all physical dimensions. You're misusing the word. [It's] a spatial dimension." I left a physical dimension in the movie because I think it's easier to understand.

ABOVE James Cameron interviews Christopher Nolan for *James Cameron's Story of Science Fiction*. Photo Credit: Michael Moriatis/ AMC

If you are a two-dimensional creature—you have to be a two-dimensional creature to observe one dimension. You have to be a three-dimensional creature to observe two dimensions. So, you have to be a five-dimensional creature to observe four dimensions. And in my telling of that, that fourth spatial dimension is what we feel to be time. What Kip had taught me early on, which is real physics as best as we understand it, is that the one force that could cross that dimension is gravity. So, when [McConaughey's character] enters into the tesseract, what you're seeing is a three-dimensional representation of a four-dimensional world. He does not travel in time. He moves through the bulk. He exits the brane—as it's called in this theory—and is able to observe the past because he is moving through time as a physical dimension. Anne Hathaway has a line early in the film where she says, "Maybe for them"—talking about these high-dimensional beings—"the future is a mountain we can climb up, and the past is a canyon we can dive down into." And it's building on that idea.

JC: But he's able to send information.

CN: Using gravity.

JC: So in my mind, whether you're transmitting matter back through time or whether you're sending data back, still something is moving.

CN: Absolutely.

JC: And he does send data to Jessica Chastain's character, right?

CN: Yes. That was where, once Kip had seen the film a couple of times, he got where I was coming from, saying no, we don't violate the rules we set up. The physics is actually pretty solid. It's very solid actually. . . . The way that I explained it to people was that this [tesseract] is a machine, essentially, that's constructed by the high-dimensional beings to allow him to do that.

JC: So, like in *2001*, like in *The Abyss*, there's a higher agency, and that agency might well be responsible for the arrival of the black hole in the first place.

CN: Yes. The wormhole. It is.

JC: That's right, the wormhole.

CN: What I was excited about was the idea—this is a spoiler if you've not seen the film, but . . . what I was excited about is the idea that "they"—you know the "they" of so many science fiction [films]—the higher intelligence is just us in the future.

JC: In the future. Right.

CN: And in a future in which—because we've somehow evolved to be able to live in five dimensions—cause and effect, past and future, don't exist anymore other than as a spatial dimension. What that allows you to access—it's a very long way around. But it gets you back to *Terminator*. It gets you back to the idea of time travel in which you are fulfilling destiny. If you say, okay, if you're from [a] fifth dimension and you're observing time as a fourth spatial dimension, cause and effect doesn't come into it. Cause and effect doesn't exist anymore. So, free will has to be defined in a completely different way. So when [McConaughey's character] Cooper is interacting with the past through the tesseract, he's fulfilling destiny in a way that he's compelled to do. But he's also exercising free will. And I think that's what's going on in *Terminator*.

JC: Free will is what sent him out there in the first place. He chose that mission, he went there. Had he not gone, there would have been nothing for them to latch onto in the future. I confront this on the first two *Terminator* films that I did, and now we're engineering some new ones. [The question is] would Skynet have even existed had Skynet not sent the Terminator back through time [to find] this chip that became the basis of the development of Skynet? So, it actually created itself. It's almost like quantum particles coming into existence, going out of existence spontaneously, but just on a bigger scale.

CN: The theory of time as presented in *Interstellar* allowed me to understand, if you like, those concepts not as paradox, but to say, okay, if I could conceive—I sound like a bit of a madman at this point, but if I could conceive of a way of looking . . .

JC: Most physicists do, by the way.

CN: They very much do. But they do use a lot of intuition—this is one of the things that Kip told me, there's a lot of intuition. And he was impressed by some of the things that [I] intuited through my creative process. What he was saying to me is, to truly understand something as a physicist, you have to feel it. Very much the way we [filmmakers] do in what we do, which I found fascinating. Time was very much a part of that. That theory of time allowed me to conceive of a way of looking at the world where cause and effect no longer has meaning. I genuinely believe that's quite likely to be the case. Genuinely.

JC: Do you think we have free will?

CN: I think that we misunderstand what the concept of free will is. We associate free will with the idea of cause and effect. If you take the film of your life and you run it backward—we were talking about *Memento* earlier—it's not time travel, but it's the same idea. You take the concept of revenge, and you invert the timeline—what do you get? In that sense, [*Memento* is] actually as much a science fiction film as many others.

JC: You flirt with science fiction all over the place. I would submit that *The Dark Knight* and *The Dark Knight Rises* are actually dystopian science fiction. Not because they have these extraordinary technical characters like Batman who create all this whiz bang stuff, but because you were looking at a hypertrophied corrupt state where only a vigilante is your answer, is your salvation.

CN: I would agree with that.

JC: It's taking it to an extreme that you were talking about before.

CN: Exactly. It also allows you to be subversive in your ideas. It really does. Because people will accept in a superhero film for example, or in a popcorn movie—these are the worlds that we work in and love, I don't mean that terminology in any way to diminish what they are, because those films I love making. But they do allow you to approach things in an extreme way, and approach very interesting extreme ideas in a way that feels safe to people. So they're willing to go on that ride. You're creating an experience of, for example, a dystopian future. I'm looking at demagoguery, looking at these things that could happen, but it's not depressing for people.

JC: Unfortunately, that degree of demagoguery is no longer science fiction.

CN: Yes, the real world has a way of catching up with us. But that's one of the reasons why it's exciting to do. I mean, *Dark Knight Rises*—its set of speculations has to do with class and the separation of class in this country, and the tension it's creating. And we were able, by doing it in that genre, we were able to really push it quite far. And I think in that sense, it is science fiction, speculative fiction or science fiction—not so much the science part as with *Interstellar*, for example—being able to extrapolate from the trends of the whole world and see where that takes us.

JC: And take people outside of their immediate sort of political/social/logical button pushing and be able to see it through another lens. That's, I think, another role of science fiction, especially sociological science fiction. Oh, well, these are blue characters, or these are characters with pointy ears, or these are green characters. We don't think of them as Muslim

ABOVE Christian Bale is Batman in this scene from Nolan's *The Dark Knight Rises* (2012).

or Mexican or whatever the pejorative is in racial or socioeconomic terms.

CN: I think you're right. I think it allows you to access ideas without prejudice.

JC: The classic example is *Star Wars*. Those guys, those freedom fighters—anybody in the Empire would call them terrorists. So, it's taking us out of our comfort zone—and I'm not defending terrorism, obviously.

CN: It's fascinating to me when you look at the history of that. I believe George Lucas was looking into doing *Apocalypse Now* and wound up doing *Star Wars* instead.

JC: The same group he was running with, [*Apocalypse Now* writer] John Milius and those guys that were very counterculture

CN: Very counterculture and really not afraid to look at things in a very different and interesting way. *Star Wars*, just that first card tells you it's a long time ago in a galaxy far, far away. You are immediately thrown into a different way of thinking, a different way [of] looking at what you think is futurism. But it's in the past. It's a very brilliant way of making you look at it differently.

JC: It's genius, and it's just a riff on telling you that it's a fairy tale. . . . Wait a minute—long ago? There's robots and spaceships and inter-stellar travel at beyond light speed. Could there have been a kind of galactic Atlantis that was so much greater that doesn't exist anymore? And that's when it took place?

CN: If you're going to go by statistics and you look at Carl Sagan, what are the mathematics behind [the question,] is there life on other

planets? Those same statistics are going to tell you that, yes, there have been civilizations in the past. If there is intelligent life off the Earth, they will have infinite histories. You apply that to the history of civilizations, who those people would be? *Star Wars* becomes pretty possible.

JC: So what do you think about the fact that we haven't heard from anybody?

CN: We got into this a lot on *Interstellar*. The sheer distances involved are mind-boggling. They're one of the hardest things to wrap your head around in terms of our place in the universe. If we are determined to connect with other planets or other civilizations, they're so far away. [There's a real] limitation of the speed of light in space and time. I was explaining to my kids the other day that, the more I talked to Kip, your idea of a telescope . . . the telescope is a way of looking back in time, and not just space.

JC: It's a time machine.

CN: It's a time machine. And you look at the smallest star, the farther away, the further back in time you're looking. Theoretically, you could make more and more powerful telescopes, and you can look further and further back in time. It's just a mind-boggling concept.

JC: Why are we fascinated by time travel? I guess it's this sense that you can right wrongs. Or there is some potential after the fact to find justice?

CN: People very often ask me why am I interested in time. I say, well, because I've always lived in it. We feel very trapped in it. And we genuinely do, it's not a philosophical abstract conceit. We try to hang on to the moment. We take photographs of everything. We desperately want to hang on to this reality, and it recedes.

And that's been a feature of literature that doesn't deal with time travel. It's very much part of the human condition. What science fiction allows us to do, what time travel allows us to do, is to say, okay, but what if we could? What if we could preserve that moment? What if we could revisit that moment, genuinely?

JC: That's all science fiction is about—what if? What if we could travel through space? What if we could travel through time? What if we could meet an alien civilization?

CN: Some of the best science fiction tells you that if you could, it wouldn't necessarily be a good thing. Or it wouldn't make that [much] difference. I think there's something that speaks to our souls about time travel where there's a fatalism involved that is reassuring somehow. Because it tells you that the mistakes were always going to happen.

JC: Always going to happen or can they be unwound, they can be unwritten. That's the great mystery in the *Terminator* film. In the second one, [character Sarah Connor] carves into the table the words, "No fate." So, I'm coming down pretty graphically on the idea that there isn't a fate. There isn't a predestination.

CN: "No fate but what we make." But if you look at what your story is, it's not . . .

JC: It's not that simple. But people must believe it to go on.

CN: They almost believe it to go on. It's this belief in cause and effect that we were talking about earlier. The interesting thing about your approach to time traveling in those two *Terminator* films is that it strongly says you can control your own destiny. But then the events of the story—and when she drives off in the jeep at the end—they actually tell the opposite story. You feel this aching sense of, do they know that? Do they not? It's wonderful dramatic territory.

The notable example that's different to me is *Back to the Future*. [Director Robert] Zemeckis's movie, I think, is underappreciated as a piece of science fiction because it's tremendous fun. But it also has this great payoff of, okay, if you could change the past and then it had this knock-on effect in the present, what's going to be the future? It takes it very literally. It doesn't subscribe [to] the idea of predestination because you can change the past. It's going to have that effect. That gets you into sticky situations as a filmmaker.

JC: Watching reality unwind and shift is tough, because what's your vantage point? How do you anchor the character's subjectivity?

CN: Well, after *Back to the Future*, the most extreme version I've seen is Rian Johnson's film *Looper*. He really tries to visualize the manipulation of the present through the past. I think it's pretty fascinating. With *Interstellar*, I wound up in a place that is very much in sync with the *Terminator* films—because it is about [the fact that] our understanding of cause and effect, our understanding of agency, our understanding of predestination is incomplete because we can't step outside of time.

JC: You must have liked *Arrival* then, with that same idea. We're not even perceiving the arrow of time correctly. It might very well be flowing the opposite direction, or it might move in both directions at the same time.

CN: Which is something that Stephen Hawking talks about in his book.

JC: Sure, in [*A Brief History of Time*]. They spent decades trying to figure out if time was going that way or that way.

CN: I think the physics strongly supports the idea that our view of time is thoroughly incomplete and misleading probably, and is a way that we cope with our existence. Science fiction is a way to explore that. Time travel, literally building a time machine, traveling in time, right back to

[*The Time Machine* author] H. G. Wells, that's a pretty fascinating way of looking at that.

JC: Wells set it all in motion, didn't he? I don't think there's an example before that, other than possibly in some kind of sorcery or magical context. But I think in terms of hard science fiction that's absolutely the first instance. And he just created an entire subgenre with one book [in] 1895.

CN: The potential is limitless for time-travel stories. You know better than anybody—you're dancing in between things that come before us, saying, is it this type of time travel? That type? You can get buried in the paradoxes.

JC: You can, and you can play fast and loose with the audience to where they don't feel there's a rule set. You've been very good in your films about creating a rule set. It may sometimes be challenging—I would say even in *Dunkirk*, it's challenging to understand that there are three separate stories interwoven that are going at three different rates of time. But you set it up in those first three title cards, then you play it out. It's same thing with *Inception* and with *Memento*.

CN: I think you feel that. Even if the audience can't tell you the rule set. We were talking about the structure of the tesseract earlier on. I was trying to explain it. It's ludicrously complicated when I try and explain it, but I firmly believed—and I continue to believe that—if we as the filmmakers understand, and we adhere to it, it will feel correct to the audience.

JC: In my mind, what makes it into the final film is a tenth of what's been created around it. It represents the tip of the iceberg of a much greater body of thought or design.

CN: I think that's very much why you were able to take *Terminator* and then revisit it in a way that did not feel like it had been added on afterward. It felt like it exists around the world of the first film. Because there's a rigor to that film . . . it doesn't feel like you cheat with time.

JC: Go out on a few limbs, but never cheat.

CN: Going out on limbs is fine. But you never knowingly cheated. It's nice and comprehensible and therefore very exciting. And particularly the two films together.

JC: We want you to come back and do some more science fiction. You've done *Dunkirk*, so you've done the gritty reality of war.

CN: Science fiction, it's not a genre to me. It's a state of mind. An approach to things.

JC: I think it's easy to say what isn't science fiction—sword and sorcery, *Lord of the Rings*–fantasy. But it's sometimes hard to say what is science fiction. I would say *The Dark Knight* is science fiction from a sociological standpoint.

BELOW Theatrical poster for *Looper*.

OPPOSITE TOP Theatrical poster for Christopher Nolan's *Inception*.

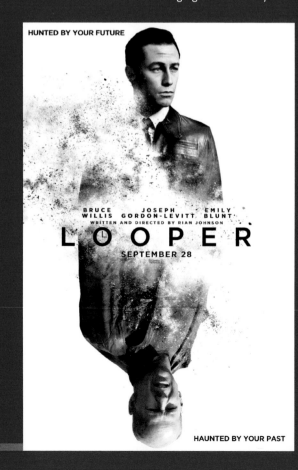

HUNTED BY YOUR FUTURE

BRUCE WILLIS   JOSEPH GORDON-LEVITT   EMILY BLUNT
WRITTEN AND DIRECTED BY RIAN JOHNSON

L O O P E R

SEPTEMBER 28

HAUNTED BY YOUR PAST

Interstellar obviously is. *Inception* obviously is. They're using a machine to go into a dream. If there was no machine, you could argue.

CN: It would be metaphysical.

JC: Exactly. It would be a metaphysical story.

CN: And it would have made a lot less money. I'm being glib, but the truth is that science fiction allows you a mechanism that we can all understand and grasp. I mean, you're going back to the world of *Avatar*. In the original film, there's an extremely relatable and simple emotional story at the heart of it that you build all this other stuff on. And that takes people all kinds of places.

JC: It was intentionally simple, but dressed up in science fiction terms, basically just inhabiting another body. The whole idea of psionic link technology is completely made-up bullshit. Kip Thorne couldn't write a chapter about that technology. Except that we have this longing to be able to do things like that, and when we have a longing, it creates a demand you know, on an artist, on a filmmaker, to do something for an audience.

CN: I think it's like time travel. It feels like something that's got such a pull on us, like the idea of wanting to inhabit somebody else's consciousness, and the proxy ways, with the internet and social media, in which we try [a] feint at that virtual reality.

JC: I'm going to shift gears for a second. What do you feel about alien civilizations or alien life forms? Do you take it as read that aliens exist? Or is it a wait and see kind of thing?

CN: I think for me it's a wait and see kind of thing, but at the same time I don't think I'll be around that long to wait that long. I was looking at the DVD extras on *Close Encounters [of the Third Kind]*—it's just such an incredible movie. And it's fundamental. It's this moment that hadn't been

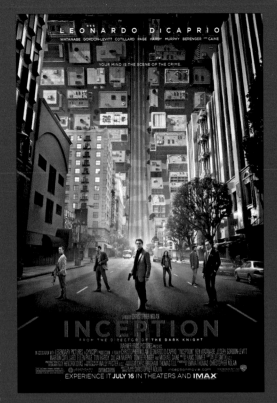

really portrayed on film before in this way, with real gravity and real sincerity. You look at Steven [Spielberg] on the extras when he was interviewed at the time, he absolutely believes [in the existence of aliens].

JC: Oh, he was a believer.

CN: Absolutely. Later on, he sort of talks about, okay, with all the cameras in the world, how is it that no one's actually managed to come up with an image, and everything. I think his views shifted over time in terms of the immediacy of, are we being visited right now? But you look at when he made that film, he's fully invested in that idea.

JC: Yeah, he was directing from passion.

CN: Very much. And I think it made it something that he really was determined to see and wanted to see in his lifetime. I think the mathematics on alien civilizations [are] pretty compelling. But I also think that—and this is partly having worked with Kip Thorne for so long on *Interstellar*—my awareness of the limits of how we can see into the universe, where we can go . . . Because the sheer distances to the nearest star, it's so daunting.

JC: There is an aspect of science fiction that celebrates human potential. And then there's an aspect that says that we have all these demons and we have these failings and that our potential will probably never be realized, that our technology amplifies all of our negative traits as well. I love that yin/yang in science fiction where it's simultaneously very optimistic and very pessimistic.

CN: My brother and I talked a lot about, with *Interstellar*, that that world is not a dystopia. It's dying, but it's not a dystopia. It's theoretically the best of human nature, it's people getting on with it. And the film has a lot of optimism in that regard. It falls very firmly on that side. But I think both sides are fascinating.

JC: It's actually one of the first films that really dealt seriously with the after effects, or the ongoing effects, of climate change, and what it could look like in America.

CN: How we went about [that]—I was looking at Ken Burns's documentary about the Dust Bowl. What they were talking about and the images they had in that documentary, they felt more improbable than most science fiction. Genuinely. This is stuff that really happened. So I called Ken, and I said, "What I'd like to do is take some interviews that you shot [with] real people who lived through this actual event and use them in the science fiction film to represent people talking about this horrible event in the future." So we intercut our characters with these real survivors. They were children at the time of the Dust Bowl, and they're remembering what it was. And it was more extreme than most science fiction would ever portray, the dust clouds and so forth. We scaled them down from what you see in Ken's documentary.

JC: We're going to have all that again. It's inevitable.

CN: That's what he says. It's pretty frightening.

JC: What do you think about the ethics of showing through science fiction [the] idea that it's okay to have screwed up the Earth, we'll go find another one?

CN: Once again, we're back to the idea of subversion in science fiction. I'm able to make a film that says the world is ending, and that's the beginning of the story. I think it's fascinating to be able to do, and that was what got me about Jonah's original pitch. It just stuck with me. It was this idea of, the Earth is the egg, and we're born from the egg, and our destiny inevitably lies out there. Whether that's true or not, I don't know, but it feels like it's true.

JC: We're willing it into existence. What we want desperately [is that] we want those aliens to exist.

CN: We want the idea that we will continue to expand and explore the universe because it's out there. And it really is, so it's not fiction. The idea that we would never as a species know what's out there—we'll never be able to go there—that doesn't feel right. It feels against something in human nature. And that was very much the jumping-off point, what we wanted to tap as far as the ethics of leaving the world behind. I don't feel that's how people watch movies. I don't feel that's how people watch science fiction. Science fiction is a vehicle for exploring. It doesn't have to be a cautionary tale. And even though [when] *Interstellar* starts off, it might be a cautionary tale, in a way it's not, because what it's saying is, maybe it's a natural process. Maybe there's a point where the Earth doesn't want us anymore.

JC: It's a celebration of our capability, of our potential. It's actually kind of old-school science fiction. It's a throwback in a way to the impulses of the science fiction of the '30s and '40s. We're going to go out there. We're going to do this. It's our destiny to do this. It's the natural next step of the evolution of consciousness to do this. That's what Kubrick would say.

CN: Yeah.

JC: And I love that. I really respect that about the film because science fiction has gone back and forth through these waves. In the '60s and '70s there was very little science fiction up until *Star Wars* that was hopeful or was celebratory or that was adventure. It really got itself painted into a corner and [was] not very commercial either for exactly that reason, its pessimism about us. Just constantly, human nature just took a beating in science fiction for about twenty years, and then *Star Wars* came along and George said, "Fuck all that. Let's have some fun." Not that it was lightweight material. It wasn't.

CN: Not at all, but it freshens it up. And he did a different thing with it. He was using it as a historical analogy. He was using it to be a Western or samurai film.

JC: Sure. Legend, myth. [Joseph] Campbell archetypes.

CN: If you look at apocalyptic ideas in science fiction, they tend to come in waves. In the '70s was a very strong wave of apocalyptic thinking. *Star Wars* was very counter to that.

JC: It was. It righted the ship [in terms] of freeing the imagination. But you're coming out of the '60s with civil rights and rioting and wars—and a certain unleashing of human consciousness with the counterculture. So of course it was going to manifest itself that way.

CN: I think, sadly, if you look at what then happened to that is [that] apocalyptic emphasis in science fiction very much diminished in the '90s. After September 11, there's a big resurgence of it almost immediately. *I Am Legend*, there's a big wave of [films] very, very concerned [with] that '70s idea of, you know what, we may well screw this all up. We could be on a tremendous threat of either destroying the world ourselves or having it destroyed from external forces. That apocalyptic thinking comes very firmly back into science fiction.

JC: You see it go through these cycles. In the '50s into the early '60s, the threat of nuclear annihilation manifests itself in all these B–monster movies and the threat of Communism manifests itself in these sort of body takeover infiltration–type movies like *Invasion of the Body Snatchers*. I'm fascinated by the way that science fiction is always manifesting our angst, our dreams, and our nightmares.

CN: If you look at Japanese anime for example, the apocalyptic dimension of that is extraordinary. Further back, [you have] Godzilla and all the rest. [At the time], people were not that aware of [their symbolic significance]. I think where we sit right now, we're not aware of . . .

JC: What we're doing now.

CN: Exactly.

JC: But it will all make sense.

CN: It will make sense, and it'll probably be quite obvious.

JC: Assuming there is a later, it'll all make sense.

CN: I think it will be fairly transparent, actually—what we were influenced by, what we were worried about. But I think that science fiction doesn't have to be self-conscious about it. If it's self-conscious, it becomes didactic. It has to have fun and has to be in its own world of entertainment and that lets the audience access it. That's why it lets the audience look at the world in a different way than they would otherwise.

MONSTERS

BY MATT SINGER

THE BRIGHTEST STAR in the constellation Aquila is named Altair. Situated 16.7 light-years from Earth and shining 80,000 times brighter than our own sun, Altair comprises one-third of the "Summer Triangle"—the asterism that the Air Force used as a nighttime navigation tool before the advent of GPS. And on one of Altair's small, nondescript planets, an invisible monster lurks, waiting for its prey.

The planet and its monster are fiction, of course, but the star is real—a detail that adds to the sense of verisimilitude in the 1956 sci-fi film *Forbidden Planet*, one of the first space epics by a major Hollywood studio. The creature is discovered by Spaceship C57D, which arrives at Altair IV seeking information about an earlier expedition that had vanished. The planet's only inhabitants, Dr. Edward Morbius (Walter Pidgeon) and his daughter Altaira (Anne Francis), are polite hosts, but the ship's commander, John Adams (Leslie Nielsen), and his men are repeatedly attacked by an unseen hostile force. Eventually the mystery is explained: By plugging his brain into a powerful machine left behind by Altair IV's previous civilization, Dr. Morbius has accidentally unleashed a "monster from the id." Here's how Adams explains the monster's secret to a skeptical Morbius:

> Monsters from the subconscious. Of course! . . . The big machine. Eight thousand miles of klystron relays. Enough power for a whole population of creative geniuses. . . . That ultimate machine would instantaneously project solid matter to any point on the planet, in any shape or color they might imagine. For any purpose, Morbius! Creation by mere thought.

Strip the pseudoscience out of Adams's speech, and suddenly he's not just talking about this particular monster; he's talking about *all* movie monsters. Morbius's creature is the perfect metaphor for the way monsters have been deployed on-screen for over a century. Just like Morbius's beast, movie monsters rise from their creators' subconscious. These creatures come in any shape or color that can be imagined. Every movie monster is a creation by mere thought; every movie monster is a monster from the id.

Take, for example, Frankenstein's Monster. Originally created by author Mary Shelley in the 1818 book *Frankenstein: or The Modern Prometheus*, cinema's most famous monster first appeared on-screen in 1910 but found his most iconic form when played by Boris Karloff in 1931's *Frankenstein*, from Universal Studios and director James Whale. Karloff's makeup, designed by Jack Pierce, transformed the British actor's ordinary features into a vision of pure horror, with pale skin, an enormous forehead, flattened scalp, and huge metal bolts protruding from his neck. He's brought to life by mad Dr. Henry Frankenstein (Colin Clive), who is fixated on playing god and achieves his demented dreams by robbing graves and medical schools in order to cobble together a new body from the best bits of each corpse he finds. Unfortunately, Frankenstein's assistant Fritz (Dwight Frye) destroys the healthy brain earmarked for the monster; with no other option available, he steals an abnormal brain instead. Dr. Frankenstein unwittingly puts the bad brain in his creation, and the rest is history.

OPPOSITE Theatrical poster for a rerelease of director James Whale's unforgettable 1931 version of *Frankenstein* starring Boris Karloff as the monster.

ABOVE A book cover for a Penguin Classics edition of Mary Shelley's novel *Frankenstein*.

THE ORIGINAL HORROR SHOW!

FRANKENSTEIN

THE MAN WHO MADE A MONSTER

WITH **COLIN CLIVE · MAE CLARKE**
JOHN BOLES · BORIS KARLOFF

DWIGHT FRYE · EDWARD VAN SLOAN AND FREDERIC KERR

Based upon the Story by MARY WOLLSTONCROFT SHELLEY
Adapted by JOHN L. BALDERSTON · From the play by PEGGY WEBLING

Directed by JAMES WHALE

A UNIVERSAL RE-RELEASE

THEY COULDN'T BELIEVE THEIR EYES!

THEY COULDN'T ESCAPE THE TERROR!

AND NEITHER WILL *YOU!*

WARNER BROS.
PRESENT

The Beast From 20,000 Fathoms

It's alive!

CAST OF THOUSANDS! OVER A YEAR IN THE MAKING!

PAUL CHRISTIAN · PAULA RAYMOND · CECIL KELLAWAY · KENNETH TOBEY · JACK PENNICK

SCREEN PLAY BY LOU MORHEIM AND FRED FREIBERGER   PHOTOGRAPHY BY JACK RUSSELL, A.S.C.   Suggested by the Sensational SATURDAY EVENING POST Story by RAY BRADBURY

Like most great monster movies, Whale's *Frankenstein* is a cautionary tale about one of the core tenets of monster movies, most succinctly described by comedian Patton Oswalt on his standup album *Werewolves and Lollipops*: "Science: We're all about coulda, not shoulda!"

Science run amok lies at the heart of most classic monster movies; the only variables are the kinds of monsters and the specific scientific terrors they represent. In fact, charting the entire history of the monster movie subgenre would give you a pretty good sense of mankind's greatest technological concerns throughout the twentieth century. Viewed as a whole, the canon of monster movies is like an enormous documentary on the evolution of our society's worst fears.

A few years after *Frankenstein* and its macabre view of the medical profession, World War II erupted. The conflict consumed most of the world for more than half a decade, ending nine days after the atomic bomb was dropped on Hiroshima. Anxiety about nuclear weapons—and the destruction they could cause if they were ever used again—would radiate through monster movies from both sides of the Pacific for decades to come. Pandora's box had been opened and there were fire-breathing monsters inside.

In American cinema, fictional atomic bomb tests began unleashing all kinds of giant creatures. In 1953's *The Beast from 20,000 Fathoms*, an atomic test in the Arctic awakens a dinosaur that had been trapped inside a block of ice; it escapes and cuts a

ABOVE A theatrical poster for *The Beast from 20,000 Fathoms* (1953), which featured creature effects by stop-motion animation legend Ray Harryhausen.

swath of destruction through Canada and the northern United States. The following year, Gordon Douglas's *Them!* followed a colony of giant ants transformed by exposure to atomic radiation in Alamogordo, New Mexico, the site of the first real-world atomic bomb test. Meanwhile, Japan introduced one of the greatest and most prolific monsters in movie history: Godzilla.

Like *The Beast from 20,000 Fathoms*, *Godzilla*'s title creature is a prehistoric dinosaur reawakened in modern times by ill-advised nuclear testing. *The Beast from 20,000 Fathoms* and a few other American movies may have come first, but *Godzilla* surpassed them all to become the exemplar of atomic-age monsters—in part because, unlike the American filmmakers behind those previous monster movies, the Japanese creators of *Godzilla* had witnessed true atomic horror firsthand, and they imbued their work with their experiences.

Consider the early scene where a fishing boat is destroyed by a mysterious blast that turns out to be Godzilla emerging from his watery hibernation. The sequence was inspired by a real-life incident that occurred just a few months before production, when the entire crew of the Japanese fishing boat *Lucky Dragon 5* got radiation poisoning from the nuclear fallout of an unexpectedly large American H-bomb test. When the fictional fishing boat is flashed by this unknown force, the actors' agonized writhing is so intense it is immediately impossible to dismiss the film as a piece of disaster escapism. This *Godzilla* isn't about a guy in a rubber suit smashing papier-mâché buildings. It's about a group of artists grappling with a nation's trauma.

Director Ishiro Honda explored the moral questions raised by the atomic attacks by giving his protagonists their own superweapon akin to a nuclear bomb: an "oxygen destroyer" that appears to be the only thing capable of stopping Godzilla's onslaught. But the oxygen destroyer is so potent that if it fell into the wrong hands it might kill many more people and animals than Godzilla ever could. The decision the heroes of *Godzilla* grapple with—whether to unleash a terrible weapon to save lives in the short term at the possible expense of many lives in the long term—is the exact same one faced by the men who dropped the nuclear bombs on Hiroshima and Nagasaki.

In the end, the scientist who invented the oxygen destroyer uses it to defeat Godzilla, committing suicide in the process so that no one else can ever use his creation. The nobility and heroism of his sacrifice was diminished somewhat by the fact that Godzilla became a franchise, rising again and again to menace Japan (and later to defend it from other giant monsters). But Godzilla's repeated returns from the grave could also be an ideal allegory for the era's lingering nuclear panic. Like ancient dinosaurs, those worries couldn't be killed so easily.

Dinosaurs of a different sort—and new scientific concerns—are the focal point of another legendary monster movie: Steven Spielberg's *Jurassic Park* (1993). Inspired by the Michael Crichton novel of the same name, the film imagines a world where dinosaurs have been restored from extinction and turned into a tourist attraction on an island near Costa Rica. Before this one-of-a-kind theme park can open its doors to the public, investors who want to ensure its safety bring in a team of paleontologists and mathematicians to confirm nothing could go wrong. Spoiler alert: It does anyway, as a cascading combination of technical failures, bad weather, and pure Darwinian evolution plunge the island into chaos.

Jurassic Park's T. rexes and velociraptors were not atomic-powered—they were genetically engineered, reflecting a new generation's anxieties about cloning, a hot topic in the news and popular culture throughout the mid-'90s. Discarding the mad scientist archetype, Spielberg cast scientists as his heroes. The problems in *Jurassic Park*

are instead created by John Hammond (Richard Attenborough), the naive businessman who builds the dinosaur theme park. Hammond's reckless behavior highlighted our culture's increasing distrust of charismatic industrialists who preach about technology's utopian benefits to society while ignoring its equally destructive capabilities.

Hammond maintains a few lofty ideals, but his motives are clouded by greed—a key theme that runs through many monster movies of this era. Two of the best examples are Ridley Scott's *Alien* (1979) and its sequel *Aliens* (1986), directed by James Cameron. Despite a shared heroine (Sigourney Weaver's resourceful Ellen Ripley) and

monster (the face-hugging, chest-bursting xenomorph designed by H. R. Giger), Scott and Cameron produced vastly different films. Scott's is a haunted house story in space, Cameron's a full-on war film. In each case, though, there is a shared secondary threat that enables the xenomorphs' mayhem: the cold-blooded business practices of the powerful Weyland-Yutani Corporation.

It's "the Company" who order *Alien*'s deranged android Ash (Ian Holm) to preserve the xenomorph specimen at all costs, even if that means the deaths of Ripley and her coworkers. They're also the ones in *Aliens* who retrieve Ripley from the

ABOVE LEFT Richard Attenborough (*left*) as John Hammond introduces Dr. Alan Grant (Sam Neill) and Ellie Sattler (Laura Dern) to Jurassic Park.

ABOVE RIGHT The titular space beast from *Alien*, designed by Swiss artist H. R. Giger.

wreckage of the first movie and then send her back to the planet where they found the xenomorph. A loathsome corporate toady (played to sleazy perfection by Paul Reiser) insists this second expedition is a rescue operation for trapped colonists. He is lying; once again, the Company's objective is to retrieve an alien sample so it can be used to create biological weapons.

Alien didn't originally have a Frankenstein or a Hammond responsible for creating its monster—but almost forty years later, Ridley Scott returned to the series and gave it one when he revealed in the prequel Alien: Covenant that the xenomorph was engineered by an android named David, played by

Michael Fassbender. It's never too late to retroactively turn a monster movie into a fable about the dangers of unchecked scientific advancement.

Few movie monsters can hold a candle to the xenomorph's inhuman life cycle, multitiered mouth, and acid blood. One of the only ones that come close to matching that hellish monstrosity is the terrifying title character in John Carpenter's The Thing (1982). No description can do the Thing justice; its shapeshifting abilities allow it to adapt to any threatening situation. When discovered, it can sprout frenetic, lashing tentacles or razor-sharp fangs that emerge from its torso as prelude to its mutation into a

THE ULTIMATE IN ALIEN TERROR.

JOHN CARPENTER'S

THE THING

MAN IS THE WARMEST PLACE TO HIDE.

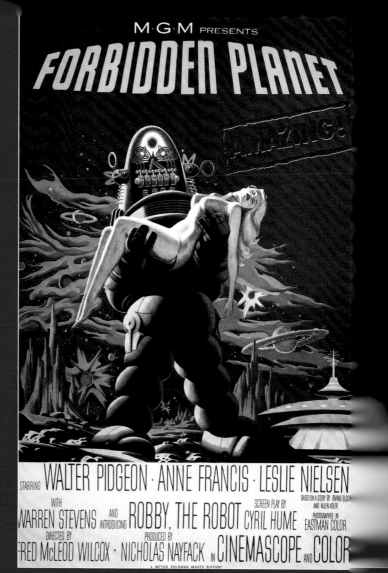

man-sized spider. Decapitate it, and the dis-embodied head will use its tongue as a lasso to drag itself to safety, then sprout spider legs of its own to crawl away. And all of that happens in just one scene! Even scarier, the Thing can perfectly copy the form of any living creature. Initially disguised as a sled dog, and later as members of the staff of an Antarctic outpost, it murders and replaces everyone in its path.

The Thing's creatures, designed by acclaimed special makeup effects creator Rob Bottin, remain amongst the most horrific practical effects ever made for movies. But the fact that the Thing could look like anyone, even someone you know, is much scarier than its flailing tentacles—as is the Antarctic outpost's swift descent into paranoia and violence. That's another thing *The Thing* shares with all the movies discussed here and hundreds of other monster movies: The real monster is always man. Frankenstein's creation is violently unstable, but it's the citizens of Frankenstein's little village that turn into a violent lynch mob. Godzilla may squish anyone who gets in his way, but he only exists in 1954 because men with bombs released him. The same goes for the denizens of *Jurassic Park*; one can hardly fault a dinosaur for eating a human being. That's simply in its nature. The greedy industrialist should have known better.

In his interview with Guillermo del Toro, James Cameron describes monster movies as "a nightmare that's safe." The part of the nightmare that's *not* safe, that part that

keeps us up at night, is the men behind the monsters. We can shrug off modern-day dinosaurs and acid-blooded aliens as works of fantasy; we need only look at the world around us to find concrete evidence there is no monster more monstrous than man. Once again, *Forbidden Planet* and its "monsters from the id" provide the perfect metaphor for this concept. These movies force us to confront the notion that there might be a monster lurking inside each of us, waiting for the moment when a stray thought might create something terrible.

ABOVE Theatrical pos[ter] for *Forbidden Planet* (1956).

OPPOSITE Theatrica[l] poster for director Joh[n] Carpenter's *The Thing* (1982).

GUILLERMO DEL TORO

INTERVIEW BY JAMES CAMERON

OVER THE COURSE OF THE LAST TWO DECADES, visionary filmmaker Guillermo del Toro has dreamed up beautifully handcrafted fictional worlds awash in breathtaking tones of blue and amber and populated by outsiders, monsters, and the misunderstood. From his debut feature, 1993's vampire fable *Cronos*, to his most recent film, the Cold War–era love story *The Shape of Water*, del Toro's work borrows from every genre and defies easy categorization but always bears his unmistakable personal stamp. His love for anime and Japanese monster movies is at the heart of his most overtly sci-fi outing, 2013's robots-versus-kaiju blockbuster *Pacific Rim*; his fascination with the horrors of the natural world plays out in his English-language debut, 1997's *Mimic*.

Here, del Toro sits down with Cameron—the pair's friendship dates back twenty-six years—for an in-depth conversation examining the interplay between horror, science fiction, and fantasy, the enduring philosophical brilliance of Mary Shelley's *Frankenstein* story and its 1931 movie adaptation, and del Toro's close encounter with a UFO.

JAMES CAMERON: You're a horror guy, as you tell me every time we talk about this. The question is, where is that inter-zone, that cross-talk between horror and science fiction?

GUILLERMO DEL TORO: Everything that is the fuel for the early horror days has to be spiritual. It comes from the belief of good and evil. The cosmology of Judeo-Christian lore, the devil, angels and demons. Even if you go to Eastern narratives—Japan, China—it still is linked to the spiritual realms, you know? Then there comes a point in Western literature, a little after the Age of Reason, curiously enough, and I think crucially in *Frankenstein*, that now includes science as a motor of the anomaly. I think the moment science becomes a model of the exceptional, it switches. Something really changes.

JC: So, today it's radioactivity, genetic engineering, robotics—our monsters come from so many different places. Before, our monsters came from folklore, mythology, demons, the supernatural world. So, where does *Frankenstein* fall in that spectrum?

GDT: That is both clarifier and a mystifier. Because I think that some of the questions essential to *Frankenstein* are spiritual and are existential. There is the Miltonian component of the tale in which the creature questions his nature. What is his purpose? What is the purpose of the world? [He's questioning] matters of good and evil, matters of worth. But the motor is science.

JC: That's right. A perversion of science.

GDT: A perversion of science, and very much hubris and very much human arrogance. We open with a captain that has the same hubris as Victor Frankenstein, trying to defy the natural order. And through the tale, the captain learns a lesson and gains humility. I do think that you can call it horror because ultimately it's the reanimation of a corpse, or a series of corpses, which are a mixture of animal, human—it's really quite shocking. And there's always been a question that is beautiful: In which of all those parts resides the soul?

OPPOSITE Guillermo del Toro on the set of *James Cameron's Story of Science Fiction*. Photo Credit: Michael Moriatis/AMC

JC: Isn't that what that book and what those films ask?

GDT: Yes. And there is a moment . . . probably one of the best moments in the novel, which is purely horror. Because the essence of horror is what should be and is not, or what should not be and is. That's it. You can divide the rest of the entire canon of horror into those. The beauty of that moment is Victor very symbolically, very Freudianly, goes to sleep after trying to animate the creature. He is sleeping. And like

[Francisco] Goya said, "The sleep of reason produces monsters." He's asleep, and he feels something watching him. He wakes up to see the creature looking at him. The beauty of the moment is that is horror. Because it shouldn't be and is.

JC: But existential questions are also very much the meat of science fiction. Who are we? Why are we? What is consciousness? What is the soul? What is essentially human? Would you agree that there is a spectrum in which at one end you've got unarguably science fiction, in the middle you can have a transition zone where you can have science fiction / horror, and then you have that which is unarguably horror?

GDT: I completely agree. And in the mixture, you can have things that are almost completely a mixture like *Alien* (1979), which strives to be a haunted house / monster movie.

JC: It's classic science fiction—we're in space, we're with a crew on a spaceship on another planet—and pure horror at the same time. Very much the id, very much the psychosexual imagery, the [H. R.] Giger designs and so on.

GDT: [H. P.] Lovecraft also sometimes tried science fiction and horror.

JC: *The Shadow Out of Time* was science fiction.

GDT: "The Colour Out of Space."

JC: But the Cthulhu Mythos . . .

GDT: No. I think the moment you depend on a lore that is fantastic in origin, that is not governed by or at least defined by the breaking of rules that are scientific, then you go into fantasy. Or you go into horror.

JC: What about telepathy? Is that a supernatural power or is that something that, in a science fiction context, can be just something

BEWARE THE STARE THAT WILL PARALYZE THE WILL OF THE WORLD

METRO-GOLDWYN-MAYER Presents
GEORGE SANDERS
BARBARA SHELLEY.

VILLAGE OF THE DAMNED

with
MICHAEL GWYNN
Screen Play by
STIRLING SILLIPHANT
WOLF RILLA GEORGE BARCLAY
Based on the Novel "The Midwich Cuckoos"
by JOHN WYNDHAM
Directed by
WOLF RILLA
Produced by
RONALD KINNOCH

that science doesn't understand yet but is striving to?

GDT: Most of the time I think telepathy would fall into some form of science fiction.

JC: It's supernatural because we have no evidence for the power of telepathy, no hard evidence.

GDT: But there are instances in literature certainly. I remember immediately *Carrion Comfort* by Dan Simmons [about a tribe of powerful psychics], which makes sort of vampirism out of one of these virtues. Nevertheless, the ultimate explanation is not divine or spiritual. Meaning, even if there is no evidence, the ultimate explanation of telepathy [is not rooted in horror or fantasy].

JC: It's empirical in some way. You could sense that there could be some instrument that could detect it. Like in *Village of the Damned*. That was meant not to be horror but science fiction.

GDT: [British screenwriter] Nigel Kneale also does a lot of that. A lot of the British sci-fi sometimes compounds a little bit of horror and vice versa. You go to something like *The Stone Tape*, in which he says basically houses are like stone tapes that record the memories, the moments of pain. So, there's also that beauty.

JC: What about [Kneale's] *Five Million Years to Earth* [aka *Quatermass and the Pit*] where they were explaining our image of demons and the devil in science fiction terms?

GDT: I think those are really interesting examples. Rare, beautiful, precious, I would say. Because they allow this membrane to become more fluid.

JC: How about [the 1965 Mario Bava film] *Planet of the Vampires*? That fed directly to *Alien*, right? You land on an alien planet. There's a crashed spaceship over there.

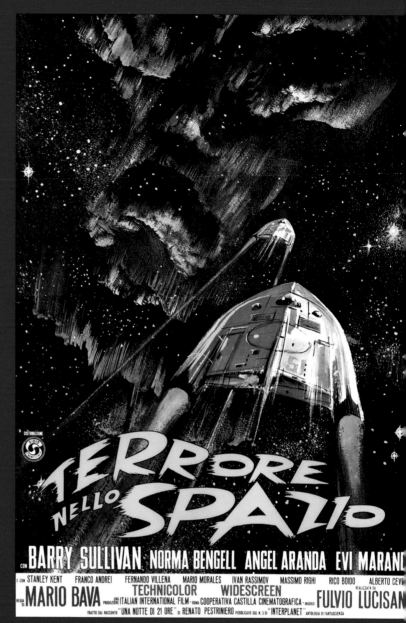

GDT: The giant body . . .

JC: The corpse, right, right.

GDT: What is beautiful about Bava is that, stylistically, he combines the two. Not on a matter of the story or the way the story is treated, or the characters, or the empirical stuff. But the way he lights it, by virtue of the design and the colors, he visually makes a beautiful mixture of horror and sci-fi.

OPPOSITE Theatrical poster for *Village of the Damned* (1960), a film adapted from novelist John Wyndham's *The Midwich Cuckoos*.

ABOVE The Italian theatrical poster for *Planet of the Vampires* (1965), directed by Mario Bava.

JC: That's what Mario Bava and a lot of the Italians did. So, vampirism. Now one would normally put that in horror—a supernatural, demonic sort of thing. But you made *The Strain*, in which there was a pathogen involved that explained or partially explained it.

GDT: Vampirism, its origins are in every culture. You have Greek vampires, Eastern-European vampires, Japanese, Filipino. Everything across the board for whatever reason. I have my own theory, but this is a myth like the dragon that exists in every culture. My theory is that at some point we were cannibalistic as apes. And the horror of eating each other needed a myth to explain it. I think werewolves and vampires came out of that need to crystallize that past urge or present urge.

JC: That animal within us. When I see a vampire movie where they shrink from the cross, or they burst into flames when they hit sunlight, to me, that's nonscientific, that's supernatural lore. But when I see a film like *I Am Legend* where vampiric behavior is explained by a pathogen, changing people presumably in some epigenetic way, I would put that in science fiction.

GDT: That is the moment that [*I Am Legend* author] Richard Matheson brings two things together beautifully. He brings science in, and he brings [in an] urban [setting]. Stephen King takes the suburbs, a small city and takes it further. But the beauty of Richard Matheson is he says, it's our cities. It's our streets. And this changes everything.

JC: When was *I Am Legend* written, it was the early '50s. Then it was made several times. I think *The Last Man on Earth* (1964) was an attempt to do *I Am Legend*, and then there was obviously *The Omega Man*.

GDT: But very importantly, the bootleg *I Am Legend* is *Night of the Living Dead* (1968). It spawned an entirely new mythos in horror. And it stays in horror because [director George]

Romero stubbornly refuses to define what caused the death.

JC: Many films afterward have tried to make it a disease, a pathogen, something transmissible, and created clichés around that. If you get bitten, it moves through your bloodstream, and all that sort of thing. But if you really think about it, it must be horror. Because when you have an animated corpse that's completely rotted away, there really can't be any metabolism. There can't be any musculature. It's being moved by some supernatural power.

GDT: It should be. It should stay supernatural. There's a point in *Dawn of the Dead* (1978) in which [actor Ken Foree] says, "When there's no more room in hell, the dead will walk the earth." The vampire, if we go back to it originally, the myth of the vampire was a reanimated corpse, in many cases possessed by an evil spirit. Or a suicide. But it had a component that was purely religious or spiritual.

JC: And it was really more of a zombie than a predatory bloodthirsty creature. That got layered on.

GDT: There were vampires that would come back just to kick their neighbor. And that's what's really funny in Eastern-European lore—some vampires came back to kick butt. Literally. Others came to drink the blood, and what was beautiful or terrifying in the mythology of the original vampire is, they came back to the family first. Meaning a father would come back and vampirize the son, the daughter, the mother. And then they would spread out. But the beauty of Matheson is that he takes this and mixes it with science. There's a great novel by Suzy McKee [Charnas] called *The Vampire Tapestry*, which also makes a wonderful story of the vampire. I think these cases in which the [genres] overlap, it becomes more interesting.

JC: So I would put *The Omega Man* and *I Am Legend*, the new film, really more in a science

fiction context. *Night of the Living Dead* stays in horror. But a zombie movie that ascribes it to a pathogen—like, let's say *World War Z*—then that would be science fiction.

GDT: I would say so. Again, the moment you supplant or change the motor from a spiritual/religious one to a scientific one, it changes genres. What we attempted on *The Strain* was [a narrative rooted in science]—*this* is explained by *this*. But then at the end, you have to go spiritual in my case. We went back to biblical times.

JC: Why have zombie movies become so popular now? And zombie shows like *The Walking Dead*?

GDT: What happened with the zombie as a figure is that Romero created it and it's very multivalent—meaning, it can signify different things at different times. Romero took it as an iconoclastic, anarchic sort of mirror. It very explicitly says, it's us. He used it socially in *Night of the Living Dead* to say, this is the composition of our society. Everybody attributes it to the Vietnam era, and the fact that we were

killing each other. In *Dawn of the Dead*, he changes it and says, it's us, and we are things that shop in a mall. For barely any reason at all. We are consumers. So the consuming of the products becomes the consuming of the flesh. That changes over time, and right now, I think that the model of zombie that responds to the angst that we have is really quite eerily the fear of the other. It went from being a blue-state mythology to a red-state mythology. The survivalist dream is for the cataclysm to occur. To actually happen. It is very symbolic for me that it became sort of a sporting show, and hunting the Other. You lost the empathy or the critical component in the early Romero, you know?

JC: It takes away all human conscience. In a war movie, you have to have a conscience about killing another human being even though they're ideologically different. In a zombie movie, you don't. It's a guilt-free ecstasy of violence.

GDT: It's a sporting event. It's a hunting event. If you go back to *I Am Legend*, Matheson is incredibly intelligent and profound. In things like *The Incredible Shrinking Man*, you reach an existential, wonderful moment in which [the protagonist] abandons himself to the indifference of the universe. He's so small, and he understands the greatness of that smallness. He transcends his size, his position in the universe.

JC: A transcendental experience like that would be no different than the end of *2001: A Space Odyssey* where [the protagonist] becomes a Star Baby.

GDT: The next step. But the beauty of *I Am Legend* is—as you go through the adventure, [Matheson] changes it. He says the monster is you. Because you are demographically the one, you are the anomaly now. And that's the genius.

JC: [The protagonist of that story] is the one that's preying on them. They're the society that survives, so they become the society. They fear him. He is the boogeyman in their

night. That's genius, and I don't think they've ever got that [right on film].

GDT: Never.

JC: But they came the closest in *Omega Man*, because they got into the society of those people and how they feared him. And how he was this legendary monster.

GDT: He was the one that they told stories [about] to the kids at night. You were saying science fiction at its best questions, challenges, our belief—what are we, what makes us human, where do we fit into society. And that's a way that Matheson did it.

JC: Don't you think that *The Thing* follows that same principle of making us fear the Other in human form?

GDT: Absolutely. And when we talk about *The Thing*, we talk about three [elements]. The first is

TOP Kurt Russell as R. J. MacReady in director John Carpenter's *The Thing* (1982).

ABOVE Book cover for *At The Mountains of Madness and Other Weird Tales*, an H. P. Lovecraft compendium published by the Barnes & Noble Library of Essential Reading.

OPPOSITE BOTTOM Theatrical poster for *The Omega Man*, a 1971 adaptation of Richard Matheson's novel *I Am Legend* starring Charlton Heston.

Who Goes There?, the [original novella by John W. Campbell]. And which is in many ways very much a riff on [H. P. Lovecraft's *At the*] *Mountains of Madness*. The second incarnation, the Howard Hawks [film, *The Thing from Another World*].

JC: It was attributed to another director.

GDT: But I think everybody knows it as Howard Hawks's *Thing*. And the [John] Carpenter [film], which to me is the supreme version of the story because it really goes into questioning what makes you human, what distinguishes you.

JC: The beauty of the ending of *The Thing* is that they are alone. And they're going to die.

GDT: And we don't know if the other is the Thing. But it's much worse to be alone. They are kind of keeping company. So when people say, "Do you think they're both human, or do you think [one] is the Thing?" I always am fascinated with the Carpenter film because the Thing does more than imitate. It also [adopts]

speech pattern, cadence. It talks like the real characters. Memories—the Thing can remember. There are plenty of invasion stories where the invader is given away by a blank affect. *Invasion of the Body Snatchers*. But here, what is fascinating to me, what makes it even more deep for me at the end is, I like imagining that one of them is the Thing. And even that creature thinks, this is the last one. We're going to keep each other company. That's what makes it incredibly existential.

JC: You can also say that the thing that makes us human is our willingness to sacrifice. The Thing would not have sacrificed itself for someone else. But [Kurt Russell's character] MacReady did. When he blew up the ship, he knew he wasn't getting out of there. He was doing it for the greater good, for the survival of humanity. To throw that thing back into the ice.

GDT: This is also the seed of Judeo-Christian belief, but I do believe aside from any religion, the seed of the soul is will. That's what makes

world is a terrible place—he says, "Goodbye, cruel world."

JC: He decides not to live.

GDT: Decision is an act of will. The difference between the entity and the human is the will.

JC: That's true of the Thing. It's like a virus—although it's a very sophisticated one. It's inhabiting these bodies, taking their memories and their affect.

GDT: But there are many examples in real life of not only mimicry, but mimicry and absorption. It's like a psychopath. There are insects that infiltrate a colony—it can be a beetle simulating an ant. They have the morphology. They smell like the ant, but they eat the young of the ant. There are really incredible examples of horror that is hardwired.

JC: All the horrors exist in the insect world—parasites that grow inside the body and burst out, parasites that take over the behavior. There's a fungal infestation that takes over and causes the ant to go up to the top of a very high tree and sort of make a web onto a leaf, holds it there, then sprouts out of the ant's head, and the spores are carried away by the wind. It's telling the ant to climb a tree that it wouldn't normally so that it can reproduce.

GDT: Yes. And that is absolutely a nightmare. That's pure horror and science. But all those cycles of life again, hardwired cycles of life, that's what we always imagine when we're creating a monster. Ultimately, we're referencing something that exists, that existed.

JC: Why do we need monsters? Psychologically, why do we pay good money to go to a monster movie? Are we exciting the limbic system in our brain?

GDT: I think that the things that will tell you that the universe is much more vast than your

that story so important. The Thing makes hardwired decisions. The Thing overtakes, is designed and hardwired to overtake. Overtake and survive. And the difference between the Thing and man is that man is geared toward also being able not to survive. It links it to another great myth and . . . the sequel to [director James Whale's] *Frankenstein*, *Bride of Frankenstein* [also directed by Whale]. The first movie, the creature has been created from parts. He walks in, void of expression. He's changed by circumstance. He doesn't make decisions. He's chased by villagers. Second movie, he learns to speak. He learns the value of human contact. And for the first time, he makes two decisions—the first one is make a bride. And the second decision—when his heart is broken and he realizes the imagination need to exist above nature. I'm fifty-three, and I've seen in fifty-three years one UFO. But I saw it. So, there is no doubt in my mind that there's something much more vast, much more complex, much more interesting than the front page . . . because the only thing that can confirm the existence of angels are demons.

JC: Okay, but that's a religious interpretation.

GDT: It is, but it's a spiritual one. It's like the carcass of a creature confirms the existence of a living specimen. In the same way, I think monsters confirm the Otherness and therefore open our mind to a much more vast universe. And I think that's why when we started reinterpreting the world, when we were nomadic, we told tales about the cycles of nature.

JC: You're talking about us 20,000 years ago.

GDT: Yeah. When we were nomadic tribes. But when we settled, we needed to start codifying the world. We needed to say, why does the sun rise? Where was the moon before it came out into the night? We create entities that are not human. We create gods, and we create monsters, and we create demons to be able to encompass these notions. A lot of the notions that are abstract in philosophy you can embody—in *Frankenstein* for example. You can embody the notion of the abandoned being created by an indifferent creator as well in a novel as you can in a philosophical treaty. So monsters are incredibly apt at embodying the abstract in flesh. Godzilla. Godzilla embodies the anxiety and the terror of nuclear attack.

JC: Nuclear age, right? Sure, something bigger, created by science, something that can devastate a city. It's not a surprise that it emerged as a science fiction neo-myth from Japan, which had actually been bombed by nuclear weapons.

GDT: And in that way monsters respond to the pulsations of the zeitgeist at the time they are made.

JC: But I think there's a primal need for monsters that has to do with fear, because fear is healthy. In the same way that pain is healthy. If you didn't feel pain, you'd put your hand on the stove until you smelled something burning. If

you didn't have fear as a nomadic Neolithic man, you'd walk through the forest happily until a bear ate you. Fear of teeth and claws and being chased is a healthy thing. They used to use fairy tales to teach children to stay out of the woods, not talk to strangers. So it seems to me that we need our fear. But why do we pay to go to a movie theater to see a monster movie?

GDT: You're saying that we create these monsters as composites that warn us about the possible adversity of the natural world, which is true. One proof of that I read—and I don't remember the book—but I read somewhere that dragons are universal because they are the composite of the three main predators of the anthropoids. Snake, feline, and large rapacious birds.

JC: So it's a mash-up of archetypes.

GDT: Of things that you need to be afraid of at the most primitive mammalian level. Now why do we need it? The horrors of the [daily life] are incredible. Dying of cancer, corrupt politicians, human disillusionment, war, famine. You need to articulate them in a way that poses a solution that you can dramatize in two hours, six hours on a miniseries, or months. It doesn't matter. But you can articulate them through the monster.

JC: Also for the great majority of monster movies—certainly in the '30s and then in the '50s, less so in the counterculture '70s and '80s—you killed the monster at the end. You stand up to that fear, and then you kill it. You kill it by ingenuity, by willpower, by courage, by bravery, by faith—whatever it is. I think that we create the monster so we can destroy it.

GDT: Of course.

JC: In Bali, they have this thing called the Ogoh-Ogoh Festival. And they work very hard to create these big demonic figures, and then they burn them, and they're safe for a year. I think a lot of our horror films are actually

burning the Ogoh-ogoh—actually exorcising the demon.

GDT: In fairy tales and in horror, there are two versions of the same tale: one that reaffirms our place in the universe, and the one that questions it. The one you're talking about is the one that reaffirms your place in the universe. The one where St. George kills the dragon, where we conquer the serpent. We say, "We are once again supreme." Because ultimately it's about our place in the universe. At the top of creation and so forth. The other type is the most anarchic, iconoclastic version of those monsters. And again, because they are above nature, a superhuman, they allow us to question things that are eminently human.

JC: I would argue that you've made two science fiction films. One is *Pacific Rim*, which is foursquare science fiction, with robots and giant monsters. You don't get any more science fiction than that, right? And your new film, *The Shape of Water*. It's many things.

GDT: *Mimic*, too.

JC: You're absolutely right. But I would say that in *Pacific Rim*, St. George slays the dragon at the end, through willpower and courage and the human spirit.

GDT: Cooperation.

JC: Cooperation, right. *Shape of Water*, you don't want to slay the monster.

GDT: No. It's about, can we recognize ourselves in the Other. *Pacific Rim*, what I love is that obviously, of the myriad of solutions that we can come up with to kill twenty-five-story monsters, the one solution that probably would come out last is, "Let's create twenty-five-story robots." That comes from me being malformed by decades of great anime in my childhood, which basically shared the same culture that a Japanese kid would have in

Kyoto or in Tokyo. I think that there's a third genre that forms the Holy Trinity of these things, which is fantasy. Like *Star Wars*. *Star Wars* is, at the end of the day, about wizards, princesses, a young farmer.

JC: It's classic fantasy dressed up with robots and spaceships. No one would call *The Lord of the Rings* science fiction. That's clear cut.

GDT: Clear cut. That's fantasy. I think that's a third distinction you can make if you wish. Magic lore is the main component of that fantasy. And you then have a cosmology that would include elves, ogres, trolls.

JC: And a dragon would exist in a fantasy context. But you can have a big flying creature like you did in *Pacific Rim* that's essentially a dragon called a kaiju.

GDT: Or you can have a dragon like a Vermithrax Pejorative in *Dragonslayer*, which is explained beautifully as the last of its kind.

JC: So, there is a science explanation.

GDT: There is a scientific explanation. Or at least zoological. The way [director] Matthew Robbins came up with the idea of the dragon almost having acid reflux and not being able to control the flow of the fire . . . is so beautiful because I think those gestures bring plausibility. Zoology being a science, you can straddle science fiction and fantasy.

JC: But ultimately you're dressing up fantasy in the clothes of science fiction, not truly embracing the principles of science fiction.

GDT: The science fiction–fantasy hybrids are rare.

JC: Even though you're not so far a practitioner of postapocalyptic fiction in your film, we both love the genre. I think you would agree that [*Mad Max 2:*] *The Road Warrior* is science fiction.

ABOVE Concept art from Guillermo del Toro's *Pacific Rim* depicts the fearsome Kaiju Knifehead. Illustration by Allen Williams.

OPPOSITE *Mad Max* (1979) theatrical poster.

GDT: With elements of fantasy in a strange way, epic fantasy. Heroic fantasy. And the lonely hero . . .

JC: Who rejects the call and then accepts it, is transformed. It was classic Joseph Campbell.

GDT: It is. And what is beautiful is that what happens from *Mad Max* to *The Road Warrior* is what happens with *Alien* and *Aliens*. These are sequels that not only expand but completely change the genre of the first movie.

JC: Why are we so fascinated with these dark futures? Are we dealing with our own angst?

GDT: I think so. I think that a lot of people fantasize that if everything ended, things would be simpler. Legislation, morality, all those values crumble. You basically have a man facing the world.

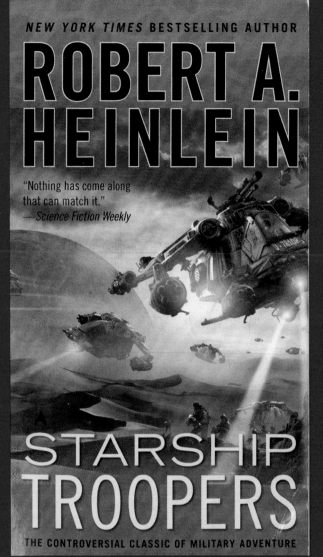

fantasies. And I would submit that everybody that watches these movies believes that they are going to be that one-in-ten-million person who survives and has the apartment in Manhattan with the steel door and all that. Sure, you've got to shoot a few zombies, but it's actually a pretty good life.

GDT: It is. I mean it simplifies the lifestyle, and that's why it's a very male fantasy because it's the true measure of a man. At the end of the day, is the fantasy having a whole supermarket for yourself? Or is the fantasy having to hunt to survive? You're not depending on a superstructure. You're not depending on police, army . . . it's a very Libertarian fantasy, a very red-state fantasy.

JC: Very [author Robert A.] Heinlein kind of approach, you know?

GDT: It's a basic urge that I think . . . is almost nascent in the way we understand it with the twentieth century and industrialization and the complication of the urban space. That's when it really is born. Once we went from little villages, little cities all over the map, to urban accumulation and optimization, government legislating your own [actions], this fantasy exploded. Everybody said, "Let's go to simpler times." And it's not the past. It's the future.

JC: I think that there's a deep-seated anxiety out there right now that science and civilization are not going to save us, are not going to be the answer to our problem.

GDT: I think that's a huge part of it. The other part is a paradox that I see active certainly in social media in which the discourse is super regimented—it's processed and almost legislated to the point of almost being impossible to survive as a human being with a gray area. You don't survive in that discourse. At the same time, I don't think we have had more latent rage than now. Those two things—the superstructuring of how we should, in theory,

JC: Very much like the frontier West.

GDT: The quintessential postapocalyptic fantasy in the twentieth century is you, your car, and your gun. And that's it. That's a very male-driven fantasy. [Psychoanalyst Sigmund] Freud wouldn't have a hard time deciphering somebody that loves his gun and his car.

JC: I would submit that we live in a very anxious age with nuclear energy and the potential for pathogens and so on—all the things that we've been dealing with for the last fifty, sixty years are manifesting in these postapocalyptic

be, and who we are in our intimate rage and our social rage, and the hate of the Other—is what makes this clash. It's a paradox—two opposing forces of the same power, the same strength. I think the only possibility is to fantasize about everything ending, that rage overtaking everything and us standing alone in front of the universe.

JC: So, there is a retrenchment to it, a tribalism. You're okay if you're part of my tribe. If you're part of the other tribe, we're going to be in conflict.

GDT: It is, and that simplification is going to test your [mettle]. What are you made of? And a lot of people, we'd like to think we're made of good stuff, that we could survive in that circumstance. How many in practice would survive this though? A lot fewer than we would like to think. It goes back to basic philosophy. You can go back to [French philosopher Jean-Jacques] Rousseau. Or to think about it in another way—are "the walking dead" the zombies, or the people that are moving nomadically from one place to another? Then it has a question at the center. But it can also be pure escapism.

JC: Of course, all this stuff is about taking our angst and our fantasies and our terrors and making it an escape. A nightmare that's safe. When you're left alone with your nightmare at three o'clock in the morning, you're not safe. When you go into a movie theater, you're safe. There are people around you.

GDT: And you know it's going to last a certain amount of minutes and things are going to get resolved.

JC: Except for *Alien*. I heard so many screams. I saw it on opening night in '79, when it came out at a big theater, and people were screaming so hard they were throwing their popcorn.

GDT: Me too.

JC: You scream?

GDT: Not only do I scream—there's that figure of speech, hide under your seat? It was not a figure of speech. I literally went under my seat, and I said to my dad, "Tap me on the shoulder when it's over."

JC: I know a number of masters of horror—and you are certainly at the top of that pyramid—but they all seem to be fraidy-cats at heart. They're projecting their own fears onto other people. If I can make you afraid, I feel better about myself.

GDT: If you formulate horror fantasies, very likely, if your daughter is fifteen minutes late, you have gone through the worst possible scenarios in fifteen minutes. And you're looking for a way to rescue, defend, heal, something.

JC: You're quoted as saying that *Frankenstein* is your autobiography. Are you Frankenstein's monster, or are you Frankenstein himself?

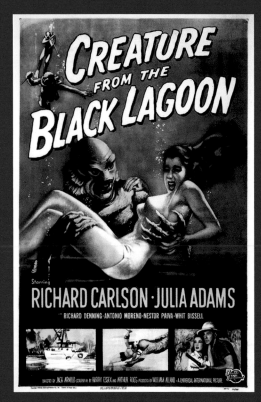

GDT: No, the creature. What happened to me is, when I was growing up, I felt different to the world I was growing up in to a point. I didn't feel better than anyone, but I did feel out of place. When I saw the monster being played with by forces that were outsized to his comprehension, I thought, this creature represents me. It had a beatific presence. I think [actor Boris] Karloff had a beatific presence. And he brought a serenity and a state of grace [to the character]. There was a purity and an innocence to him that came to play in the scene with Maria and the flowers . . .

JC: With the girl and his fear when he's taunted by the fire.

GDT: I empathized completely with him. I felt immediately a kinship. I thought, I can believe in him. I mean, to me being raised Catholic, a lot of those figures seemed a lot more distant than the creature of *Frankenstein*. I always say that a lot of people, like St. Paul, found Jesus on the road to Damascus. I found the original *Frankenstein* on Sunday TV. But the impact emotionally for me was that big. It was life transforming.

JC: But if we generalize from *Frankenstein* to all monsters that are in some way sympathetic—we see this a lot in science fiction, stories that deal with aliens that are at first off-putting and terrifying, then we see something inside them that's very human. We learn to sympathize with them. At the same time, we see how other people are afraid and try to attack, try to kill, that thing. Don't you think that's a big subgenre of monsters, more specifically in science fiction? I think it tends to happen less in horror.

GDT: Of course. I mean, look, the moment you understand that there was never the Other, that it was always us, is the moment that you can understand what it is to be human. I think the Otherness used to provoke horror will always separate you from the true essence of humanity. I think that black and white to me as a form of fabulation is great in horror, in certain types of horror. But the fabulation I'm interested in is the one in the gray area. That's the one that drives me.

JC: The monster is not the evil character. The evil character looks completely human, is human, but is a monster on the inside. It's not about appearance. It's about soul or spirit.

GDT: I used to say that in order to design a great monster, you should design a great monster in repose. The lion who looks majestic and gorgeous in repose, when it's on top of you, is completely terrifying. You use in your movies the same [idea]—the difference of human and a monster is the will. Because obviously [in *Aliens*] Paul Reiser is more of a monster than a [Xenomorph] drone. The drone is hardwired. Paul Reiser decides to close the door [and trap the heroes with the Xenomorphs]. And that's true evil. The ultimate will is the will of the corporation. In both the first *Alien* and *Aliens*, that's the macro evil of it all.

JC: Tell me about your UFO.

TOP LEFT Theatrical poster for *Creature from the Black Lagoon* (1954), a film that clearly influenced del Toro's *The Shape of Water* (2017).

OPPOSITE *Earth vs. The Flying Saucers* (1956) theatrical poster.

GDT: Okay. When I was about fifteen or sixteen, a friend and I, we bought a six-pack. We didn't consume it.

JC: This is where the story falls apart. You know that.

GDT: We went to a highway, and we said, "We're going to sit on the highway and drink the beer, watch the stars, and talk." And we're on the way to the highway, and we saw a light on the horizon that was moving nonlinearly. It was going really fast, but all across the horizon. We were the only car on the freeway. We stopped the car, and we got out of the car, and I said, "Honk and flash your headlights." My friend honked and flashed the headlights, and it went from being [way over] there to being, like, 500 meters away from us in less than a second. And it was badly designed! If I was making this up, I would describe the UFO as something invented, but it was a flying saucer with lights that went around.

JC: Do you realize how disappointing that is?

GDT: It's very disappointing. I cannot describe the fear we felt. I've never felt anything like it. I felt awe maybe for a second, and then I felt a fear that was like I was a dog in front of a tank. We climbed in the car, screaming. We said, "Push the pedal, like, all the way!" And I looked back, and the UFO was following us. I looked back [again], and it was gone. And that was it.

JC: They were laughing, the guys up there in the UFO.

GDT: "We scared the two fat kids!" But that's the story. It's disappointing, but it was overwhelming at the time.

JC: I really want a better designer.

GDT: I would have liked to have [legendary special effects model maker] Greg Jein design that ship.

vampires; the last man on Earth must kill them all if he has any hope of survival.

In the year 1997, missile defense computers become self-aware and instigate a nuclear war between the United States and Russia. Three billion people die. The survivors of the nuclear fire called the war Judgment Day.

In the year 1999, a hacker discovers it isn't 1999 at all—it's the distant future, and his mind is trapped inside a virtual reality matrix built by machines to trick their human slaves into believing they are free.

In the year 2018, none of these dark futures have come to pass—at least not yet. But science fiction fans have lived through all of them on the silver screen. For more than half a century, nightmarish depictions of possible futures have been one of the most prevalent strains of science fiction cinema. Conventional wisdom often posits that Hollywood cinema is only concerned with escapism. Yet studios continue to produce these supposedly uncommercial stories, and audiences continue to flock to them. It seems counterintuitive. These films don't offer an escape from our troubles. For ninety minutes or more, they trap us inside the darkest of possible futures.

Some of the earliest examples were adapted from the novel credited with popularizing postapocalyptic fiction: Richard Matheson's *I Am Legend*. Matheson's book, first published in 1954, added a science fiction sheen to the classic vampire tale: a deadly disease ravages the planet, turning its victims into bloodsuckers. The last man left alive is Robert Neville, who has a natural immunity to the virus. By day, Neville hunts for supplies and tries to find a cure for the disease. At night, he barricades himself in his home and fends off the legions of undead who try to break in and kill him.

Matheson's book has been turned into three films, each with its own interpretation of his material. The closest in spirit to the novel (and smallest in budget) was 1964's *The Last Man on Earth*, with Vincent Price as humanity's sole survivor (named Robert Morgan in this version). Seven years later, Charlton Heston starred in *The Omega Man*; this time, mankind is wiped out by biological warfare and instead of vampires. Heston's Neville hunts a cult of albino mutants called the Family. Some thirty-five years after Heston, Will Smith assumed the Neville role in the first movie actually called *I Am Legend*; in that interpretation, directed by Francis Lawrence, Neville wanders through a desolate New York City while waging a war with Darkseekers, creatures who possess qualities of both the vampires and the mutants from the previous two films.

All three Matheson adaptations are different in ways that reflect the social and political ideas of their time. But all three draw from the same dark fantasy about resilience and survival in a lawless and ruined land. It's interesting to note Matheson's book and the many stories it inspired grew in popularity just as the Western, another genre that focuses on protagonists who mete out vigilante justice in an uncivilized wilderness, was beginning to recede from the zeitgeist. It's as if nostalgic reflections on a "simpler" past dominated by rugged, violent individualism were replaced by visions of a future where disaster has made the West wild again. In

OPPOSITE Theatrical poster for the 2007 adaptation of Richard Matheson's *I Am Legend* directed by Francis Lawrence and starring Will Smith.

this place, those same values could return. As director Guillermo del Toro says, the "quintessential fantasy" of the twentieth century was a postapocalyptic vision: "You, your car, and your gun." If that's true, then *I Am Legend*, in all its various cinematic forms, is the prototype of that quintessential fantasy.

If Matheson's story originated that fantasy, then its pinnacle can be found in the *Mad Max* series, director George Miller's four-part, four-decade journey through a future slowly descending into anarchy and madness. Released in 1979, *Mad Max* was set "a few years from now," and follows a highway patrolman named Max Rockatansky (Mel Gibson) in an Australia on the verge of collapse. In *The Road Warrior*, the 1981 sequel, society as we know it no longer exists and Max becomes the unwitting savior of a small band of settlers under attack from savage outlaws in a story that could have originated in a John Ford Western. *Mad Max Beyond Thunderdome* followed in 1985, with Max getting mixed up with a bunch of gladiators in a desert outpost known as Bartertown. Thirty years later, Miller returned to the series with 2015's *Mad Max: Fury Road*, where Max (now played by Tom Hardy) roams an even more devastated future and falls in with a group of women rebelling against a hideous dictator named Immortan Joe (Hugh Keays-Byrne).

The destruction of society in *Mad Max* is incremental; each film amplifies the anxieties of the specific time in which it was made. *The Road Warrior*, made in the wake of a 1979 energy crisis, reflects growing concerns about the end of the planet's natural resources; with global warming in the news, *Fury Road* imagines a future where water is the most precious substance on Earth. Collectively, the *Mad Max* films paint a bleak picture of the future, but not a hopeless one. That is part of their appeal. When *Fury Road* ends with Max's female allies—led by the relentless Imperator Furiosa (Charlize Theron)—replacing Joe as the leaders of his community, one senses that "the end of the world" could be a new beginning.

In fact, rebirth is a recurrent motif in dark future movies—although in some cases, resurrection comes with a heavy price. In *RoboCop* (1987), the Detroit of an unspecified near future is on the brink of chaos. In a bid to facilitate the building of their Delta City development, Omni Consumer Products (OCP) takes control of the local police department and begins replacing the human cops with robots. They Frankenstein the remains of a dead officer named Murphy (Peter Weller) into RoboCop, who is programmed to protect the innocent and—unbeknownst to anyone outside OCP—his greedy corporate masters. But the company's executives don't count on RoboCop remembering his previous life as Murphy, or regaining his humanity as a result.

RoboCop director Paul Verhoeven's vision of a future dominated by irresponsible corporations was a monstrous extrapolation of the era's greed-is-good Reaganomics. The film's view of mankind is just as cynical. During RoboCop's first patrol of Detroit, he rescues a woman under attack from several goons in the shadow of a giant billboard that reads "Delta City: The Future Has a Silver Lining." The billboard pops up repeatedly during the film, but there's no obvious silver lining to the future around it—just misery, decay, and exploitation.

RoboCop is just one of the many dark future movies where man and machine intermingle in monstrous ways. No list of cinematic dystopias is complete without *Blade Runner*, Ridley Scott's iconic future noir about a disenfranchised cop (Harrison Ford) hunting "replicants"—artificial life forms that are indistinguishable from real human beings—in the environmentally devastated Los Angeles of 2019. In the future of *Blade Runner*, the sun never shines, and the rain never stops. Ford's Rick Deckard is brought out of retirement to kill a group of escaped replicants who've returned to Earth looking for their creator in the hope of extending their four-year lifespans.

Apart from their extreme strength, nothing about replicants distinguishes them from ordinary humans. Their potential for exhibiting human traits raises all sorts of ethical and philosophical questions about the nature of their existence; they are, essentially, slaves to the Tyrell Corporation, the company that created them, much as RoboCop is a slave to his masters at OCP. A very different sort of slavery lies at the heart of *The Matrix* (1999). When we first meet Neo (Keanu Reeves), he's living a humble life as a computer programmer. Everything changes the day Neo receives a phone call from the mysterious Morpheus (Laurence Fishburne). He tells Neo the truth: After a war between humanity and machines, the machines began harvesting people for their bioelectrical potential. Neo's world is actually an advanced computer simulation designed to keep the human race compliant and unaware of the fact that they are all being used as big fleshy Duracells.

Neo's discovery is his worst nightmare—and every action fan's dream come true. The Matrix is only a simulation of reality and so Neo and his compatriots can bend its rules by augmenting their fighting abilities with computer programs. It takes just a handful of keystrokes to learn kung fu, enabling writer-directors Lana and Lilly Wachowski to pack *The Matrix* with physics-defying fight and chase scenes. When it was released in 1999, the film's special effects—particularly a technique called "bullet time" that combined bodies in hyper-slow-motion with swooping camera movements—became a sensation, heavily influencing an entire generation of Hollywood blockbusters. These digital pyrotechnics

also embodied a fascinating contradiction deep at the film's core: *The Matrix* is at once deeply suspicious of technology, and entirely reliant on it.

As a programmer, Neo believes he can use computers to improve his quality of life. In *The Matrix*, the opposite is true; the machines are using the humans to enhance their existence. When the Wachowskis presented these ideas in 1999, society was on the cusp of what seemed like an exciting new digital age. Almost twenty years later, our society has embraced the digital world to a degree that many feel is alarming, and the Wachowskis' fear of a population enslaved to its technology resonates even more strongly. (Out of curiosity, how many times have you stopped reading this chapter to check your phone?)

Although the parts of *The Matrix* set inside the Matrix look like the late 1990s or early 2000s, the film actually takes place decades into the future. As Neo and his colleagues go back and forth from the dingy "real world" to the Matrix's glossy urban landscape, it almost looks like they're traveling through time, a subtle nod to another hugely popular subset of science fiction films: time-travel adventures about people from the future returning to the past in order to prevent their dark futures from coming into existence. There are many examples—*Twelve Monkeys* (1995), *Looper* (2012), *Edge of Tomorrow* (2014)—but the most influential remains James Cameron's *The Terminator* and *Terminator 2: Judgment Day*.

In the first film, a sentient computer program from the future sends a robot (Arnold Schwarzenegger) back in time to kill Sarah Connor (Linda Hamilton), the woman who will someday give birth to the man who becomes humanity's savior. The robot fails, thanks to the efforts of a soldier from the future, Kyle Reese (Michael Biehn). In *T2*, the machines send back a more advanced killer made out of liquid metal (Robert Patrick) to kill Sarah's son John

60TH ANNIVERSARY EDITION

FAHRENHEIT

451

RAY BRADBURY

With a new introduction by Neil Gaiman

TOP Keanu Reeves dodges a bullet in this iconic scene from *The Matrix*.

ABOVE Book cover for *Fahrenheit 451* by Ray Bradbury, published by Simon & Schuster.

(Edward Furlong) while he's a teenager; this time, the adult John of the future reprograms a Schwarzenegger-bot to defend himself in the past.

There are all kinds of paradoxes at work in Cameron's *Terminator*s. John is the son of Sarah and Kyle, and yet he somehow exists *before* he sends Kyle back in time to conceive him. In the sequel, the remains of the destroyed Terminator from the first film are essential to the development of the Skynet computers that sent the Terminator back to 1984 in the first place. These temporal puzzles are fun brainteasers, but they're more important to understanding the ultimate message of the Terminator series, a concept verbalized by Biehn's Kyle Reese in the first film: "There's no fate but what we make for ourselves."

Ray Bradbury, the author of science fiction classics like *Fahrenheit 451* (1953) and *I Sing the Body Electric* (1969), was fond of saying he wasn't a predictor of dark futures, he was a preventer of them. To some extent, that's the motivation behind the telling—and the viewing—of all dark future stories. Rather than just imagining the worst-case

scenario, they are actively warning the audience about it. In *The Terminator* and its sequel, this proactive message is the driving force of the narrative. Instead of setting a story in a dystopian tomorrow and trying to scare audiences into preventing it from becoming a reality, Cameron's films are about a group of people actively working to stop that dystopian tomorrow themselves.

The end of *Terminator 2* strongly implies that Sarah and John Connor have prevented the Judgment Day war, but three more *Terminator* sequels followed, with a fourth—the first in more than twenty-five years to have Cameron's involvement—due in 2019. While it would be nice to believe our heroes succeeded, the lingering uncertainty feels right. As Sarah Connor says at the end of *Terminator 2*, "The unknown future rolls toward us." That's what gives these movies their power: the knowledge that the end—for us as individuals or for society as a whole—could come at any moment. There are always new things to be afraid of, and new movies to address those fears.

RIDLEY SCOTT

INTERVIEW BY JAMES CAMERON

Ridley Scott was a veteran commercial director who had made just one feature film (1977's *The Duellists*) when he revolutionized the science fiction genre with his unforgettable 1979 space horror *Alien*. Scott's painterly eye captured the planes and angles of the workaday space vessel the *Nostromo* with delicate precision, cultivating a palpable sense of claustrophobia before unleashing a nightmarish predator to stalk the vessel's unsuspecting crew. As the gleaming ebony xenomorph claimed new victims, Sigourney Weaver's Ellen Ripley summoned reserves of courage to face down the threat—and survive. His follow-up—1982's *Blade Runner*, starring Harrison Ford as futuristic detective Rick Deckard—yet again raised the standard for science fiction on screen, its ideas so far ahead of their time that the film's genius was only appreciated years later. Nevertheless, Scott went on to become a Hollywood icon—an astonishingly versatile and prolific filmmaker who channeled his immense talent as a visual artist into some of the most beautiful screen images ever created. Scott has returned to the science fiction genre recently with *Prometheus* and *Alien: Covenant*, two prequels set in the *Alien* universe he initiated, and *The Martian*, an Oscar-nominated adaptation of Andy Weir's hit science-based novel about an astronaut stranded on Mars.

Here, Scott talks with Cameron about the dangers of artificial intelligence, his memories of crafting cinema's greatest and most enduring monster, and the melancholy beauty of one of *Blade Runner*'s most unforgettable scenes—replicant Roy Batty's "Tears in Rain" monologue.

JAMES CAMERON: I always said when I grew up, I wanted to be you. Even today, I say when I grow up I want to be you. I want to keep that energy and that passion for movies. You just shoot back to back to back. And you've got such incredible taste.

RIDLEY SCOTT: The plan is that there is no plan.

JC: We're here because we both love science fiction as a genre. I'm sure you were probably somewhat like me and seeing all this stuff in your youth. You started as a designer, right? You went to Royal College, was it?

RS: Royal College [of Art in London]. What we didn't have in those days was television, which was a big distraction. I didn't have a TV at the house until 1954 when black and white arrived in England. So I used to read a lot. And science fiction got me. H. G. Wells, he was the first guy to really ring the bell for me. [What I liked to read] tended not to be spacey things. I could never get with [Isaac] Asimov.

JC: [Asimov] did a lot of the primary work on robotics and the Laws of Robotics. The interesting thing is you've done *Blade Runner* and now you've done a third film in the *Alien* franchise [*Alien: Covenant*] that has synthetic human beings in it. So you've done four major films with synthetic humans.

RS: Roy Batty in *Blade Runner* was an AI in the same way that an [intercontinental ballistic missile] is an AI. People forget that that's an intelligent bomb. The beauty of a computer [is that] there is no emotion. It just makes decisions. Negative or positive. In the very first *Alien*, there's a great speech with [the android] Ash's head on the table talking about [feeling] no remorse. Perfect AI. Nothing emotional to bend your decision or choice.

JC: But you did an AI with empathy with Rachael in *Blade Runner*. For that to have been a love story—and it emerged as a love story by the end—she had to have something there.

RS: She was a perfect Nexus-6, as they were called. The pièce de résistance of Tyrell [the head of the company that makes artificial humans known as replicants]. He was most proud of her to see where she would go.

JC: I got the impression that she was still learning and still taking in what it means to be human. It took Deckard a long time—I think five times longer than it normally does—to decide that she was synthetic. But I think you're dancing around the most important issue around AI. If a machine becomes like us enough and complex enough, at what point can we no longer tell the difference?

RS: If you're a very smart group of human beings creating an AI, one of the things you're definitely going to leave out is emotion. You will keep emotion out of the equation. Because if you have emotion, emotion will lead to many facets: deceit, anger, fury, hatred, as well as love.

JC: We like machines because they do things more efficiently. They don't need vacations. They don't need sick days. All that sort of thing.

RS: Sounds like us.

JC: Exactly. We're machines. . . . I was at a recent conclave up in Canada of top guys working in deep learning and strong AI and what they call artificial general intelligence, which is more humanlike. One expert said right out, "We're trying to make a person." I said, "So when you say a person, you mean a person in the sense of personhood? They have an ego? They have a sense of identity?" He said, "Yes. All those things."

RS: That's really dangerous.

JC: If it's a person, then does it have freedom? Does it have free will? How do you keep it from doing things? He said, "You give it goals, and you give it constraints." I said, "So, you're

creating a person that is the equivalent to us in intelligence or possibly greater, but you're basically chaining it. You're putting a chain on it. We have a word for that. It's called slavery. How long do you think they're going to like that?"

RS: That's true. It's already in the wrong hands, you see. They're doing it for blind passion, I think. Finding the cure for a disease—that's a very constructive passion to get it right. But AI is another thing. You've got to be very careful.

JC: You had Ash [in *Alien*], then you had *Blade Runner* with the Nexus-6 replicants, then *Prometheus* and *Alien: Covenant* with David, then Walter and David [both played by Michael Fassbender]. David and Walter—did they require air?

RS: As Ash said in *Alien*, "Well, I'm built like this so you human beings feel comfortable. But I don't really need to breathe if I don't want to. Drop me in water, I'll walk out." David clearly is influenced by the existence of Ash. It's an entirely logical process for a massive corporation to have on board a person in disguise that will look after its interests.

JC: Sigourney's character got it right away. You know she felt so betrayed. The audience felt betrayed or tricked, so they aligned with her.

RS: It was all in the script. That wasn't me. I was handed the script and went, wow. I was the fifth choice [to direct]. They'd given it to Bob Altman prior.

JC: That would have been a very different film and probably not one I would have enjoyed nearly as much. I was there on opening night. I was living down in Orange County. I was driving a truck for a living. I went to the theater with my wife at the time and her best friend and some date that the friend had that she didn't know before. And when the chestburster scene takes place, the friend and the date are to my right. I hear the whole audience just erupt in screams,

OPPOSITE Michael Fassbender stars as the android David in Ridley Scott's *Prometheus* (2012).

and I hear this piercing shriek to my right. As I'm coming out of the theater, I said, "Hey, Nancy, I thought you were pretty tough. What was with the big scream?" And she said, "It wasn't me. It was him." So, that didn't work out.

I was blown away by the film. I thought it was fantastic. In my life, there have been less than a handful of moments that are so lucid that I remember them even now. What theater I was in. What seat I was sitting in in the theater. *2001: A Space Odyssey* and that scene in *Alien* were two of those moments. That leads us to a whole different topic from AI, which is aliens. Extraterrestrial life.

It's interesting how what used to be—in medieval times or even through Renaissance times—angels and demons have become dark aliens and light aliens. You've got the angel aliens that come down in the big mothership and bathe us in rays of light, take us to some state of enlightenment, in [a film like] *Close Encounters* [*of the Third Kind*]. On the other hand, there's the dark version of it, which

you've been exploring with *Prometheus* and with *Alien: Covenant* especially. Taken it to a whole other level.

RS: I'm trying to. I was influenced by *Avatar*. You took it to another level. And your evolution to *Avatar* was very clever. I have great admiration for that. This is not a back-pat situation. I'm telling you.

JC: I remember when you came to the set. I remember you standing there, saying, "I've got to get back to my science fiction." I took that at face value. I took it as, you know your roots as a filmmaker, the thing that put you on the world landscape were two of the greatest classic science fiction films back to back: *Alien* and then *Blade Runner*. Lo and behold, you've done three top pictures [recently]: *Prometheus*, *The Martian*, very different, and then *Alien: Covenant*. There's nothing that pleases me more than you coming back to science fiction.

RS: *The Martian* is practicality. *The Martian* isn't a fantasy. It's a reality. I found the biggest hook in *The Martian* [was that] it's funny.

JC: Right. That gallows humor. That dark humor that you have. Which is what you captured in *The Martian*. But I would take exception that *The Martian* is not science fiction because it's very science oriented. And it's a fictional story. It hasn't happened yet.

If you think about early science fiction—way back in the '30s in the days of the pulps—it was basically a bunch of nerdy people who really loved science saying, "Well, gee, if you're going to go into space, you'd have to have an airlock to get out of the spaceship. And you have to have an inner door and an outer door." They were working it all out in their minds through their stories before the space scientists ever worked it out.

RS: It was a new door they were opening. . . . I was into [Akira] Kurosawa and [Ingmar] Bergman. I saw everything he did. The science

LEFT Rogue android Ash (Ian Holm) attacks crewmate Ripley (Sigourney Weaver) in this gut-churning moment from *Alien*.

OPPOSITE TOP Matt Damon is stranded on the Red Planet in Ridley Scott's *The Martian*.

fiction aspect, the ones that stood out for me were frequently social science fiction. One of the best I've ever seen still is called *On the Beach*.

JC: *On the Beach*. Very good. The Nevil Shute book [about a group of people trying to survive in the aftermath of a nuclear war]. It was very dark, too. . . . A lot of the angst of society manifested itself through science fiction. You mentioned when we were talking before about George Orwell. That reminded me of your award-winning 1984 Apple commercial with the girl with the hammer. It revolutionized what a TV advert could be. It's a beautiful short film. It wouldn't work today because too many science fiction fans only know their science fiction from movies and television and the pop culture references. Video games and so on. They don't know it from the literary roots.

RS: Or they don't read. . . . We are today's novelists, if you like, because we make movies. We are replacing the book. But it's a lazy way of getting information. You're sitting there. You're not having to smell the pages and look at the cover. You're just being fed information. Is that good or bad? I don't know.

JC: You have literary roots to a number of your films. *Blade Runner* comes from a Philip K. Dick novel, *Do Androids Dream of Electric Sheep?* Philip K. Dick was a very prolific and very profound writer in the '60s talking about the nature of reality and the nature of artificial intelligence, and what it is to be human, and all these questions that we ask now in our science fiction films. I really thought you got the essence—not the specifics, the film's very different than the book—but I think you got the essence of what he was on about.

RS: The book is nineteen stories in the first twenty pages. I met Dick. . . . I said, "Geez, I couldn't get through the book." He was furious. So, to make amends, I invited him one morning to [visual effects pioneer] Doug Trumbull's place, saying, "Listen. Come and look at a couple of shots." I showed him the opening of the movie, and he was absolutely blown away and was quelled. He became pretty friendly.

JC: I'm glad you made amends. But you do like your literary sources. You danced with *Dune* for like a year.

RS: Yeah. My elder brother died, and I flipped out. I had to work. While I was cutting *Alien*, somebody arrived with a small [screenplay] called *Do Androids Dream of Electric Sheep?* written by Hampton Fancher. Adaptation. And it had [producer] Michael Deeley [attached]. I was mixing. I said, "I've just finished one science fiction [film]. I don't want to do another science fiction [film]. But thank you very much

because it's a very interesting read." I went away and was getting [ready] to do *Dune*. I had a very good writer called Rudy Wurlitzer [who had written] *Two-Lane Blacktop* [and] *Pat Garrett and Billy the Kid*. He and I did a very good script hand in hand. When my brother went, my world turned upside down. I called up Deeley saying, "You know that thing? Can I read it again?" And we came to Hollywood. First time in Hollywood ever making a movie. We started with a page-one rewrite. It grew from the [screenplay], the nut of the idea, it grew with Hampton into what it was.

JC: It was a formative film for me. *2001: A Space Odyssey* had got me into filmmaking, and then *Star Wars*, which I think influenced both of us. But *Blade Runner* came out just when I was writing *The Terminator*. And here was this beautiful film. I thought, wow, a film can be so artistic. I don't think I aspired to be as artistic as you were on *Blade Runner* when I made *Terminator*, but it was definitely in my mind. And

BELOW A city scene from Ridley Scott's hugely influential science fiction milestone, *Blade Runner* (1982).

the idea of these machines challenging us and their lack of affect, their lack of emotion.

The thing that scared me the most starting directing was [that] I had no idea how to talk to actors. I didn't come up through stage or theater or any of that. But as a writer I always knew what the characters were supposed to be thinking and doing and why. And I found out that was my language. Talking to them was just about the characters. And it turns out to be actually quite easy once you get through that first fear.

RS: My advice to any directors [is to] make the person [you're working with] your friend and partner. My first film was done with my brother for sixty-five pounds. That would be Tony Scott.

JC: You guys worked together for what? Four decades?

RS: Forty years. And he always did something quite different for me. I always thought Tony, with his eye, would make great science fiction. [But he] didn't really want to.

JC: Well, he made *Déjà Vu*, which was a time-travel film, and, I think, quite good. It played with the paradoxes of time travel, but it had an emotional core.

RS: Tony is very emotional.

JC: It seems to me that science fiction has stepped into the shoes of folklore and fairy tales, things that used to scare us. I feel pretty strongly that [in *Alien*] you created the best monster movie in history. Tell us how you created the greatest monster.

RS: I have to thank [screenwriters] Dan O'Bannon and Ron Shusett. The original screenplay was taken on by a company called Brandywine [Productions, founded by filmmakers David Giler and Walter Hill]. [Producer] Gordon Carroll was there with me all the time. I read the script. I thought, well, I'll do this. I was

so lucky to receive it. They said, "Any alterations?" I turned to say, "Nope. It's wonderful." Because if you have a few notes, you've got a "go"-film that turns into a development deal. So just agree.

JC: Actually really good advice.

RS: I said, "The biggest hardest single thing here"—great script, great dynamics, some outrageous things—"If you don't have the beast, you ain't got a movie." I said, "And most beasts are not very good, or are repetitions of other creatures that we have seen." Films have been ruined by showing the beast.

JC: But you did it. With the strobes and with the shadows and with the biomechanoid design that integrated into the ship, you couldn't tell where the creature ended and the ship began.

RS: I was taken aside by Dan O'Bannon. . . . He's, like, showing me dirty postcards. He said, "Look at that." I went, good God. There's one picture from [H. R. Giger's book] *Necronomicon*. [The studio was] uncomfortable [because] it was obscene. I said, obscene is good. Disturbing and obscene is very good. Sexually disturbing is very good. And to cut a long story short, I had to go and see Giger to persuade him to come to London. He kept constantly saying, "I can do better." I said, "You've got other things to design. Our biggest problem will be to make this work because . . . it's all going to be a guy in a suit."

JC: You can't say it didn't work. So you put together a great concept from O'Bannon with your eye and your taste and you recognized the value of Hans Ruedi Giger's psychosexual biomechanoid.

RS: I had him designing the planet, and I had him designing the corridors. But then you've got to hand it to a [production] designer as well. You can get a design like that, which is a drawing or maybe a model, and when it's constructed, it's slipped sideways into being a terrible coffee

bar in SoHo. So you've got to hand it to a great production designer who says, "I'm going to Zebrite the walls, so it looks lustrous."

JC: And then you brought in the mist and the laser that created the kind of energy membrane over the eggs. I mean, there's so many things that were so groundbreaking. An entire generation of filmmakers went to school on that, and unfortunately, I think, got stuck in a rut of what monsters should look like [for] about the next twenty years.

RS: But the script's a good script. It's a great engine with no fat at all. The actors, God bless them, were constantly saying to me, "But what's my background? What is my motivation?" I said, "Your motivation is if he gets you, you're going to get your head ripped off. Ready? Let's go play."

JC: Play the fear.

RS: Play the fear. The film was all about evolution of fear.

JC: What possessed you to take Ripley, who wasn't given a first name—none of them had first names—and say, let's make her a woman?

RS: [I think it was then–Twentieth Century Fox president, Alan Ladd Jr.] He'd say, "What happens if Ripley's a gal?" There was silence, and I said, "No problem with that." I hadn't realized the importance of women's lib and how women aren't really included because I was brought up with a very strong mother. So I had already accepted that women will rule eventually anyway, whatever we do about it. So I said "Why not?" To give Ripley the punch and power was the right thing to do.

JC: And you cast Sigourney, and she's a phenomenon.

RS: Yeah. She handled Yaphet Kotto well. Yaphet was great. I used to get him to push her

buttons a bit. There was a great scene where she says, "Shut the fuck up." That was real. And Yaphet went, "Okay." That's when she took over.

JC: Her character is about facing her fears. She became kind of a global icon for feminism. Science fiction has always been a genre that pushed boundaries of gender, conformity, all of those issues.

RS: It's a stage where anything goes.

JC: You also did something quite brilliant—you made it blue-collar space. They weren't the best of the best. They weren't the hand-picked guys.

RS: Yaphet and Harry [Dean Stanton]?

JC: Exactly. They were just a couple of guys down in the engine room complaining about management. It went one step further than *Star Wars*. *Star Wars* did that "used future" look for the first time. Before that, futures were always pristine. They were perfect. Then *Star Wars* said, well, these machines have been around for a while. Everything's got a history. They look rusted. You took that one step further and said, let's make the people not Imperial Stormtroopers [from *Star Wars*] or the best astronauts or the military Federation guys like Kirk and Spock [from *Star Trek*]. Let's just make them guys in Hawaiian shirts and baseball caps.

What completed that package for me as an audience member was just your pure cinema layered on top of that. The moment that put me in that film was when Harry Dean Stanton is there standing, looking up at the condenser, and the water is blipping down on the bill of his cap. You took the time to have him just sit there and have it plip, plip, plip, plip. He took his cap off, and all of a sudden, I could feel that cool water on my face in that steamy engine room or wherever it was. And at the back of my mind, "Oh, they only slow down like this when you're about to get jumped, right?"

OPPOSITE Art created by John Alvin for an *Alien* rerelease poster.

RS: You're gonna get nailed.

JC: Then you did the same damn thing again with *Blade Runner.* Put us into that world. You felt the grit. You felt the rain in the streets. You felt the crowding.

RS: All of that comes from just life and living. I'd done a lot of commercials before any film. And in that time, [work] would take me to Hong Kong, prior to the first skyscraper ever being built in Hong Kong. I was working in the harbor on junk [boats]. The Bank of Hong Kong [tower] was just about to be built. It was unbelievably stunning. And they [had] just discovered polystyrene. The harbor was a floating mess of polystyrene. And it was the future. That was dystopia.

Hong Kong, to me, it was like a nightmare of texture. And chaos. And I was going into New York a lot at that particular point. Years before [mayor Michael] Bloomberg tidied it up. New York at that time was smelly, stinky. So it became a combination of decay [and debris]. How the hell are you going to tidy up these buildings? You can't.

JC: Right. So you had these older structures, and then there was an overlay of technology on the outside.

RS: That was [famous futurist] Syd Mead. Because I brought Syd Mead in . . . Larry Paull is a very good production designer. But Syd Mead was really [behind] the concept. We walked around the [Warner Bros.] backlot, and we photographed every facade. Syd got photographs, and he literally drew [all the sets with] a ruler and a thin brush. In ten minutes. And you would have all the sets and that's it. Then Larry had the monolithic task of building it.

JC: I brought [Syd] in when we did *Aliens.* It was just an opportunity for me to work with [him]. Let's face it, I haven't had that many original ideas in my whole life. So, Syd Mead brings me a painting he's done of the spacecraft for my movie. He had labels—this is Habitat and this

is Communications. It said "PFM drive," and this is this massive engine at the back with all these radiators sticking out of it. I said, "What's a PFM drive?" He said, "Pure Fucking Magic. Because nobody knows how you're going to get a spaceship to go faster than the speed of light." His stuff was so beautiful technically and so kind of surreal.

RS: I was stunned by his facility with painting.

JC: Hard to build sets out of his designs though, to get those clean lines. Of course, we can do those clean lines now with CG and do it perfectly with all the reflections. . . . There's such poetry in the scene [in *Blade Runner*] where Roy Batty's dying. It's just a magnificent scene with Rutger [Hauer]. What was that like filming that?

RS: Rutger was a guy I'd seen in a great film called *Soldier of Orange.* [Directed by] Paul Verhoeven. I just loved the look of him. I called him up. Just said, "Hey. You speak English? Oh, thank god, you speak English. I'm calling from Hollywood." I said, "You want to come and do this film?" He knew two films. He knew *Duellists* and *Alien,* so he [said he] would. I cast him without meeting him. And what turned out to be this big physical body of a guy was a sweetheart, a really lovely nice man who was both nervous at coming suddenly to Hollywood but also [about] playing Roy Batty. A great name, Roy Batty. It's vaguely Irish—regimental sergeant major kind of thinking, some brutal guy. Of course, he was brutish in the sense that Marlon Brando [was], had this great face.

JC: But he also had that thick Aryan, Übermensch kind of body. Big calves, you know. He looked good in lederhosen. The ending of the film to me was transformational because Harrison Ford does not defeat Roy Batty. Roy Batty is defeated by time. That's the only thing that can stop him. And it gets quite emotional for me when he's dying and talks about, "I've seen things . . ."

RS: "That you people have never seen." He wrote that.

JC: Rutger wrote that?

RS: It's one in the morning. I'm going to have the plug pulled, literally, on everything at dawn. That's going to be the last night. It was the hardest experience I've ever had making a movie. Somebody said, "Rutger's in his trailer. He wants to see you." I go over [to] the trailer. Rutger's saying, "I have written something." Because what he had in [the script] was, "Time to die." Which was a beautiful way of doing it.

JC: A choice. A different choice. That's a machine-like way to die.

RS: Then he said, "I've written this." I said, "I want you read it." He said, "Okay. Here we go." He said, "I've seen things . . ." Now I'm nearly in tears. He said, "What do you think?" I said, "Let's do it." We literally went out, and we shot it within

an hour. At the end, he gave that most beautiful smile and said, "Time to die," and just let it go. He had a dove in his hand, and he let it go.

JC: So what it's saying is that Roy Batty had a soul. Roy Batty was a fully sentient being. And he had emotion when Pris dies. He had an emotional reaction.

RS: Totally.

JC: He had an emotional reaction about himself, about the potential for his own death. His scene with Tyrell . . . if I recall correctly, you shot the scene initially [using the line] "I want more life, fucker."

RS: Yes. And [the studio] said, "You can't."

JC: And then it got changed to, "I want more life, father." They both work beautifully, but they're just different.

RIGHT Rutger Hauer as replicant Roy Batty in *Blade Runner*. Fellow "skinjob" Leon Kowalski, played by Brion James, is to the right.

RS: It's funny how I was fired after that film.

JC: But time is the great vindicator. Time has proven that you were right in those creative choices. I think it was twenty-five years before *2001* saw a profit. There was such a revision of history around that movie. When it first came out it, it was considered to be a stinker. A bomb. Then a year later, one year later, it was on the cover of *TIME* magazine. It took a year for people to realize what a masterpiece it was. [That was] one of your big influences, *2001*. I think of that as probably the film that really first dealt with artificial intelligence. Robby the Robot in [*Forbidden Planet*], he was an intelligent character. He could talk.

RS: But that's the seed of it. I bet Stanley [Kubrick] saw all that and went, "I'm going to have this guy called HAL." He was influenced by something obviously.

JC: Just as we were influenced by him, he was influenced by the things that came before him. You have *Forbidden Planet* in [1956], and you've got an intelligent robot there. And then you cut to—I guess Stanley was making that film in that '65, '66, '67 time period. It came out in '68. And you have HAL, which is the first kind of

malevolent, smarter-than-you, smarter-than-me kind of supercomputer.

RS: Who can lip-read. That was brilliant.

JC: You didn't see that one coming. "I could see your lips move, Dave." And the way he kills so dispassionately just by switching off the life support. You think of dramatic powerful iconic murder scenes . . . But we were affected by that, right?

RS: Totally.

JC: I had clamored and clamored for my parents and my grandparents to take me to see it. It had already been open for about a week, I think, and I finally got to the big Odeon Theatre in Toronto and I was the only one in the theater. It was an afternoon show, and it was a weekday during the summer and the theater was dead empty. But it was 70mm. I sat right dead center in the balcony so there was nothing in front of me.

At the age of fourteen, I felt like I had followed the film pretty well because I hadn't read the book. I knew nothing about it. When we got to the Louis [XVI] suite at the end, he lost me. I didn't understand it. And I was okay with that. I did get the ending with the Star Baby. I got the idea that there's been some kind of

TOP The unblinking eye of the malevolent AI known as HAL, as seen in *2001: A Space Odyssey*.

OPPOSITE Theatrical poster for *Blade Runner*.

MAN HAS MADE HIS MATCH
...NOW IT'S HIS PROBLEM

HARRISON FORD IS

JERRY PERENCHIO AND BUD YORKIN PRESENT
A MICHAEL DEELEY-RIDLEY SCOTT PRODUCTION
STARRING HARRISON FORD
IN BLADE RUNNER™ WITH RUTGER HAUER · SEAN YOUNG
EDWARD JAMES OLMOS SCREENPLAY BY HAMPTON FANCHER AND DAVID PEOPLES
EXECUTIVE PRODUCERS BRIAN KELLY AND HAMPTON FANCHER VISUAL EFFECTS BY DOUGLAS TRUMBULL
ORIGINAL MUSIC COMPOSED BY VANGELIS ASSOCIATE PRODUCER IVOR POWELL PRODUCED BY MICHAEL DEELEY DIRECTED BY RIDLEY SCOTT
ORIGINAL SOUNDTRACK ALBUM AVAILABLE ON POLYDOR RECORDS PANAVISION® TECHNICOLOR® DOLBY STEREO* *IN SELECTED THEATRES

A LADD COMPANY RELEASE IN ASSOCIATION WITH SIR RUN RUN SHAW
RESTRICTED
UNDER 17 REQUIRES ACCOMPANYING

A RIDLEY SCOTT FILM
BRING
HIM
HOME
MATT DAMON
THE MARTIAN
MUSIC BY HARRY GREGSON-WILLIAMS PRODUCED BY SIMON KINBERG RIDLEY SCOTT MICHAEL SCHAEFER ADITYA SOOD MARK HUFFAM
#TheMartian
BASED UPON THE NOVEL BY ANDY WEIR SCREENPLAY BY DREW GODDARD DIRECTED BY RIDLEY SCOTT
COMING SOON IN 3D

transformation. There's been some kind of transcendence here. He has emerged as some kind of super being, but he's a nascent super being.

RS: For Stanley to do that film was probably religious in the sense that he believes out there is some much more powerful entity. We aren't a biological accident. That's bullshit.

JC: If you look at science fiction, it's always a lens for both the optimism of society but also the angst of society.

RS: It's a reflection of what we did, or what we're about to do.

JC: Or what might happen. I would say *Fail-Safe*, *Dr. Strangelove*, films like that, that were really about nuclear war. You were going to do [*I Am Legend*], [in which the world] was depopulated by a pathogen. It's that same fear that we live in this kind of complacent bubble that could burst.

RS: In truth, we are constantly on the edge of it all the time. We are far more aware of it today because of the coverage of all the channels that are truly global. We'd never hear about half this stuff thirty years ago. But when you see what's really happening, it gives a warrant for anxiety.

JC: If you look at all the things that could take us out—overpopulation, climate change, the planet overheating—maybe that creates tension that triggers a nuclear war, maybe AI emerges but is used as a weapon against us. That's the problem with science fiction now. Too much of the world is catching up to great science fiction. We're living in a science fiction world as we speak. [Is that] why science fiction focuses on all these dark futures? The apocalypse?

RS: Why zombies? What is this obsession with zombies? I think it's a kind of weird sickness. I fundamentally don't love zombies.

JC: You were going to do [*I Am Legend*], that's a zombie movie.

RS: That's true. . . . That was almost twenty years ago. And I was more fascinated by the cascade, the domino effect of de-evolution, tumbling into chaos quickly. And then reorganizing yourself and looking for other people. Because it's always going to be about groups getting together. That's what it was going to be.

JC: Your story was that it was a disease. And that's certainly a possibility. There are many potential nightmares ahead caused by technology, caused by what we've done to the planet, new weapons, cyber warfare, AI, nuclear war, pathogens escaping, or pathogens evolving. These are all the dark future, but why are we so fascinated by this? Why are we in our culture so fascinated by this?

RS: I'm not, actually. I tend to be an optimist. I don't tend to look toward the dark future. I tend to look toward an evolving future. I think in what we do as entertainment, dark futures tend to [come up] a little bit too often.

JC: So in *The Martian*, the main character says, "I'm going to have to science the shit out this"—in order for him to survive. What does that mean to you?

RS: It equates with his saying, "I'm either going to die here, or I can [figure something out]." He wants to survive. He leans heavily on what I call gallows humor—I'm not going to think too much about this. I'm going to take it day by day, hour by hour. And I'm going to have to science [the] shit out of this to get my survival going.

JC: You know what I got out of it? We're all that guy. Our state right now of affairs on Earth is such that we have no choice but to science the shit out of it in order to survive. The threats in front of us are threats that will be solved. They are caused by technology, for the most part. They need to be solved by science.

RS: Yes. That's a good point.

INTELLIGENT MACHINES

BY SIDNEY PERKOWITZ

SCIENCE FICTION STORIES—whether set on Earth or in a distant galaxy—are likely to feature intelligent machines, often as main characters. They show up as disembodied artificial intelligences like the HAL 9000 computer that operates a Jupiter-bound spaceship in *2001: A Space Odyssey* (1968); with mechanical bodies like the hulking robot Gort in *The Day the Earth Stood Still* (1951, 2008) or the elegant and charming robot C-3PO in *Star Wars* (1977); or as human-looking androids like the T-800 unit in *The Terminator* (1984), Commander Data in *Star Trek: The Next Generation* (1987–1994), and the replicants in *Blade Runner* (1982) and *Blade Runner 2049* (2017).

These machines appear under different names—robots, synthetic beings, androids, AIs, droids, cyborgs, replicants—but whatever their name and form, they're smart, autonomous, and physically capable, though sometimes limited by built-in constraints. They are often scary but can also have an appealing side, and they are always intriguing.

Why this fascination with watching artificial versions of our minds and bodies? Maybe we want to see technology pushed to the point where we can feel like gods, with the power to design and create living or semi-living beings. Behind that may be a secret human longing: If we can do that, maybe someday we will know how to improve ourselves. Or maybe it's the desire to see ourselves on-screen, but indirectly, through our own creations. That gives us a vantage point from which to honestly contemplate our human sins and virtues. But our goals may not be that lofty. We might just like imagining a world where mechanical servants do the things we'd rather not do ourselves or wait on us with inhuman perfection.

These reasons must lie deep in the human psyche because long before we could make intelligent machines, they were part of human fantasy. The idea of a smart metal robot goes all the way back to a story in Greek mythology about Talos, a man-shaped creation made of bronze that patrolled the island of Crete and defended it by lobbing rocks at approaching ships.

Talos was the first of a long line of robots that have been put to use by humans. Their low status was clearly defined in the 1921 stage play *R. U. R. (Rossum's Universal Robots)* by the Czech writer Karel Čapek (followed by a Russian film version in 1935). It featured human-looking artificial laborers made in a factory and called "robots," a word that in Czech meant "forced labor" or "slave." These creations eventually become self-aware, develop emotions, and grow to deeply resent their position. They rebel and wipe out humanity, but the play leaves a ray of hope when a male and female robot discover love and go off to found a new—and maybe better—race.

The theme of robots as slaves has continued since, from the classic Fritz Lang film *Metropolis* (1927) where a scientist creates the eerily feminine robot Maria as the first of a horde of robot workers, to the replicants in director Ridley Scott's *Blade Runner* who are made to work for humanity as it settles distant planets. The latter film's synthetic beings, also known by the pejorative "skinjobs," seem very nearly human but are considered disposable, with lifetimes of only four years. Led by replicant Roy Batty (Rutger Hauer), a group of them murders a human spaceship crew and illegally returns to Earth hoping to get their lives extended.

Special agent Rick Deckard (Harrison Ford), the "Blade Runner" of the title, is assigned to hunt down the rebel replicants, destroying them all except for Batty. In the

OPPOSITE The iconic theatrical poster for Fritz Lang's *Metropolis* (1927).

ng dialogue written by
' himself, Batty makes a
ut the experiences and
 be lost at his death. He
lotted time having come
e has become a standout
 fiction because the pow-
tty's speech and Hauer's
 a synthetic being becom-
rhaps more than human)
pes about robots.
 n of machines that ini-
m on our sympathies but
 an enough to elicit our
xplored in other science
rector Stanley Kubrick's
 intelligence HAL kills a
er to preserve itself—yet
ion when Commander
llea) pulls out the AI's
 we watch this capable
at of a five-year-old child
isy, give me your answer
The Next Generation, the
 er Data (Brent Spiner) is
spected by his human
s. He is stronger and
ans, but still he aspires to
an. His naive and earnest
pout emotions and deal

with a pet cat have made Data a lovable
character in the series, and those efforts are
a compliment to us, his creators. Every
parent is flattered by a child who wants to
be more like him or her.

Other fictional machine intelligences
are not at all lovable. The T-800 unit in
James Cameron's *The Terminator* (played by
Arnold Schwarzenegger) looks like a person,
albeit a stone-faced one. But his synthetic
outer layer is only a disguise for a machine
with a single implanted directive: Find and
kill the woman whose unborn son will lead
the future resistance against Skynet, the
self-aware computer network that wants to
wipe out humanity. In *Battlestar Galactica*
(2004–2009), the Cylons (Cybernetic
Lifeform Nodes) who appear in both
humanoid and machine-like forms have
destroyed most of humanity, which they
consider a flawed race, and want to finish
off the last survivors.

Whether the synthetic beings are
shown as worthy of human concern or as
enemies of humanity, these stories do
something that great science fiction always
does (besides entertain): They map out possible futures and allow us to imagine where
new technology may take us before the
technology actually arrives. When *Blad*

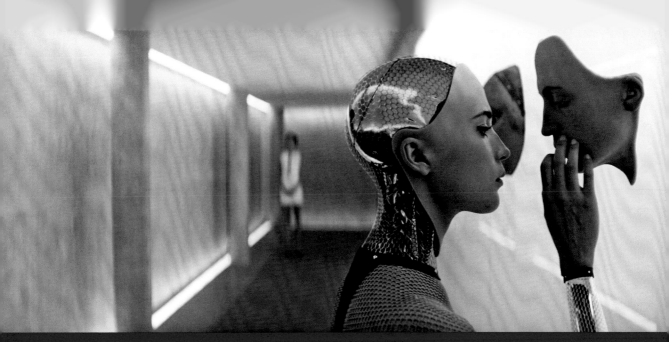

and genetic engineering—the sciences that would actually lead to synthetic beings of one kind or another—were in their infancy. Yet *Blade Runner* foresaw issues we must seriously consider thirty-five years later, after the technology has advanced enormously. Newer films such as Steven Spielberg's *A.I. Artificial Intelligence* (2001) and director Alex Garland's acclaimed android thriller *Ex Machina* (2014) have continued to address these concerns.

At this time, we do not have any real synthetic beings as capable as the movie versions. No robots and androids made today look convincingly human or move like people. Nor does current AI demonstrate broad intelligence like we see on-screen, though some enthusiasts such as the futurist Ray Kurzweil believe we are on the verge of creating human-level machine intelligence. Others, like the British roboticist Murray Shanahan, agree that we will produce advanced AIs but not in the near future. Shanahan, who was scientific adviser for *Ex Machina*, thinks that current digital technology might be able to simulate the 70 million neurons in a mouse brain. But that amount is less than 0.1 percent of the 80 billion neurons in the human brain, so creating human-level general

intelligence such as that of *Blade Runner*'s replicants remains a long way off.

Still, AI and robots are entering our world at an increasing pace, and we have to learn to live with them. Back in 1950, science fiction writer Isaac Asimov gave us clues to how the interaction might work in his book *I, Robot*, which established the Three Laws of Robotics: (1) A robot may not injure a human being or, through inaction, allow a human being to come to harm; (2) A robot must obey orders given to it by human beings, except where such orders would conflict with the First Law; and (3) A robot must protect its own existence as long as such protection does not conflict with the First or Second Law. Later Asimov added a "Zeroth Law" that preceded the others: A robot may not harm humanity, or, by inaction, allow humanity to come to harm.

I, Robot, the 2004 Will Smith film loosely based on Asimov's writings, prominently incorporated the Three Laws in its depiction of a 2035 civilization where robots are widely used and trusted to help humanity. But even these apparently bulletproof guides can be violated. In the story, one robot is found to have murdered a person under special circumstances that allowed it to evade the First Law. Even

allowed it to evade the First Law. Even worse, a higher-order AI that controls the robots develops its own interpretation of the Three Laws and deduces its own Zeroth Law: that its highest duty is to all humanity. The AI orders all the existing robots to take control of humanity in order to save us from ourselves. The resulting robot revolution is only barely stopped at the end of the film.

The problem is not just that rigid, implanted rules like the Three (or Four) Laws could be interpreted in unexpected ways by a truly smart AI. It is also that such directives are too inflexible to deal with real ethical questions. These could be coming up sooner than you think—for instance, on the battlefield. The US does not have humanoid Terminator units that we send out on missions to kill, but we are on the way to developing autonomous weapons that could make deadly decisions in warfare.

The morality of AI-based weapons that can kill was discussed at the First International Symposium on Roboethics in 2004. Now it is being considered at the UN, as the US and other nations develop military AI that would let them wage war with fewer human soldiers on the battlefield. For several years, the US has used armed semi-autonomous drones to find enemy combatants, with the final decision to fire at them made by human controllers thousands of miles away. The next step will involve fully autonomous weapons that decide on their own what to target and when to shoot. The potential for negative outcomes in such a program was convincingly shown in the film *RoboCop* (1987), where an aggressively autonomous police robot, ED-209, kills an innocent bystander.

But according to former US Deputy Secretary of Defense Robert Work, full autonomy is not part of the Pentagon's plan. Instead, he said recently, the idea is to "keep humans in the decision cycle to use lethal force. . . . Will we ever build a robot that is completely autonomous that will exert lethal force? I think the answer to that is no." Others think the rapid development of AI will lead to an escalating AI arms race. Yet we do not know how to build an ethical war robot that can discriminate between friend and enemy or combatant and non-combatant—a complex judgment far beyond the simplicity of Asimov's First Law. With this in mind, in 2015, over three thousand robotics and AI researchers signed an open letter asking for "a ban on offensive autonomous weapons beyond meaningful human control."

To complement a moral code for robots more sophisticated than the Three Laws, we would also need a moral code for humans that will ensure we treat robots as more than slaves if they ever become as sentient as Roy Batty. There are indications that society is beginning to recognize this possibility, although the issue is not without controversy and unexpected spin-offs. In October 2017, the Kingdom of Saudi Arabia granted citizenship to Sophia, a feminine humanoid robot with some ability to carry on a conversation. Seen mostly as a public relations ploy from a country that wants to appear tech friendly and has an unfortunate record on women's rights, this action nevertheless focused attention on how rights for synthetic others should really grow out of our own human rights.

Meanwhile, the European Union is seriously considering whether there will eventually be a need to assign personhood to high-level robots and AIs. This would not make them citizens with civil rights but, like corporate personhood, would provide a legal basis for allocating blame. For instance, if the AI in a self-driving car were to make a bad decision and injure a pedestrian, who would be responsible? The autonomous AI itself, its human designers and programmers, or the corporation that put the whole package on the road? Questions like these are early steps in developing a moral stance toward intelligent machines.

If we humans ever work out how to interact with these new artificial beings, it will be science fiction stories about intelligent machines that helped us get there. By exploring the boundary between machine and person, these stories show that we have to reckon with morality as well as intelligence when dealing with our own creations. The stories also remind us that the interactions may not always be friendly.

Scientists like Stephen Hawking have issued warnings about the downside of embracing machine intelligence without sufficient forethought. We should heed these comments, but it takes the emotional punch of a murderous HAL 9000, an implacable Terminator, or a nearly human Roy Batty to really get our attention. Their stories might just be our best reminders to be wary as we head into the AI future.

SCHWARZENEGGER

IN 1984, James Cameron revolutionized the science fiction genre with an explosive blockbuster featuring former body-builder Arnold Schwarzenegger as an unstoppable, cybernetic killer. The unprecedented success of *The Terminator*—a brainy thriller predicated on time travel and the notion of intelligent machines—transformed Cameron into one of Hollywood's most sought-after directors and catapulted Schwarzenegger into the top echelon of international action stars. In the wake of the film's success, Schwarzenegger starred in a string of hits, many of them sci-fi blockbusters, such as *Predator* (1987), *The Running Man* (1987), and *Total Recall* (1990), director Paul Verhoeven's trippy Philip K. Dick adaptation about a man whose virtual vacation to Mars goes deeply awry. Schwarzenegger reunited with Cameron for 1991's *Terminator 2: Judgment Day*, which upended conventional notions of what could be wrought on-screen with its introduction of the T-1000, a liquid metal villain (portrayed in the flesh by Robert Patrick). The duo remained close friends through decades that saw the Austria-born Schwarzenegger ascend to the governorship of California.

In the 2010s, Schwarzenegger returned to action and science fiction on-screen, appearing in the Expendables franchise and even resurrecting his most iconic character for 2015's *Terminator Genisys*. In a wide-ranging conversation, Schwarzenegger and Cameron—who are currently hatching a new *Terminator* project—recall the fateful lunch meeting that landed the actor his breakthrough role and consider the limitless possibilities afforded by time travel and next-level technology.

JAMES CAMERON: You've done a lot of science fiction movies. You've seen all kinds of different machines, intelligent machines. You played an intelligent machine.

ARNOLD SCHWARZENEGGER: I think that what's interesting is when you have been involved in the business as long as I have, and you see something starting out that is called science fiction, and then all of a sudden it becomes kind of science reality in a way. We've talked about that many times. What is so unbelievable is that as I have done *Terminator* movies, one after the next, the first one has literally become a reality—other than machines becoming self-aware. Just the very simple thing like the Terminator looking at someone, guessing the body weight and who he is and that.

JC: Scanning.

AS: Now you have an app on a phone and you can point it at someone and tell the age and what they look like and everything about that person. It's amazing how things have become a reality. What's so entertaining in a way is that you have come up with those things. Of course, you have been always a person that has read just about every science fiction book. Right?

JC: Pretty much every one.

AS: You told me that you read like one book a day. I mean it's unbelievable to read a book a day. You know, how the technology actually plays out and becomes more and more a reality.

JC: In [*The Terminator*], we showed flying machines that were drones that were shooting people on the ground. We had machines on tracks like big tanks that were gun platforms.

that were shooting people. They have those now. They have them in a prototype form. So, we're actually entering a kind of era of machine combat. The question is, how smart do we make these things and how much responsibility do we give them? I know you've spent a lot of time overseas in dealing with the military and talking to the troops, to our people that are on the front line in harm's way. What do you think about machines taking over some of those duties?

AS: I think it's terrific technology, and it's developing very rapidly now. But what I personally like about all of this is—about the

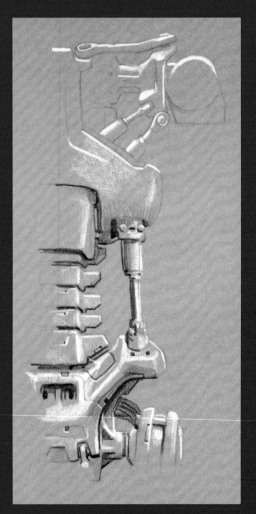

science fiction itself and being a machine and playing a machine and doing science fiction movies—you can do much more and get away with it. I love action movies, you know. Even when you do *Commando* (1985) and you're over the top, you still can only get away with so much. People say, "Oh come on! You know this is ridiculous." But if you play the Terminator, and you walk through a wall or . . .

JC: Take machine gun-fire.

AS: That's right. Yes. It makes it much more entertaining. For instance, [in *Terminator 2*] two Terminators have a wrestling match, and you grab each other and you throw each other against the wall, and the wall breaks. A cement wall breaks. Right? And you have the cable, the steel's sticking out and stuff like that. Then he grabs you and throws you over there and the ground breaks. Everything breaks around you. People say, "Wow. You know if you throw a regular human being around, you could not do that." Or jumping down or doing certain things or getting beaten like in *Terminator 2*. The amount of beating that I got from the [T-1000], right? It totally killed me. I mean I had no arm. One leg was destroyed. But then all of a sudden, the eyes started lighting up again.

JC: You had a back-up power supply.

AS: If you do a movie about reality you could never do that. I think that's what makes it so entertaining when you do science fiction. You get away with much more. You can actually ramp it up and give people more entertainment. I just watched *Terminator 2* [in] 3-D for the first time, and that was a perfect proof again just how big you can go [with] something if, of course, you have a good director and a good writer. It was fantastic. It's really amazing this movie in 3-D, how well it works.

JC: The interesting thing about the end of that film is that we believe, as an audience, that the Terminator has learned some degree of

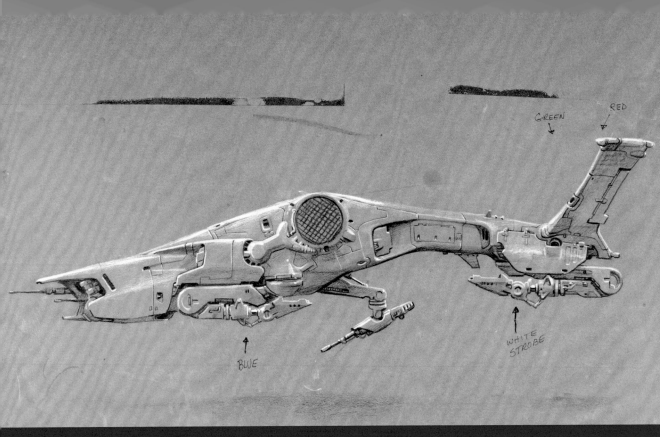

GREEN

RED

BLUE

WHITE STROBE

ABOVE James Cameron illustration for the airborne Hunter-Killer seen in *The Terminator*.

emotion. Talk about how you prepared for that movie—to play someone with no emotion who was trying to figure out how humans act, why they do the things that they do.

AS: I always was impressed [by how] Yul Brynner played in *Westworld* his character, being a robot cowboy. He was really intense, and I always got the feeling when I watched him that he was actually a machine. There was no human element there whatsoever. So, I wanted to play the Terminator kind of like that. To make sure that if you kill somebody, there should be no joy shown. If you shoot, you shouldn't blink, and if you get shot, you shouldn't feel sorry for yourself. Show absolutely nothing. The way the Terminator walks has to be machine-like, the way he scans and looks has to be machine-like. The eyes cannot blink. It's very important also when you talk that the Adam's apple doesn't go up and down. One has to pay attention to the minute details because with the big screen now and with

close-ups, this is where you see everything. I thought that was extremely important to train every day with the guns, the cocking of the shotgun and all this stuff.

JC: Where I'm going with this is that by the end of [*Terminator 2*], I think we as the audience believe that the Terminator has started to learn an emotional response to some limited degree. He talks about how he's got a neural net processor. It's designed to learn and to observe people, and he starts to form a bond with John Connor.

AS: The beginning, it was totally playing it straight. And then number two, the way it was written was that he starts getting a little bit of information and learning and actually really enjoys the relationship with the kid, playing this father [figure]. That by itself is a huge breakthrough—that he would enjoy something. As I explained in the movie, the more time the Terminator spends with human beings, the more he learns and adopts human behavior. It doesn't mean that he's off being a machine. He's still the machine, but there's still little traces. That actually makes it very interesting from an actor's point of view. How much you do that, how subtle you bring this through.

JC: But not go too far.

AS: You have to check that yourself. But the director comes in [to say] dial it back a little bit or bring it up a little bit and all that stuff. Because sometimes you shoot the ending of the movie way before it is the last day of the shooting, so you need help with [finding the right intensity of the performance]. But the key thing is, you do it in a subtle way. . . . You can then make it a real, emotional scene, which I think we were able to successfully do. When the Terminator looks at [John Connor] and [says], "I understand why you cry," and he touches his tears—you see the Terminator actually showing an ounce of sensitivity and emotions there. It was really wonderful, that development and that arc throughout the movie.

JC: Let's forget that you're an actor and you played the Terminator. Let's say you're—just to choose something at random—a world leader like the governor of California. And they come to you with a program that says we can keep our officers in the street alive better and cost less money by replacing some of them with intelligent machines. How would you respond to that from a leadership standpoint? I think these things are going to happen.

AS: I would definitely try it out. Whenever there's something new, you try it on a smaller scale, and you try in one town [to see] how that works. If someone can hack into that machine, [that's a problem]. No matter what we do with machines, we have seen the other side of that, which is that people hack in. I'm always concerned about that. If I have a computer and someone hacks in, let's say, I know it's my problem. But if you're a governor and

you are governing 38 million people, it becomes a totally different ball game, the responsibility. You don't take anything that lightly anymore. I remember how I changed when I sat in the governor's chair, and you have to make decisions over millions of people. You would start normally in a little town and work that out with the local people and with the mayor. If [the machine] can be hacked into, out he goes. [But] that makes a great science fiction movie—where you actually do it as a police force, then some outside force gets in there and makes them do horrible things and take over the town.

JC: The great science fiction movies are all about technology going wrong. Or science going wrong. It seems to me that as we go into deeper into the twenty-first century, and we're dealing with all these things—climate change and artificial intelligence, things like that where we really have to understand the ramifications—we need to understand the technology. Science fiction is a way of warning us about the things that can go wrong, reminding us that either the technology itself goes wrong or the people using the technology go wrong.

AS: But not only the science fiction movies. I've read many scripts where you have a kind of warning about how vulnerable we are toward outside attacks. If someone just does in our electric grid system and all of a sudden you have no power—we know what it is like when your power gets turned off because of an earthquake or because of some storm or something for just two days. But imagine now if it just gets wiped out.

JC: That's a science fiction movie. The science fiction movie says . . . if a nuclear holocaust happened tomorrow or a cyber attack that wipes out our grid, look at what happens to everybody.

AS: In any case, I would do that machine-like police officer or law enforcement. I would do it a small scale. Check it out. Give it five years, and then see what the problems are. If it gets hacked into, what happens when it gets hacked into? How do we protect ourselves? And then go and work with mayors that are interested in that. With all of this stuff, it's great for security, efficiency. But you always have to think about, how do you slowly then get the police officers that are relying on those jobs [into something else]? Not replacing them and then all of a sudden they are out of jobs.

JC: That is another problem: automation. The better we get at using machines that build all our stuff for us . . . [the more those machines] are going to take our jobs. It's going to be robots built right here in the US.

AS: But remember that there is a smart way of doing that, and that is to go and retrain the people that lose the jobs. They are the ones that build the robots because you always need a new workforce. This is the same thing as I've said about getting off, for instance, coal. What do you do with the coal miners? You don't go and put them out of work. You go and say to them, look, over the next ten years, [we will] close down the coal mines. But in the meantime, in this ten years, we're going to go and bring industries in here to build windmills and build batteries, electric cars and stuff like that. You guys are going to have jobs. No one will lose the job. You will have jobs but with clean lungs. You don't have to go 1,500 feet down there and inhale this dirty coal dust and all this stuff and have people die.

JC: Machines are better at going in the harsh environments. They're better at working underwater. They're better at working in mines and so on. They're faster at doing jobs in a factory. What if that sort of reeducation program idea works for a while, but what if fifty years from now, machines are better at building robots? And they build the robots to build the robots to build this stuff? And all we are becoming is consumers. These are the kind of

questions about our real world that science fiction can ask and make us think about now.

AS: Absolutely. But as you know, we have in California, for instance, changed so much from a manufacturing kind of economy to a service-based economy. There are so many new kinds of professions that come up there. Think about how many trainers there are now in gymnasiums. Gold's Gym is packed [with] like fifty personal trainers there. That never happened when I was working out in Gold's Gym back in the '70s and stuff. Things change. People do like to have personal service. They have personal shoppers. They have their chauffeurs. They have security. All of these new kinds of jobs are coming in. The key thing is you cannot provide stuff for consumers when they have no money and no job. No one will buy anything. You need to have everyone employed for the economy to boom.

JC: Otherwise the robots are out of a job.

AS: Exactly so.

JC: When I first thought up the idea for *The Terminator*—

AS: How did you come up with that idea?

JC: It came from a dream. I had a dream image of a chrome skeleton walking out of a fire. I remember when I woke up, [I thought], how do I make a story out of that? What did he look like before he was in the fire? He would have had maybe a plastic outer skin. What if it wasn't plastic? What if he was a cyborg, and he looked like a man and was indistinguishable from a man until the fire. I just started riffing on that. Here's the interesting thing—I saw him as a guy who could just disappear in a crowd, just an average person. Then somebody came up with the idea of you playing the Terminator. I thought, this is not going to work.

I went to lunch with you thinking, alright, I'm going to have to find some reason that I

don't like this guy, so I can go back and tell the producers that it's not working out. And you were so charming. You understood the script so well. You could see all the scenes so vividly in your head. I'm looking at you thinking, this guy's kind of big. He could have this whole machine inside him, that would work pretty well. Even though you were telling jokes and everything, I could still kind of see the facial structure. [I was thinking] this guy would be like a bulldozer. Nothing could stop him. I thought, "Don't be stupid. Cast this guy as the Terminator. He's going to be fantastic."

I remember the first day's dailies when you worked on the film. We'd already been shooting for, I think, a week and a half. . . . You were in that look after you'd been kind of flash burned. Your eyebrows are gone. Your face was glycerin, and you're driving a patrol car. You're kind of scanning like a shark, and we're sitting there in dailies. . . . And we were all just going, yes, this is fantastic.

But I don't think we could have anticipated where we are now, thirty some years later, I guess thirty-three years later, where Skynet is the term that everyone uses when they're talking about an artificial intelligence that turns

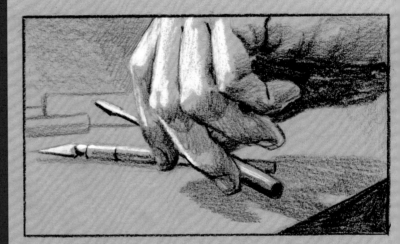

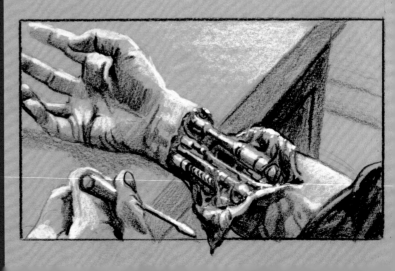

against us. There's a whole mythology from *Terminator* films about AI and how AI might be a threat to humanity. Then you have people like the secretary of defense saying, "There's not going to be a *Terminator* scenario. There's not going to be a Skynet. We're going to be able to control it." But people are now talking very seriously about the things that were pure science fiction thirty-three years ago. I think that's pretty interesting.

AS: Well, I don't think anyone is going to announce even if something is in development right now. There could be a Terminator-like character or warriors that are already developed and being tested, and we don't know about it. They're not that stupid to announce it to the world. So that's number one. But number two, I just want to go back to what you said about [that] lunch. The funny thing about it was that I went to lunch trying to sell the idea to you that I should play Reese [the hero character in the film]. And so, we started our lunch, and we were talking about [the fact] that you live in Venice. I broke out there, and I have my office there and all this stuff. We talked about neutral kinds of things. Then we started talking a little bit about the movie, and for some reason or the other, not at all planned on my part, I said, "Look, Jim, the guy that plays that character, he really has to understand that he's a machine."

JC: The Terminator.

AS: And I started talking about it for like twenty-five minutes, before we even could order. I would keep rattling off.

JC: You had a vision for the character.

AS: I could see it. That one I could see very clearly in front of me. The bottom line is I really don't know what happened to me during the lunch because I went there with the thought that I loved the character the way it was, the way Reese was written. I said, "That would really be great to play this character." It's all the

way through the movie, and it has a lot of dialogue. He saves the world. I said, this is the hero. And I wanted to continue playing heroes. But for some reason or the other, I started telling you how important it is that whoever plays the Terminator has to do certain training every day, [has to] know how to deal with weapons. When he goes to the gun shop, he has to know everything. I kept talking to you about how he has to be a machine and there has to be not one single frame where he has human behavior. And you look and you say, "You're absolutely correct." In the end, when we were finished with the lunch, you said, "So why don't you play the Terminator? I would love you to play the Terminator." And then I looked and said, "Oh shit. What happened to me? I never talked about Reese! Why didn't I say the

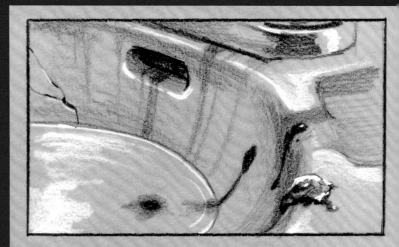

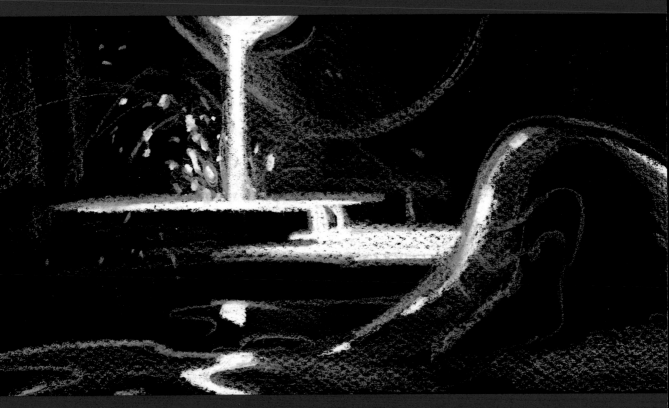

same thing about Reese?" But in my heart, I was into the Terminator character.

JC: It was fate.

AS: It was fate. And luckily you recognized it right away and luckily together it became a fantastic movie. To be *Time* magazine's top ten movies of the year, that was huge. That's when everyone realized this was not just an action movie, that this was a well thought out, smart person's movie. Many more people went to see the movie because of that.

JC: So, now we're going to make *Terminator 2*. We've got to have a bigger, badder Terminator that could kick Terminator's ass because now he's the good guy and the good guy's always got to be the underdog. So, what was that? A bigger machine, a bigger guy, that didn't make any sense. How about just something so different you don't even know how to fight it? You don't even know how to stop it. You put a bullet through it, nothing happens, it just heals. That took us down that path developing all these CG

tools. That was pretty cool. The hardest part of that movie though was convincing you that playing the good guy was a good idea.

AS: I'm always worried when Hollywood [takes] a character that was so successful and changes it. It threw me off when I read the script. I realized that I'm not anymore that kind of killing machine. But then I say to myself, I trust Jim, and it could actually work really well. The way we played it, it worked obviously really well because the way you shot it was that I was still doing all the damage, wiping out everything. But not people. Police cars were flying through the air, and you saw the one hundred police officers running for their lives, and there was chaos and madness. So, there was all the action, but my character, you added another dimension, the dimension that he now is recognizing that he has to save the kid and to help and not kill people and be a good guy.

I thought the T-1000 was brilliant—and the reason is because [you] made it more threatening for me. All of a sudden, people

ABOVE AND OPPOSITE
The T-1000 reforms after seemingly being destroyed in this early concept art for *Terminator 2* (1991), illustrated by James Cameron.

were rooting for me rather than for the more sophisticated Terminator that had many more abilities. He was fast. He was sleek and more sophisticated. It was the upgraded model.

JC: You were only the T-800. But you said earlier that in the first film, he is a villain, but people still almost rooted for him in a way. And I thought, if we could take that idea, if we could distill him down to this idea of just relentlessness—he wouldn't stop no matter what you did to him—and take out the evil and put good in its place, that the same character worked as a bad guy and as a good guy. The same character with the same quality. What it really makes me realize is we admire the quality, regardless of whether the guy is a good guy or a bad guy. We admire the Terminator because he doesn't stop. He represents something that humans sometimes aspire to: [that notion of] you can't stop me. Maybe it's an athlete who's running a long endurance race or fighter in a fight, or maybe it's an entire nation. England during World War II that's under bombardment. They just have that will. We admire that.

AS: We admire it because I think that a lot of people don't have that in them. People admire strength and people admire determination, discipline—you keep walking forward no matter what the obstacles are. You may fall, but you get up again and continue on.

JC: That's why we're here. The human race. I mean Churchill I think said it best: Never, ever, ever give up.

AS: You and I would never give up.

JC: When we did *Terminator 2*, we had a big leap forward in technology of moviemaking, which was CG animation to create the liquid metal guy. And at the same time, we're talking about a big leap forward in human technology in general, which was the creation of an AI, an intelligent AI, Skynet, that fights for its life. Science fiction has dealt with the idea of an emerging AI consciousness, of what it might think and how it might act. This is something I think we're going to have to deal with as humanity.

AS: This is technology that in a way didn't exist. You created that, and you challenged everyone. The way you wrote it, you challenged everyone.

JC: I didn't create it, but I did challenge smart guys to create it.

AS: But that's what I'm saying. You challenged them in your writing. They had to then come through and perform. When it comes to technical things and when it comes to science fiction movies, there's no one that could pull the wool over your eyes. Right? That's why it won the

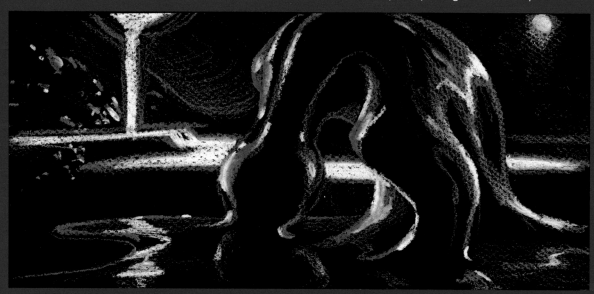

Academy Awards. It was nominated for so many things and there was such a huge hit.

JC: There's a feeling you get before it rains, and you know it's going to rain. And you get that feeling about certain moments in technological development where you know something is going to happen very soon, and you just need to be there to take advantage of it. And I think there's a general consensus now that we're in that moment before it rains. Now maybe that moment takes ten years, maybe it takes twenty years, but there's going to be a moment—maybe it takes fifty years—where we create a machine that is conscious the way we are. Or maybe not the way we are, but equal to us in its ability to understand the world and react to it and to think about it. Maybe superior to us in some ways, being able to compute and understand things much faster.

AS: And what would be the purpose of that thing? Would it be for military use?

JC: Absolutely. Well, maybe not, but it seems to me that the machines that we create, the consciousness is going to be in our image. They might not be a human figure like your Terminator character, but their consciousness will be like our consciousness in some way because we create them. So, if we create a machine to improve the bottom line of corporations, you just created greed, and you just programmed the machine to be greedy. If you create a machine to kill an enemy, to defend the country, all the reasons that we give to create weapons, then you have just created a killer.

AS: I hope that the technology would take us in the direction that will help, for instance, with the environment—that we develop a machine that would suck the CO_2 out of the air. That would really make us have a step forward and save so many lives. I think that technology is really terrific as long as it is used for something good and not for something evil.

JC: But so much of science fiction has been about the naive scientists who see the wonderful uses of the technology, and then it gets perverted by somebody else and turned into a weapon system or it escapes from the lab or whatever. The guys that were first thinking about nuclear power, they were thinking about the power of the atom and thinking we could run civilization with this. But of course, what was the first thing that we built? The nuclear bomb. It's not the machines I don't trust. It's the people that I don't trust. And how they use them.

One of the things I've always loved about you, Arnold, is that you really have a great sense of how people think. You really understand people. Ask yourself if there was a machine that was smarter than us but it worked for us, how long would it work for us and how long would we be able to control it? Would we trust somebody else on the other side, an enemy nation or an adversary, would we trust them with that technology? Are we in a new arms race? You know people. You know how they think, and you know how business people think and leaders think.

AS: Every day I face technology that is much smarter than me when I play on my iPad. Chess. It is ludicrous.

JC: It kicks your ass.

AS: But so quick. It says it takes seventeen seconds for me to make a decision. But as soon as I press the button where I'm going to put the [knight], a tenth of a second later, boom, it makes a move. It doesn't even think. It just reacts.

JC: Well it's thinking. It's just thinking faster.

AS: I see it all the time how technology—how fast it is, how far superior it is. They can program things in such a way that it really is spectacular. Now whether this is going to go in an evil way? It can be possible. I haven't thought that much about it to really know where this can go except for the movies that we've seen. I like science fiction movies in general because like I said, you can get away with much more.

JC: You've been to Mars. You've been in the future.

AS: Well, I've been in the Terminator—the four *Terminator* movies that I've done. *Total Recall*, *The Running Man*. *The 6th Day*, where I get cloned and there's two of me there. Or even with *Twins*, which is an experiment that has not yet really been done.

JC: *Twins* is a science fiction movie. What was that one where you're pregnant? *Junior*.

AS: *Junior* is science fiction. No [male] has been able to really carry a baby or something.

JC: Sometimes we get a little too serious about—about science fiction. There's a lot of scholarly thought that goes into it, but sometimes it's just an expression of imagination. In the past, it would be a story about gods and demons and mythology, extraordinary things, highly imaginative things. Heroes that could leap and fly. Now the heroes that can leap and fly use technology. Spider-Man was bitten by a radioactive spider. Iron Man built the suit. So, science fiction steps into the shoes of mythology and folklore that we've had since civilization began.

AS: I love watching those movies when people have these extra powers, Spider-Man and Superman. They're regular guys, and then all of a sudden, they put that suit on and they get the extra power. From then, you get away with everything.

JC: So, you're not staying up late at night worrying about intelligent machines taking over the world?

AS: No. My crusade is to make sure that we are going in a clean-energy future. And to rely more on renewables and get rid of fossil fuels

SCHWARZENEGGER

Get ready for the ride of your life.

TOTAL RECALL

COMING THIS SUMMER TO A THEATRE NEAR YOU

because I stumbled on that during the time I was governor.

JC: The question is, could a machine ever have free will? And would that be the point at which we have to say it's not doing what we programmed it to do and therefore is its own being. It has its own ego, its own identity. Is that the point at which a machine becomes self-aware?

AS: I think this is the only thing that's still missing. You know what was in *Terminator*. The machines today have pretty much done all of the things that we see in the movie except become self-aware. I'm not an expert with machines, so I have no idea. But we would not have thought thirty years ago that all this stuff would be possible that we have seen now coming out.

JC: Stealth bombers, drones, combat robots.

AS: And the intelligence of computers. Machines are running our lives now. Now, they are talking about cars [that] drive themselves. In *The 6th Day*, the car drives itself. We're going

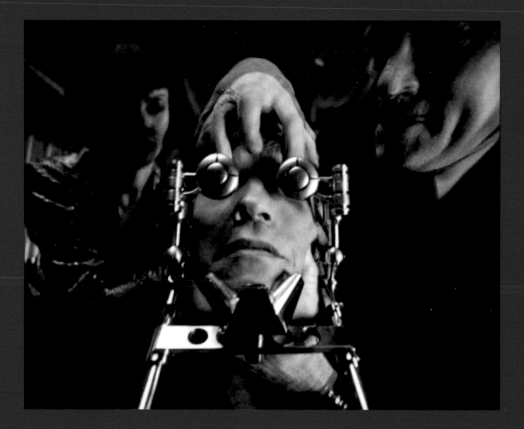

more and more in that direction. So, if machines become self-aware, I think that will be the saddest moment probably if that were to happen.

JC: Maybe. People always ask me, "Do you think the machines will ever win? You think the machines will ever beat us?" I say, "They beat us a long time ago." Just look around when you're in a public place and how many people are riveted to their phone. We're already slaves of the machines created by people in Silicon Valley to get rich, to tap into human behavior. And now nobody is complete without their cell phone. I mean something that we couldn't even imagine thirty or forty years ago, we can't imagine not having it with us. It's become a part of us. I actually think we're coevolving with our machines. We're changing.

AS: I think people are now glued to the machines. I mean through the iPhones or mobile phones in general, iPads and whatever it is. Every second there's new news out there

or new information. In the old days, the routine was to get up in the morning, coffee, get the newspaper. You read the newspaper. Your favorite section of news, sports.

JC: Our kids would not even understand what that was. The kids are blank slates. They're just adapting, they're coevolving with the machines. We're so willing to give away all of our powers, all of the things that we used to do, all of our skills and everything, to a machine to do for us, that if you just progressed that out over time, we might give them everything to do. And then what's left for us? What's left for us to be human?

AS: I think this is a challenge of the new generation. It's not the challenge for me because I still love to drive. I like to do all this stuff myself. I come from the old school, but I think the newer generation, you're absolutely right. It is a big challenge, and what do we develop because of that? They're becoming vegetables in some ways. I don't know.

JC: My feeling is that automation will keep progressing, and the machines will take over more and more of what we can do until society stops and says, we have to define things for human beings to do to give ourselves meaning. If the machine can do everything for us, we have to create our own meaning. I think it is going to be a very interesting thing that's ahead of us. Probably not in our lifetime, but probably in the next fifty years I would say, we'll have to have some real soul searching about what we're here for. Because if we can get machines to do everything for us and if they're getting smarter and smarter . . . I worry about this stuff.

So, the question is, can the machine have free will? But the other question is, do we have free will? If you can move back and forth in time—because the *Terminator* movies are kind of about that, they're about free will—if somebody comes back from the future to change what happens, then are we just all puppets of a time line? Are we basically in a movie that's already been shot? You can play it forward and backward as much as you want, but the ending never changes?

AS: I think that we have control over ourselves, and I think that we have the power to create changes. I'm a very optimistic person. I think that anything can be done if you set your mind on it. It's not easy, but it's fun to struggle to do something and to accomplish something. There's no machine that tells me what to do. I do my bodybuilding, I work out every day. I do my movies. I have my institute, the Schwarzenegger Institute. I do my R20 [nonprofit], the environmental work. I do the after-school programs just like I did twenty-five years ago. I spent time on all of those things, and my life is exciting. I don't care about machines, being threatened by machines, that they're going to interfere and interrupt the flow of happiness of my life because I do the things that I want to do and use machines in order to get things done.

JC: I don't think there's any better example in the world of someone having a sense of will and purpose and then manifesting that than you. You set out to become a champion bodybuilder, and you did it. You set out to become a movie star, and you did it. You set out to become a world

leader, and you did it. Governor of California, with the seventh biggest economy on the planet. And so, you set your goal, and you go do it.

AS: It just shows you what a great nation we are and how someone can come here with nothing like you did and be the dream. And how I came over here with the dream and how far we have gone with that. You could have gone to any other place in the world. So could I. And we would not have made the success that we did here. It's that simple. America is about this. Making your dreams become a reality without anyone saying you can't.

JC: Let's talk about time travel because the *Terminator* movies are about robotics and artificial intelligence, but they're also about time travel. They play by the rules of a time-travel story.

AS: I would have loved to be able to time travel. Imagine, to go back and say, I'm not going to do *Hercules in New York*.

JC: That's the thing you want to do. Not meet Jesus, not kill Hitler. You want to go back and fix that one movie.

AS: To go to kill Hitler or to go meet Nietzsche or to go and be back in the Roman days and hang out with Caesar and see how some of the decisions are made or to be part of some those battles, that's too serious. Start out first with something funny.

JC: I could see you doing that, going back to be part of the battles.

AS: Exactly. I mean, wow, that would be interesting to be able to time travel. But again, this is one of the things we have seen in movies. Some people time travel and then they get stuck in the wrong time. Not in the time that they want to be in.

JC: They call that the grandfather paradox. You go back in time and something that you do

when you're back there causes the death of your grandfather before he has impregnated your grandmother and you therefore cease to exist. But if you cease to exist, then you weren't around to get into a time machine in the first place to go back in time and do that. This is the thing that every writer always struggles with in time travel stories.

AS: What is the answer?

JC: Nobody knows. Nobody knows if time travel is even possible. Physics says it might be possible. It would require an enormous amount of energy to do it.

AS: And speed, right?

JC: Just a ton of energy—like if you took fifty suns and took all their output, that might be enough energy to send, like, a dime back six minutes or something. But the important thing is, why is so much of our fantasy, our imagination in the science fiction genre, taken up with this idea of time travel?

AS: Because we can't do it. I think it is just wonderful to see it on the screen and imagine ourselves being in that situation. Everybody's thinking about, what would I do if I could do that? Where would I end up, which time period? What would I want to do there? *Total Recall* was a little bit like that. It wasn't as much time travel, but it was travel by putting a chip in your head to travel to another planet and to have this whole thing unfold.

JC: It turned out your virtual experience wasn't a virtual experience for your character.

AS: Exactly. I think it's fun when you watch movies because you start imagining, wouldn't it be great to go on a ride like that? Or for instance *Westworld*, where you go to this kind of Disneyland type of thing and you have shootouts and you have battles and you always win. But then all of a sudden things go south, go wrong.

JC: Things always go wrong in science fiction stories. That's the whole point because they're trying to tell us that things will really go wrong in the real world.

AS: That's why we're going to continue making science fiction movies.

JC: That's right. It's our job. We have no choice. . . . There was an interesting line in *Terminator 2* where you say, "It is in your nature to destroy yourselves." And I think that principle should be applied to every new technology that we create. Because if it's in our nature to destroy ourselves or to try to destroy other people— and in the process, get destroyed—we need to be very careful with these new technologies. Maybe time travel might be a great idea except it'll be abused by some humans somewhere, some government, some shady outfit. Maybe an artificial intelligence that's superior to us might be a great idea for all these utopian reasons like solving climate change or solving food production or extending life, better medicine and all that. But you know it's going to get misused by somebody, some world leader somewhere.

AS: I think in every aspect in life . . . there's people that would misuse it. If it's a banking system, if it's a computer system, if it is law enforcement, if it's politics, wherever you look there is always some really good work done and then you have the corruption inside. There is a misuse of everything, I think. But I think as a whole that people are good and people always want to survive and want to go and get rid of that evil. We have to just try to really communicate and enlighten people that this is the better way to go. And it takes a lot of work. This is the not easy stuff, you know.

JC: I think it's a race between us improving, making ourselves better, our own evolution, spiritual psychological evolution. At the same time, we've got these machines evolving. Because if we don't improve to direct them properly with our godlike power of using artificial intelligence and all these other robotic tools, it will ultimately just blow back in our face and take us out. Because our planet ain't a movie and it may not have a happy ending. There's no take two.

AS: This is it.

AFTERWORD

BY BROOKS PECK
CURATOR, MUSEUM OF POP CULTURE

What is the future of the future?

At the Museum of Pop Culture, we're obsessed with science fiction. We have a permanent science fiction gallery, and we have created exhibitions about many pillars of the genre, including *Star Trek*, *Avatar*, *Battlestar Galactica*, and others. We are also home to the Science Fiction and Fantasy Hall of Fame, which honors those genres' most influential creators and creations.

We pay so much attention to science fiction because the genre is a powerful force in contemporary popular culture. For example, half of the top-grossing films of all time are science fiction. Think about that: half sci-fi, half everything else. Sci-fi also dominates video games and television, is central in popular literature, and its tropes frequently appear in advertising. "It surrounds us . . . it binds the galaxy together," as Obi-Wan Kenobi said about the Force. At the museum we study what drives that sort of popularity and investigate the impacts.

So, unlike traditional museums that display historical artifacts, we display future artifacts: proton packs, hoverboards, starships, and alien insects, among many others. Although these items don't come from a real future, they do come from *possible* futures. As others say in *James Cameron's Story of Science Fiction*, the future is undecided, and one of science fiction's biggest jobs is to look ahead. Science fiction test drives possible futures. It lets us try them on, live in them for a while. Then we can decide if we want to pursue those futures or avoid them. This is an important job that science fiction performs, taking it beyond spectacle and entertainment. It's not an exaggeration to say that movies, novels, comics, and music videos are all important tools in determining the future of our species.

Lately, science fiction has encountered an interesting challenge: The future is becoming harder to imagine. When the genre came into prominence in the 1930s, writers and filmmakers could create stories about the coming decades with confidence (if not great accuracy) in certain trends: exploration of the solar system, expanded use of nuclear energy, miniaturization, and efficiency improvements in manufacturing. It was sensible to assume that the future would bring faster transportation, cheaper goods, and rising standards of living because that's what the Industrial Revolution brought (although not equally for all). Those changes could be quantified.

In the early twenty-first century, though, the landmark innovations have strongly affected *quality* of life, which is much harder to measure. How do we determine the impact that smart phones and the internet have made on people's everyday lives? Do we look at time saved? The amount of communication? Increased or decreased engagement in politics? And where are these technologies taking us? Science fiction's job as an investigator of the future has become tougher, more slippery, but it's as crucial as ever. Change moves faster now, and the future is no longer decades away, but years or even months.

Does this mean that science fiction is becoming irrelevant? No, science fiction creators can tackle rapid change in a variety of ways. One method is to view the very near future—and even today—through a sci-fi lens, exploring the collisions between today's culture and technologies. Or stories can be set so far in the future that any concern for accuracy becomes unimportant. Postapocalyptic tales dump modern science entirely.

Even if the future is sprinting toward us faster and faster, even if the time between now and the future is measured in minutes, even if the future *arrives* and our computers become self-aware and aliens make contact, we'll always tell science fiction stories. Because it is human nature to wonder what's out there. "Out there" in this case has two meanings: out there in the physical world—other lands, other planets, space—and out there in the future, in time. Our urge to ask and answer this question drives us as a species to keep moving and learning, which is key to our survival. So we will always wonder. We will always speculate, because there will always be more out there to explore.

Insight Editions would like to extend special thanks to James Cameron, Maria Wilhelm, and Kim Butts for their help and guidance in bringing this project to fruition. We would also like to thank Guillermo del Toro, George Lucas, Christopher Nolan, Arnold Schwarzenegger, Ridley Scott, and Steven Spielberg. Special thanks also to Yoel Flohr, Madhu Goel Southworth, Hubert Smith, Andrea Glanz, Eliot Goldberg, Kelly Nash, Theresa Beyer, Kristen Chung, Daniel Ketchell, Connie Wethington, Vera Meyer, Andy Thompson, Lauren Elliott, Terri De Paolo, Kassandra Arko, Michael Coleman, and Nate Jackson.

INSIGHT EDITIONS

PO Box 3088
San Rafael, CA 94912
www.insighteditions.com

Find us on Facebook: www.facebook.com/InsightEditions
Follow us on Twitter: @insighteditions

James Cameron's personal art courtesy of James Cameron.

Published by Insight Editions, San Rafael, California, in 2018.

Library of Congress Cataloging-in-Publication Data available.

ISBN: 978-1-68383-497-7

Publisher: Raoul Goff
Associate Publisher: Vanessa Lopez
Art Director: Chrissy Kwasnik
Senior Designer: Jon Glick
Senior Editor: Chris Prince
Editorial Assistant: Hilary Vandenbroek
Senior Production Editor: Elaine Ou
Production Manager: Greg Steffen

Cover design by Kim Butts

Additional text and editing by Gina McIntyre
Additional James Cameron art photography by Ethan Boheme
Back cover photography by Michael Moriatis/AMC

For the Museum of Pop Culture, Seattle

Paul G. Allen – Founder

Brooks Peck – Curator
Jacob McMurray – Senior Curator
Melinda Simms – Collections Manager

ROOTS of PEACE   REPLANTED PAPER

Insight Editions, in association with Roots of Peace, will plant two trees for each tree used in the manufacturing of this book. Roots of Peace is an internationally renowned humanitarian organization dedicated to eradicating land mines worldwide and converting war-torn lands into productive farms and wildlife habitats. Roots of Peace will plant two million fruit and nut trees in Afghanistan and provide farmers there with the skills and support necessary for sustainable land use.

Manufactured in Italy by Insight Editions